A NEW LIGHT OF MYSTICISM.

AZOTH;

OR,

THE STAR IN THE EAST.

EMBRACING THE FIRST MATTER OF THE MAGNUM OPUS, THE
EVOLUTION OF APHRODITE-URANIA, THE SUPERNATURAL
GENERATION OF THE SON OF THE SUN, AND
THE ALCHEMICAL TRANSFIGURATION
OF HUMANITY.

BY

ARTHUR EDWARD WAITE.

British Library Cataloguing-in-Publication Data
A catalogue record for this book is available from
the British Library

ARTHUR EDWARD WAITE

Arthur Edward Waite was born in Brooklyn, New York, USA in 1857. His father died when he was very young, and his widowed mother returned to her home country of England, where he was then raised. Waite was educated at a small private school in North London, and St. Charles' College. After school, he became a clerk, and wrote verse in his spare time.

In 1874, the death of Waite's sister saw him become deeply interested in psychical research. He began to read regularly in the Library of the British Museum, studying many branches of esotericism. Not long later, Waite became editor of an occultist magazine called *The Unknown World,* and in 1891 joined Aleister Crowley's Hermetic Order of the Golden Dawn. A decade later, he became a Freemason, and entered the Societas Rosicruciana in Anglia. Waite had a lifelong rivalry with Aleister Crowley, who presented him as a villainous wizard in his novel *Moonchild.*

Waite was a prolific author, and many of his works were well received in academic circles. He wrote occult texts on subjects such as divination, esotericism, Rosicrucianism, Freemasonry, Kabbalism and alchemy; he also translated and reissued several important mystical and occultist works. His works on the Holy Grail rank amongst his finest publications.

However, Waite is best-remembered not for his scholarly work, but for his co-creation of the popular and widely used Rider-Waite Tarot deck, and his authoring of its companion volume, *The Key to the Tarot.* First published in 1909, the Rider-Waite-Smith tarot was notable for being one of the first tarot decks to illustrate all 78 cards fully, in addition to the 22 major arcana cards. The work made him famous, and Waite spent much of the rest of his life lecturing and speaking on the topic of the Tarot. He died in 1942, aged 88.

AZOTH; OR, THE STAR IN THE EAST.

PERFECTION CONSISTS:—

In the physical order: In the realization of the dream of beauty.

In the moral order: In the realization of the dream of love.

In the intellectual order: In the realization of the dream of poetry.

In the spiritual order: In the realization of the dream of the mystics.

But these four orders are fundamentally one order, and the four dreams constitute one reality.

ANALYSIS OF THE CONTENTS.

CONTENTS.

CONTENTS.

CONTENTS.

CONTENTS.

CONTENTS.

PROEM.

We know that on some summit, far away
  Within the Soul, a beacon-light uplifted
Makes on the mountains round eternal day;
  By its bright beams the clouds beneath are rifted,
And for awhile is glorified the grey
  Life-sea, whereon so long mankind hath drifted;
That single flash will oft new strength create,
And then the Spirit conquers time and fate.

To all at times these golden glimpses come;
  The clouds roll back; the deep, supernal blue
Is arch'd above those mountains like a dome;
  The revelation of the great and true
Comes with those glimpses from the Soul's far home,
  And the Soul knows her lineage and her due;
But most have striven to reach the source in vain
Whence come those beams, or bid their flash remain.

Yet for life's fever and the mind's disease
  The only refuge for the world is there;
Before they reach it none can taste of ease,
  There all are sphered beyond the range of care;
Wrecks toss'd in scorn upon the scourging seas,
  Our sails are set to find a haven fair,
But, from those mountains shrinking, still we strive,
And drift for ever where the winds may drive.

We dream of islands lapp'd in amber light,
  Of pleasant groves and wilding woodland bowers,
Where morn unclouded follows starry night,
  And starry night on evening's pensive hours;
We see no beauty in the frowning height—
  That awful altitude the mind o'erpowers;
Yet the Soul's home is in its purer air;
Soul-glory, majesty, and might are there.

PROEM.

But there are many, could they see their way,
　Who would the summit by their toil attain,
Who not in vain would pour their lives away,
　Achieving conquests for their brethren's gain;
But whom doubt weakens, who in tears delay,
　And contemplate life's spectacle of pain;
Who to do something yearn, yet pause and ask
Some high encitement to so hard a task.

And therefore have we written, O man, for thee
　The book that follows, here its plan proclaim—
Help for thy Soul—help that the Soul may see
　In evil days her best, her noblest aim,
And ever faithful to that end may be,
　Though faith should fail, though truth her hope disclaim.
And, 'mid the general lapse from light, may find
No impulse left for the exalted mind!

What inspiration from the heaven came down
　To fill the brain? What angel bade us write?
Oh, in the green fields, in the crowded town,
　And in the sunshine or the starry night,
Those thoughts descended which in Soul are sown,
　And ripen'd in us, as the flowers in light—
Their strength supports us, from the ample store
We scatter; may they number more and more!

Oh, may this book, by our own heart created,
　Be life in all to whom its dream is told—
To draw the world up God's steep path be fated,
　Till all the splendid prospect shall behold,
And on those heights all Souls be reinstated,
　From which perchance they lapsed in days of old;
Or those attain whose altitude till then,
Though dimly dream'd, was never known by men!

PREFACE.

I N the books of the old physical Mystics, who conducted the experiments of transmutation and investigated the possibility of Nature in the world of metals and minerals, we find frequent reference to an all-permeating and sublimating principle, which, of the many forces dealt with or referred to in occult chemistry, appears most potent and most universal. It is "the essential and final principle of the Great Work"; its analogies in the intelligible order are to be found in the Divine Will; it is, allegorically speaking, the hand of God in Nature, and therefore in its symbolical aspect, as the outward sign of a withdrawn and unattainable potency, it has not been inappropriately designated the God of the Sages. This force is the alchemical Azoth, the Catholicon, Magnesia, the Sperm of the World, Mercury, and the Universal Medicine of things, endowed with a most intent and concentrated virtue. "It contains within itself," says the *Book of the Wood of Life*, "all other Medicines, as well as the first principle of all other substances, their accidents excluded. Unto this all things are alike; it uncovers every species, and imparts an immense strength, and catholic, central virtue." By its intervention the *corpus vile*, the chaotic substance, the black and crude mass, that nameless First Matter of positive philosophy, which was veiled by a thousand names, is affirmed to have been ameliorated successively through seven prismatic stages, corresponding to the seven colours of the solar spectrum, the scale of the planetary system, and the connected natural sequences, until it was exalted, developed, and transmuted into the Son of the Sun, into the dual Child of Light, into the splendent Stone of Wisdom and Stone of Power, by which all minerals, all metals, and all other substances radically homogeneous, could be also tinged and transmuted.

Faith and Reason have been poetically compared to the gold and silver sides of one divine shield. The parables of alchemy seem also of a twofold kind, and their more concealed and interior significance, in comparison with their first significance, has the relation of Sol to Luna, of the auriferous solar shining to the paler argent beam; they are physical and spiritual. Their spiritual meaning admits of being freely rendered in the language of modern science, and the Azoth of the Sages becomes manifested under this process as a

a

Principle of Universal Development or Evolution. If we exclusively consider this principle so far as it is at work in the Kingdom of Humanity, we shall see that the Great Work is the amelioration, exaltation, or transmutation of the formless human race into the dual child of the Mystic Cross of LUX—to make use of Hermetic terminology—or, in other words, into the Perfect Man. And as the development of one such being out of the whole chaos of individuals, ever manifesting and vanishing with the ebb and flow of generations, would provide a transforming instrument, a living *Sulphur Tingens*, to adopt another alchemical phrase, we thus find that the conception of a transmuting and colouring stone, and of a projecting powder which can exalt into its own nature any adaptable substance, irrespective of magnitude—things which are continually referred to in the allegories of the Philosophers—have a secret significance which points in the same direction, unto "the Blessed Isles of the Elect Children," which the alchemist prayed to behold in the parabolic vision of Mercury.

A book which derives its inspiration from the physical and spiritual Mystics, from Geber and Flamel, from Lully and Valentinus, the illustrious Benedictine; as also from Plotinus, Ammonius, Iamblichus, Dionysius, Bonaventura, and Vaughan; which founds upon their illumination and their knowledge a delineation of the principles which are now at work in the evolution of the human Flower of Paradise, as well as of the additional and intelligent forces which can be applied along the lines of those principles—that are also forces—in order to secure the end; a book which provides for the first time a philosophical forecast of the many-splendoured glories in the conditioning of the man to come—we submit that such a work does not inappropriately bear upon leaf and binding the profound but veiled suggestion which is focussed from many quarters of the intellectual heaven into the pentagrammatic term of AZOTH. Without being methodically a religious treatise, it constitutes a new light of religion; without being interwoven with any creedal system it is an interior *Lumen Christi;* and so also, without plunging into the tenebræ of transcendental physics, it deals with a universal law which was known to the transcendental physicists, which we have been taught by them, to whom, in all devotion and in all truth, we desire to dedicate our labours and to refer our knowledge. And the Star in the East, by which the Wise of old were led to the higher light of Bethlehem—the *Oriens splendor lucis æternæ et sol justitiæ;* to the key of truth in Juda—the *Clavis David et sceptum domus Israel;* to the divine virility of Jesse—*qui stat in signum populorum;* that Star also shall be a part of our emblazonment, for it is the complement of Azoth, it represents the force of evolution concentrated and fulfilled in humanity, and it is truly that fair planet in the orient of happy promise which prefigures the Great Fulfilment for which we yearn and pray—*Adveniat regnum tuum*, and yet again, with a full heart of earnestness—*Veni ad liberandum nos, jam noli tardare.*

Unto those who, like ourself, are Mystics, in the main, we address this work, not because it is written in a strange tongue which will be intelligible to the specialist alone, for it is written in all simplicity, and in the tongue which our mothers have taught us; not because it speaks in parables, or conceals 'an interior meaning, for it speaks openly, assuming no guise, and tricked with no devices of affectation. But there have been at all times certain men who, in a marked and special manner, have been in advance of their age, and in this century of intelligence and culture, of informed minds and reformed bodies— when the drift of all currents is setting towards grace and beauty, when the philosophy of the pessimist has been delivered over with other theatrical properties to the professional attitudinizer, and no longer deceives any one, when the amelioration of life and its conditions is in some sense the work of us all who have brains to think, hearts to feel, and pens to write with—even here and now, there are men who see deeper, whose intellectual instruments have been tuned into more perfect accord with the essential harmony of being. These are of that "bright Temple of Knowledge, which is the abode of the Hermetic adepts," as we learn from the physician's commentary on the *Triumphal Chariot of Antimony*. Plato to the age of Aristotle, though Aristotle prevailed in the schools; Plotinus to the Alexandrian period; Dionysius to the fourth century; Erigena to the scholastic epoch; Paracelsus to the sixteenth century; Saint-Martin to the ruddy day-star of the French Revolution; Emerson to America; Fichte to Germany; Berkeley to Ireland—all these men were the seers of their periods, and most accurately visionaries for the vulgar, whose intellectual sight penetrated above, beyond, beneath, the reach of common eyesight, and of common mental discernment. And all these men were Mystics. We too at the latest day of all the world, which is so many ages nearer to the day of Christ, for which every age has yearned, than was anything best and brightest in the times of Pythagoras or Trismegistus—we also are the seers of our century, in the sacred pride of truth and not in the conceit of vanity, and we do well to realize the fact. Unto you, therefore, O friends, who are joined with us unworthy in the bonds of transcendental knowledge, we address this book upon development—within and without—and upon the perfection of the man to come, because ye are partakers in advance of that sacrament of Light Everlasting which will ultimately be communicated to all in the great supper of the Lord. Distinguishing between the phenomenal and the real, ye are acquainted with the pathway by which man enters into real science. Transcendentalists in the super-substantial significance of that abused term, ye have distinguished between the phenomena called transcendental, and the divine and noumenal universe wherein abideth ever the withdrawn glory of the Absolute and the Ideal. Ye have outgrown the childhood of wonder, and ye have the freedom of the Fairyland of Knowledge. So, therefore, being magicians, ye no longer evoke spirits; being experimentalists, ye no longer seek understanding in tables; being mediums, ye are entranced no longer. The philosophical doctrines of the Light, and the interior religion of the Light, as they have been expounded by the children of the Light, who are the mystic seers of old, are the sources of your wisdom and the illuminators of your understanding. Ye look for "the time of the joy of the Philosophers," when the subject of philosophers has become white, clear, and shining, in the words of *The Code of Truth*. And ye look for the day of Christ, who is the eternal spring, the new world, the Paradise to come. We have crucified the Lord of Glory; we have violated his sacred person in the excesses of our youth; we have shamed him in the wantonness of our speech; we have forsaken him in the Gethsemane of the senses; we have denied him in the night of matter; we have crowned him with the thorns of our pleasures; we have scourged him with the scourges of our lusts; with the lust of the flesh, the lust of the eyes, and the pride of life, as with spears, have we pointed his path to Calvary; we have crucified him in the extinction of our aspirations; and all that is mortal of him has died terribly within us, and all that is immortal we have driven from our sight into heaven. But we have recalled him in the day of our necessity, when the scales fell from our eyes, when we knew the thing which we had done, and we have found that he is still with us, that he is still within us, whom we must manifest without us, and then we shall rest in him. This is now the bond of our faith, as it is the sum of our joy, and the end of our pilgrimage. Salutation then from the Centre of Peace to all peace-loving Mystics in this contentious age, to all who know and confess that there are many names, but one Lord, many attributions but one Spirit, one Comforter, one loving order which we know not how to name, the Power and the Glory, wherein the Closed Eye of the Unknown Darkness opens in benediction upon us, and we partake of the divine *Aniada* which are described in *The Path of Sol*, "the fruits and powers of Paradise and of Heaven." Even as in the mellow light of an autumn sunset, we behold the splendour fall; it invests the world about us; it glorifies the ripe tree of the life of wholesome fruit, and the vine which the Lord hath blessed. We have not to escape from Nature in order that we may find in Nature the one thing which we supposed to be above Nature, who is that bright spirit, the *Beata Pulchra*, celebrated in Rosicrucian romance, and adored in Rosicrucian ritual. The world holds all things that we can desire outside ourselves, and we

ourselves hold all things which we can desire beyond the world, not only the
Power and the Glory, not only the secret means of opening the "Closed Eye,"
not only the true knowledge concerning the else unknown darkness, not only
the fruits and powers of Paradise and of Heaven, but Heaven also and Paradise,
and that Christ who is above all Power and beyond all Glory. Now, there
was a time when it was impossible to write publicly concerning the philosophy
of the Mystics without being regarded as mad. There was afterwards another
time when one might indeed venture to speak, but it was necessary to feel the
way carefully, step by step, with the most guarded and clear definition, for it was
discoursing of an almost unknown subject, having a terminology which was to
all intents and purposes an unknown language. There is possibly no very real
cause for fervent gratitude because this time has also passed away, for if the
wheel of fashion, which is for ever turning, has brought us for a moment to an
upper point from which all men can see us, it is, after all, but the wheel of
fashion, and if it be the whim of the hour to talk Mysticism in our drawing-
rooms, as we have before talked æstheticism, this is no indisputable index of
a deep-seated desire after true knowledge; but it is easier to us at the moment,
for at the moment, till the wheel takes another turn, it is to some extent the
correct thing, and to some extent a test of culture, to be passingly conversant
with the speech of the Mystics, so that there is less than there was to define.
Perhaps, therefore, it is not necessary to answer once again the time-honoured
question: What is Mysticism? And why mystic? Almost every educated
person is now aware that Mysticism claims to be the synthesis of those arcane
methods and processes by which the divine in man is brought into immediate
communication with the divine in the universe. That is Mysticism, if we
regard it in its highest aspect, and if there be anybody still to enquire: Why is
Mysticism mystic? Why is the esoteric arcane? Why is the occult secret?
which questions are all about as likely to receive a satisfactory answer as are
some of another category, for example: Why is mustard hot? Why is sugar
sweet? Why is salt pungent? we shall answer: Because it is an essential part
of its nature, and it is really idle to prosecute the point further. We have
indicated times out of number in other places, as occasion continually required,
the fact that there are at least two kinds of secrecy which are connected with
Mysticism. There is one of a merely accidental character, which is concerned
with times and seasons, or the dictates of prudence at the moment. Thus, in the
long ages of persecution, when it was dangerous to differ from received opinions
on religion, the Mystic dissembled his knowledge and concealed his aims, and
acted in doing so completely within his rights, for it is legitimate at any time
to pursue a sacred intention under the veil of secrecy when the ignorance

and intolerance of the period prevent it from being pursued in public. In this sense, there is no need for Mysticism to be any longer a secret, and accordingly we find that it is being everywhere proclaimed by its professors—some think with too much zeal, and with the incautiousness of an almost extreme haste. We do not ourselves think so; we are inclined to the belief that in spite of the fickleness of fashion, and in spite of the shallowness of most modern interests, and in spite of the thin quality of conviction which is possible at best to the indifference of the world we live in, the time has come when we are called upon to speak as plainly and fully as the nature of our embassy will permit. Man, generally regarded, is as ripe and ready for the reception of truth as it is likely that the general man will be during either this or the next century.

There is another sense in which Mysticism is essentially secret, and, so far as can be seen, must continue ever to be secret from the multitude, as such. It is concerned with a sequence of experiences which is unknown to the ordinary man, and cannot be translated into the language of the ordinary man. When the Mystic speaks of the multitude and the ordinary man, he should not be understood to do so with the least accent of disparagement. We are all of us, to a very large extent—to a far greater extent than the profoundest sociologist has yet appreciated—the issue of our heredity and our environment; if some of us have a clearer vision, and some of us a stronger grasp, and some of us a further reach and a longer range—if, in a word, we are the issue of a more favourable environment, and of a higher quality of heredity, all this is no ground for presumption, but rather for a deeper sense of humility, since we are in a better position to understand how little we have made ourselves. "The subject of the Art," says Raymund, "requires its proper earth." Well, as we have affirmed, there is a range of experience which constitutes the field of Mysticism, and of which the Mystic cannot speak because there is no one to hear him. It is a distinct circle of experience, it is real and sure experience, it is the highest quality of experience, but it is only very imperfectly translatable in the language of normal experience. If there be any among the readers of this book who have an ardent love of Nature, an ardent appreciation of her beauty, and a consciousness that this Nature and this beauty can and do speak to them at times an intelligible language, though not in a tongue that can be rendered, and if ever they have tried to convey the sense of their impression to another who has no such love, no such appreciation, who has never heard that language, and if they have failed utterly in the attempt, as, in such a case, they must utterly fail, then will they understand Mysticism when it speaks of a sequence of experience which is a sealed and secret thing for all those who have never shared it. Not more withdrawn is the mystery which is named in *The*

Marvel of Marvels, the "work of divine wisdom," the composition of the Perfect Elixir. It is in like manner with those who love poetry, who have touched hearts with the essentially undefinable, yet sure and living spirit which is the energy and the life of poetry; if they have ever tried to communicate that love, and we may say that life, to another who is devoid of both, then again they will understand what is meant when it is said that, with every anxiety to communicate, there is a hindrance and a barrier for the Mystic which it is not possible to overcome, which exists in the nature of his hearers, which makes his language foreign and his thoughts inevitably arcane. "There is a golden branch," say the alchemists, "which must be consecrated to Proserpine before any one can enter into the Palace of Pluto." So far as it is possible to speak, we believe that every sincere Mystic is ready to say anything which is likely to be understood, nor in so acting does he desire to attitudinize as a being set apart from inferior creation, and possessed of a power of comprehension which lifts him into the royalty of understanding. He may be personally of opinion that there is only one circle of the sciences which is ultimately worth investigating; he may have accordingly investigated it, and, as a natural consequence, may have a special knowledge within that circle. But this does not of itself indicate the possession of an imperial intelligence. Other men have made greater progress in other branches of enquiry, and there are many subjects of useful research for which Mystics, as a class, are notoriously incapable. In speaking of transcendental subjects, the transcendentalist cannot too carefully avoid the suspicion of addressing his hearers from the edge of an exalted platform pitched high over earth and sea. His subject is sufficiently difficult without unnecessary difficulties occasioned by the pitfalls of vanity.

THE GATE OF THE SANCTUARY.

WE have heard of the charity of the new life, we have heard of the
Crown of Life, and in the first breath of inspiration, and in the
first influx of mystic love, we came among you, O illuminated
congregation, and laid upon the altar of your sanctuary, and upon the white
cloth of the altar, the chaplet or rosary of ISRAFEL, and the wreath of the
litanies of LUCASTA. Among the leaves and the flowers thereof we would
believe that there is still lingering a gentle fragrance which is sweet in the
nostrils of some of you who do worship and minister in that most interior
sanctuary. Perchance in the scrolls of those litanies, and among the song-
tablets there are hidden chords of melody, such as linger in deep sea shells and
in withdrawn recesses of cliff-honeycombing caverns, whereof the gates open on
the windy and solitary ocean. But the stars in the eyes of Israfel, and the
jewelled glittering of Lucasta, which are the Lights of the New Age, are the
transfiguring glory of the perfect man and of the perfect woman; Israfel and
Lucasta are types of the joy to come, of that joy whereupon our hearts are set,
and in such direction are unified with all law and all providence, with the
desire of the day and the night, and of the stars in their gyration—the delight
of the "day of compensation," attained by the writer of *Diana Unveiled*, in the
"Manifestation of the Hermetic Swan." Oh, not more faithfully does the dread,
grand sea follow upon the splendid pageant of the moon in her beauty, than do
our hearts, our thoughts, our dreams, for ever follow upon that vision of all
high thinking which is the end of universal development, till that which once
ranked as a mere law, discovered and expounded by science and expressed in
the imperfect language of the physical gnosis, is invested with a sacred aspect,
impinges upon the sphere of religion, and helps us itself to God by all that it
reveals to us of the God within ourselves!

> It comes, the beautiful, the free,
> The crown of all humanity.

We have heard of the religion of geology, and many other branches of
knowledge have been pressed into the service of theologies; but there is in all
truth a supreme religion of evolution, for holy, holy, holy is that law, working

within and without us, which develops us unto the full stature of the perfect man. It is a mode of progressive manifestation on the part of our latent possibilities, our potential divinity, and on the part of that indefinable quality of good will towards man which constitutes the favourable element of his external environment. In the vital and essential sense of an oft-misapplied term, does the religious principle enter into any conscious attempt to put in force that law, whereof the ultimate end is a perfect and permanent correspondence between God, man, and the universe.

"That is far distant, that is far removed," but there is no true way of life, or of blessedness, which leads in another direction. The higher certainty which transcends the narrow limits of evidence does ever, in our higher moments, show forth such end, and overwhelms the rational faculty by a decree of positive intuition; at the moment we know that it is true, that it is without error, that it is the sum of verity;

> We feel the wish across the mind
> Rush, like a rocket tearing up the sky,
> That we should join with God;

and yet if the wish should shape the will, if the will should create a way, and ever the divine magnet should draw the true metal of the desiring mind, far, oh, how far even then is the grand event, though the whole mechanism of the vast creation may be moving, with the man, to meet it. But in our present sphere of environment there is also a desired event, and here it may be truly said, that the perfection of humanity is the sole and only end. "Man," says the Quietist, St. Jure, "is the king and prodigy of all things visible." He is also the mystical Aristolochia, "the splendid white flower which is red inside, like the Stone of the Philosophers itself," as it is affirmed in the *Astrum Solis*. There is indeed no good begun which has ultimately another object. Is it the researches of science? They are for the amelioration or instruction of mankind. Is it the aspirations of religion? They are nourished for his interior exaltation. Is it the glory of God, which theology dreams can be increased in its accidental aspect? Then man is magnified in a process which institutes a peculiar relation with Deity, and represents him as an instrument in the extension of divine beatitude. Is it, once more, the poet's vision? Then, assuredly, its object is to beautify the life of man, to transfigure his environment, to idealize his form of subsistence, to actualize, about him, and in him, all that is most transcendental in the transcendent creations of sublimed intelligence. The "splendour of wit which springs a thunderbolt," the "satire which burns and purifies the world," the "true aim," and the "fair purpose," all forms which thought may take, all principles which may energize action, all laws which may rule in expression, exist and act with man for their end, as he is also their agent. From whatever point on the horizon of possibility we may elect to start, we must end in man.

In a particular and eminent way the transcendental philosophy deals with the one, universal, and eternal subject, for ever beginning and never ending, in its highest aspect; and in this book of philosophical transcendency we have laboured, O Sons of the Doctrine, to focus all that has been conceived and dreamed under the prophetic influence of the "far hyaline of light" concerning the grandeur and beauty and perfection of the supreme summit of evolution whereon Man shall one day stand; to enquire also by what processes it may be possible to attain that beatified subsistence. But there is the race, and there are the individuals who compose it, and our mystic research is concerned with both, with the race here manifested, insphered here among the fluxional pageantry and emblazonment of the phenomenal world, yet not less with the permanent individualities that lay aside ever and continually their vanishing personal part, their conditioned and exterior manifestation, and are withdrawn into the noumenal world, into the realities which subtend, into the sphere of the Heaven of Paracelsus—the eternal "quintessence." Of them what?

> Travellers, in what realm afar,
> In what planet, in what star,
> In what vast aerial space,
> Shines the light upon their face?

To both sections of the supreme question Mysticism can offer reverently the philosophic breadth and fulness of a perfect answer; it offers what all can test who will, what all can attempt who dare, what all can achieve who try. For the work of this magic all men are natural magicians, who, at least, are children of aspiration. So is it for the children of aspiration alone that we indite this book, which, in abasement of ashen humility, is presented as some attempt towards a rectilineal way unto the realization of Christ on earth, and on the plane of the timeless towards the communication of Nirvana in Christ. We offer it to them alone, for they only will comprehend the method, having been illuminated with the royal light of violet which is suffused in the superior heaven of mind. They also will understand the position which, as a Mystic, we borrow from the aureoline inspiration of a cardinal poet of the Teutons, who said, "Life is not a dream, but it ought to become one, and perhaps will." Life also is not a romance, but it can be transfigured by the spirit of romance. Life, finally, is not a poem, but the demiourgos of the life to come will breathe upon the waters of existence, and they will run in song. On that day there will be a marriage of the Bridegroom and the Bride "among the lilies and pomegranates of the Paradise of God." So will the children of aspiration appreciate the appeal to the poet:

> Bard of the future! Master-Prophet! Man
> Of men, at whose strong girdle hang the keys
> Of all things.

Who but the masters of songcraft have heard amidst the vague vastness of the organ measures which reverberate in the auditorium of futurity, those flute-notes, pitched high above the hearing of unawakened ears, of that new song which is the setting of the new name that no man knoweth? But we are Mystics, and we aim at the realization of poetry, at the concrete manifestation of dream, at the attainment of the ideal state.

At this point, then, we may fittingly plan the groundwork and fundamentals of the philosophic edifice which it is our purpose to erect.

The creation of the perfect man can be accomplished solely by correspondence with evolution, which is the abiding law of life.

The law of evolution may be subdivided into—

The laws in the development of physical beauty and perfection.

The laws in the development of the higher morality.

The laws in the development of intellectual aspiration, and the realization of intellectual ideals.

The laws in the development of the spiritual principle in the direction of the perfect rest and the perfect activity in God.

To accomplish the end of evolution in the physical order, it is necessary to transmute environment.

To accomplish the end of evolution in the moral order, it is necessary to transfigure conditions.

To accomplish the end of evolution in the intellectual order, it is necessary to derive illumination from the fontal source of light.

To accomplish the end of evolution in the spiritual order, it is necessary to know God.

The true, certain, and absolute knowledge of God is not of faith; it is not to be distilled from the substance of things hoped for, nor to be construed out of the evidence of things not seen; it is the manifestation of divine subsistence to the sensations of the concealed man, or third interior being.

For the purposes of this book it will be useful to regard man as possessed of a tetradic nature, though it should be understood that in this, as in other classifications, the distinction is for the sake of convenience, is admittedly of a conventional character, and is interpreted in a fluidic sense.

There is the exterior manifestation on the plane of time and space, which constitutes the phenomenal humanity, and is the result of a contact between our least or impermanent portion and the conditions of the phenomenal universe.

There is that which, in the philosophical order, is called the moral man, which is the first interior nature, and is the result of a contact with the elementary laws of life.

There is the intellectual personality, which is the outcome of a partial immersion in the veridic light. This is the second interior nature.

There is, finally, the spiritual being, which is the third interior, and the Concealed Man. It is the radical seat of reality; it is that portion which is most remote from the phenomenal, and is therefore the least realized in physical life; but it is also the side of our being which has a contact with infinity. It is the Supreme Monad in the microcosmic world which rules the inferior Triad, and the Triad must be absorbed, permeated, and dissolved by that Monad to attain the end of evolution.

This unification of man must be accomplished in each of his natures by a parallel process of evolution, under proper natural law.

INTRODUCTION.

THE CREDENTIALS OF MYSTICAL PHILOSOPHY.

I.

THE AGNOSTIC STANDPOINT AS THE THRESHOLD OF MYSTICISM.

THOSE persons who admit that the great problems of life are insoluble, and that every attempt to extract some intelligible answers to the eternal questions of the sphinx, ultimately proves to be inadequate, more especially in the case of religious systems which are based upon arbitrary revelation, not infrequently find themselves in a position of considerable logical difficulty. They still recognize—possibly still feel—the necessity of religion, for "deep in the heart of all men," says Böhme, "there is the hunger after the *Mysterium Magnum;*" they are still, it may be, conscious of spiritual aspiration, are intellectually aware that religion is inseparably bound up with morality, and that the secularization of morals has failed. Thus, they are constrained to accept what is false in the interest of what is good. For the practical morality which regulates social life, the underlying sense which is the foundation of ethics, the aspiration which elevates existence, illuminates the world with beauty, and can alone read any message of significance into the chaotic puzzle of existence, have acquired their shape and direction as much as they have obtained their credentials from dogmatic religion in chief. In the enormous majority of instances, it is to the influence of authoritative teaching on the things of the spirit, and on the mysteries of that world which underlies the sphere of the phenomenal,

> Where day is darkness to the starry soul,

that the birth of individual endeavour towards the perfection of the unattained must be traced.

The inseparable bond between religion and social morality was recognized by the infidel Diderot when he educated his daughters as Catholics; but his mind, which was thoroughly representative of the coarseness of French materialism on the eve of the Great Revolution, was probably insensible to the higher pleadings of aspiration for the maintenance of the nobility of religious ·

beliefs. Eliphas Levi, most finished of the French Mystics, who, having completed the conquest of his passions, found his aspirations transfigured into
emotions which themselves were passionate in their nature—Eliphas Levi,
Mystic by aspiration and desire, intellectually a complete sceptic—after ex-
ploring the most withdrawn penetralia of the occult sciences, could discover
within the whole range of Hermetics nothing which could express his aspirations so fully as the "sacred and beautiful kingdom of the sky, Jesus the Man-
God, and Mary the Mother of God, Angels of Fra Angelico, Saints of the
Golden Legend, Virgins of the Paradise of Dante"; in a word, the entire scope
of the "severe and incorruptible dogma which distributes the elect upon the
golden ladder of the hierarchy"; while the *haute convenance* which actuated him
in his pretentious submissions to the faith of his childhood had its source in
anxiety to avert the social chaos which would ensue upon a definite disruption
of religious beliefs.

With others of the class we have mentioned, with those, namely, who have
sufficient intellectual strength to keep faith with the truth under all issues,
though for them there is no "invention of verity," as it was understood in the
wisdom of Geber, the "adept of the eighth age"; who not even for a moment
can permit themselves to palter with it, whether for the life of individual emotions, however precious, or for the safety of society at large, it bechances occasionally that a certain forlorn consolation is derived even from the inscrutable
nature of the mystery which involves life and her problems. Hope, destitute
before the closed door of the Unknowable, minds which can glimpse no light
beneath "the Closed Eye of the Unknown Darkness," hearts for whom there is
no "open entrance" to the "Palace of the King," take refuge in the darkness
itself as a promise of the dawn to come, in the impassable solidity of the barrier,
and, with the chief martyr of alchemy, permit "their hearts to fill with joy for
the good of all Israel"; and though

> On the tideless seas in the middle hour
> Of the savage and measureless night,

they are now driven hardly, yet upon the further side of the great water they
"look to see the good things of the Lord in the Land of the Living."

Now, this consolation, forlorn as it is, has a firm philosophical basis. It
illuminates the agnostic philosophy with a gleam of light and hope. It is, in
fact, a key of knowledge which opens the door of that philosophy, and behind
the last conclusions of material science, we receive the first message of Transcendental Religion. Were it otherwise, the prospect before us would be dark
indeed! Were it otherwise, the wisdom of this world would indeed be "full of
sad experience"! And such in the ultimate has it ever been to those who

possess not this key, which to the *Radix Philosophorum et Mundi* is as a *Lampas Vitæ et Mortis*, even that lamp which was trimmed at *Lugdunum Batavorum* by an alchemist-scrutator of Nature at the end of the seventeenth century. Let us regard it for a moment in this aspect. Surrounded by an insoluble mystery, and being a mystery also to ourselves; unable to say whence we come or whither we are going; ignorant of the purpose for which we are placed here; ignorant whether we are working out that purpose or frustrating it; ignorant, moreover, whether our present environment does indeed serve any purpose—dark, dark, dark upon the one circle of science with which it is really worth while to be acquainted—is it any wonder that a sensual philosophy arises, and cries out to us: "Take no thought for the morrow, whether you die or live—live only in to-day! No one can count upon to-morrow!" And the sensual philosophy is heard, for it speaks to us with an appealing melody; consciously or not, the larger part of all the world conforms its life to the text, lives as it can and may, dies as it does and must:

> Scornful, and strange, and sorrowful, and full
> Of bitter knowledge.

And, by the God of our life, we take it that with that great band of black night encircling our one little space of pale daylight, it would seem well if we could narrow our natures down to the breadth of our sunbeam, taking delight as we are able while we pass along that one mellow shaft which shoots straight from the unknown whence to the unknown whither! Most of us, after our own fashion, and at one or other time, have made the experiment, but we have been tricked without mercy in consequence; because in material life, as such, there is insufficient to repay the liver. The story seems too old for repeating, and we can say nothing new about it, but it is here, it is in our midst, it is true, it is our daily experience, it is the sum of all experience, it is the quintessence of all philosophy, and it does not need books to elaborate it. Life, except as a preparation for something higher, deeper, broader, beyond it, is ultimately worthless to its possessor. "If thou hast not the secret of the Stone," says the *Golden Violet*, "the Mercury shall be only thy poison." And again, "the Matter of the Wise is worthless and less than nothing for him who is ignorant of the regimen of the Quintessence." It is a small stream, passing down through sand and through rock. Does it make for the great open ocean—deep, urgent, flashing, with an infinite capacity of strength and life? Why then, good! If not, if it be to stagnate in morass or in marsh, or if it be ultimately lost in a cesspool, then better the wand of Nature had never struck that rock which was its source, high up in the Land of the Morning. *Vanitas, inquam, vanitatis ubique reperta est, et omnia miseria et vanitas*, says the Rosicrucian adept and apologist. It is true, it is without error, and it is the sum of all verity. Sensuality at the moment cannot feel it, joy denies it, youth comprehends it not, love defies it, strength is ready to do battle with it; it has a thousand enemies, and no friends, for it is detested by those who profess it; but the doctrine of vanity is true, and it survives everything. We may erase it from our dictionaries, and purge it from our thoughts; we may leave no space in our life for *ennui;* we may open no door to satiety; but it is written ultimately in the last testament of us all. We do not know anything in life which, for itself, is worth achievement; for if we seek knowledge, as an agnostic, it is only that we prefer the quintessence of bitterness to the gross flavour of the coarser cup. It is certain that the wealth of all the world would be over-valued at ten years of the struggle to purchase it. There is fame truly—"the splendid spectrum of immortal fame"—which is counted as a lesser degree of vanity; but whether sought at the cannon's mouth, or at the pen's point, sooner or later "the bubble reputation bursts," the kaleidoscope takes another turn, and our brilliant pageant is forgotten. Art and charity remain, but art, God knows, is not happiness, and the greatest art master of all the modern world has told us that it is only a refuge. Charity is another refuge—it is a method of escape from ourselves, for if we speak as an agnostic, we would say that the highest form of charity is to teach men how they may die easily and quickly, and not to prolong misery by its amelioration. If anyone should discourse to us of duty, we would answer, as an agnostic, with Lucretius: What is Duty? and should receive in return the reply which was given to that later question: What is Truth? For there is the region of law as there is that of fact, but outside these spheres we know nothing of truth and duty, nor is there a living voice than can tell us, until we are acquainted with the Daughter of the Voice—Bath Kôl, the mystic —who speaks only to the Sons of the Doctrine. "I testify unto you," says Pythagoras, or the adept who assumes his name, "that there is a voice in the silence which comes *postquam mundi clamores*, and is heard by the true chemist; it instructs him in the desire of the wise."

Concerning the value of life, this is how it strikes an agnostic. Now, is there anywhere an error in the judgment which makes void the entire calculation? Yes, it is the old error which has placed a positive construction on an essentially negative position. There is a way of escape, and, at the same time, there is but one way, and it goes only in one direction, because there is but one method of interpretation which can read value and interest into life. And that is the construction of eternity. There is only one sun which can shine through the midnight of mystery. "I have beheld the sun at midnight and I follow the Path of Sol. The radiance of his light is on my face, and mine is the way of truth," says Artemis in the parable of Maier.   Let us take the problem at first from its lowest standpoint.   Agnosticism defines strictly the limit of our science, and suppose for a moment that it is indeed right when it affirms that there is no possible avenue to knowledge, no penetrable point, beyond that limit.   Well, even then, where there is no room for knowledge, there may, as we have seen, be at least a space for hope; nor is it an unreasonable hope, though it is one that no science can encourage, because there is no science that can throw light. But the doctrine which defines for us the limit of our knowledge can deal only with the instruments of knowledge with which it is itself equipped.   What if there be another instrument besides the five senses and the thinking brain? What if there be

> A higher faculty than reason? . . .
> . . . Of brightest revelative power,
> As the snow-headed mountain riseth o'er
> The lightning and applies itself to heaven;
> A faculty which meaning gives to time;
> Sanctity to man's kingliest blood.   .

That is the contention of the Mystics, and it is with the extension and development of such a faculty that their science deals.   For the moment, however, we may be contented with the lower ground of reasoning.

The hopes and aspirations which are concerned with the survival of the soul after that separation of the gross from the subtle—wherein, says Rulandus, is contained the whole art of alchemy—which has been falsely described as the greatest of all changes, but which may have been paralleled many times before in the history of individual evolution, and if so, on any analogical theory of psychology, will be repeated many times after in the progress from state to state through the golden chain of existence; the desire of a world which can surround its inhabitants with an environment corresponding to the dreams and conceptions of our highest and clearest moments; the hunger and thirst after justice which do not have their fill here, through the imperfections of the human vessel, and the consequent yearning for that far country which is illuminated by the Sun of Righteousness—these and all other aspirations towards "the unseen, unknown," towards

> The great world of light that lies
> Behind all human destinies,

towards the life which is beyond life, the goal of perfection, the mountain of the Lord, are aspirations which may be legitimately cherished in complete independence of every creed, and of any determinate revelation.   Dream, aspiration, and desire are the monopoly of no theology and of no formal religion; they are

3

the leaping outward of what is best in man at his own best towards the possibilities which are outside experience; for us they are evidence and index of the
splendour and scope of the possible which ever is developing into the actual,
and the expectation of their fulfilment is grounded on facts in our ignorance
which have been strangely misread by philosophers, who insist on the strict
limitation of our entire range of knowledge to the region of phenomena alone,
and while positive in proclaiming their materialism, forbid us to hope that we
shall ever become acquainted with the ultimate nature of the material world.
In admitting the truth of these statements, so far as the ordinary methods of perception are concerned, but admitting also that there is another method leading up
to the *Magnesia Catholica*, and the divine visions of Khunrath, it is astonishing
indeed that their inevitable outcome should be so completely overlooked.   If
the ultimate nature of matter be to us a sealed book, if no particle of evidence
be forthcoming to establish so much as a correspondence by analogy between
that substance which underlies, and this flux of appearances, where is the value
of our great scientific disputes on the connection between matter and mind?
Surely the materialism which would identify them is as barren a squabble of
the schools as the theology which is bent upon establishing an eternal division
between them.   The terms of a settlement are totally outside our capacities.   If
we are in ignorance of the nature of mind, and if matter in its ultimate be unknown to us, how immeasurable then is the folly which denies the existence of
mind apart from organic structure—separated from that which is material—
affirming that it is impossible for something in its nature unknown to exist
independently of another thing also in its nature unknown!   How commiserable
is the shallowness in radical thinking which has assumed to itself the name of
materialist to indicate the possession of a positive and comprehensive gnosis,
undisturbed by dreams and imaginings, when the supposition of positive knowledge on a subject so completely unsearchable is the wildest license of dreaming,
and among the most fond of all possible imaginings!

   It is evident that the philosophy which denies us an absolute science has
ipso facto annihilated its claim to affirming or denying anything in the region of
the fundamental; and, having regard to the mystery which surrounds us, it is
in no respect more improbable that our aspiration after Goethe's "serene and
solemn Spirit Land," after the "rich world unseen," the "Mystic Harmony" of
Lagneus, where the according wisdom of the Hermetic Philosophers is like the
melody of "a choir invisible," and after "the curtain'd realm of spirits," have a
foundation of truth and an avenue through death to realization, than is the
counterview.   Everywhere encompassed by a hopeless and insoluble problem,
nothing can be rejected as impossible, nor can anything be accepted as of pre-

ponderance in the scale of probability. Here is the legitimate agnosticism, un-adulterated by the positive element, and completely dissimilar from the scientific licence of fraudulent dogma which masquerades in that philosophical name.

If in the face of this utter discouragement, this stony indifference which is imprinted on the lineaments of the sphinx, it is possible for hopes and aspirations to survive at all, then to those with which we are concerned the tolerance of an extra-human impartiality is extended in rigid silence. It is evidence of their strength that under such circumstances they can and do survive, and it is curious to note how, from the conflicting significance of the contradictory message of life, they derive a certain nourishment. The beauty of existence, the loveliness of imperfect humanity, the advanced degree of moral grandeur which exists in the midst of so much unfavourable environment, the good that is found in all, the extraordinary evolution of misfortune into joy, the fruit unto beneficence which is produced by the greatest calamities, occasionally in entire independence of the disposition of the sufferer, the possible perfectibility of all men, are indications of a discernible movement in the direction of "some far-off, divine event, towards which the whole creation moves"—a progress as slow as the motion of our planetary system through the space of stars, but still certain, still faintly traceable—

> On to the bound of the waste,
> On to the City of God—

the *Paradisus Aureolus Hermeticus*, bright as the City of Hud, which Figulus, the blessed Master, beheld from afar, and was content.

The quality of undefined faith which a sense of this progress begets in the mind is perhaps at best but the "thin optimism" which ministered to the spiritual necessities of Emerson, but it is peaceful and permanent, and the world is transfigured under its influence by a slow and equable process. The insoluble problems are informed by the gentle lustre of hopes devoid of extravagance and aspirations exempted from the many errors of enthusiasm. Consciously or otherwise, the agnostic passes towards the Mystic, not by accretions to his philosophy, but because, under the guidance of that philosophy, he is emancipated from the bondage of words. Unobsessed by the nightmare of materialism, he does not see matter everywhere; uninvolved by the dreams of the spiritualist, he does not see spirit everywhere; but behind the veil of appearances he intellectually recognizes the Grand Reality—the *Sapientia Dei* of Mercurius—which is the source of appearances; he is aware that there is the same foundation, the same universal truth at the bottom of all manifestations, and, in this sense, like the fairy-gifted poet of "Phantastes," he "beholds the same thing everywhere." Now, that there is but one substance infinitely differentiated in the universe is a principle which is the heart of Buddhism, philosophically considered, of Spinozism, of the system of Berkeley, and of pure Mysticism.

Then, seeing that within the whole range of the phenomenal universe, there is nothing which seems to have struck its roots more deeply into the underlying reality than the manifestation which is the conscious mind, it is but one step forward to seek the reality within, and another fundamental principle of Mysticism is at once developed. It is then, so to speak, that the one thing permanent looks forth from the eyes of man upon the universe of illusions, and the appearances with which he is surrounded group themselves gradually into symbols which become truly "shows that show," parables to interpret, the language of the Mystic writ large upon the entire Cosmos. In the mantle of this poetic influence, under the magic of this roseate idealism, which dissolves all things in weird dream light, the thinker at this point occasionally drifts into avowed Mysticism. In some instances he becomes absorbed in the interior life, like Saint-Martin, the *philosophe inconnu*, Saint-Martin, *qui se cacha toute sa vie*, and then indeed he has entered upon the way of life and benediction, the *semita rectitudinis de Alchemia*. In others, he is drawn to the external, and begins among the phenomena of modern psychology the long search for the soul, which he pursues amidst sorrow, toil, and disappointment, ultimating commonly in the dissatisfaction of a negative conclusion. Of course, it is only in rare instances that a solid conviction is attained. The agnostic, even when modified by Mysticism, frequently remains to the end a "thin" optimist, condemned to reservation of judgment upon every vital question, and conscious to keenness of the utter incapacity of any negative philosophy to provide vertebræ for morality on the collapse of dogmatic beliefs. Thin optimism is not a gospel, undefined aspirations and indeterminate hopes are insufficient to humanity at large; if he decline to identify himself with doctrines in which he has ceased to believe, he at least will lift no hand against them, having nothing to offer in their place, and being sadly aware that they are less inadequate than his own vague uncertainties.

This is no mere fancy sketch. It epitomizes the history of a section of radical thinkers who have, metaphorically speaking, discovered the universal dissolvent, the Hermetic "Liquor of Alkahest," which reduces to philosophic water its own vessel as well as all other substances, and leaves nothing solid in its neighbourhood. Their history is to some extent coïncident with the history of all who have come to recognize that old world answers are no longer adequate to questions which in modern times have assumed a new aspect.

Now, the radical agnosticism, to which reference has been made above, is a philosophical principle which within its own lines is impregnable, and as it is a principle, moreover, which lends itself readily to Mysticism, we regard it as a preface or prolegomena to all transcendental metaphysics. And seeing that, in some or other form, the personal element is rarely absent from any earnest work, we need make no apology whatever when we explicitly desire to be included among the number of those persons whose original religious impressions have been profoundly modified by the action of this philosophy; but the aspirations which are compatible therewith have led to the extension of our researches into the fields of experimental psychology; so have we come to discover in mystic doctrine a certain arcane door which opens into the dim highways of the interior life; and have penetrated a sufficient distance to perceive that there is a world within us wherein those aspirations may be realized.   When the mystery of the universe is contemplated through the mesmeric medium of a moonlit night upon the sea; when the imagination is dilated under the spiritual influence of Nature, and the mind's mood is unified with the world's mood, it is then by a natural transition that the Mystery is transfigured into Mysticism, and the aspiration of the soul towards that beautiful reality which is behind this sheeny veil of shining sea and star-sprent heaven above; the light which is behind this tawny light "of the orb'd moon aureoline" is the aspiration of the veritable Mystic towards the "sovereign balsam," the "saphiric medicine," and the Grand Totality.   Thanks be to God for those moments of inspiration and of unclouded insight!   Thanks be to God for those brief electric contacts with the inmost heart and centre of real being! He who has never known them has never truly lived.   Who counts their revelations as delusion is devoid of all faculty for truth!

Now, pure Mysticism, understood in its proper sense, is unencumbered by arbitrary dogma; it aims at the union of that which is highest in man with that which is supreme in the universe, and its methods are strictly experimental.   But it claims to be in possession of an instrument of transcendental cognition which is unknown to modern science.   The nature of this instrument will be delineated in its proper place.   Here it is only needful to notice the logical elaboration of the possibility in so far as it affects the agnostic philosophy, and this chapter may not unfittingly conclude with a tabulated resumption of our mystic claim in its connection with the teachings of a fashionable and accredited philosophy, which regards itself as radical in character.

(a) Agnostic doctrine admits that there is a reality which subtends all appearances—in other words, that the universe is a phenomenal manifestation, which covers a concealed *noumen*.

(*b*) But man also is an appearance, a manifestation, and a part of the phenomenal world. He, like all other phenomena, must have, therefore, a reality which subtends, and behind the outward man there must also be a hidden *noumen.*

(*c*) It is unnecessary here to affirm that there are many *noumens,* or that there is one *noumen,* but if there be any path by which man can enter into the noumenal world "that is best which lies the nearest," and the nearest side of approach must be the one which subtends himself. Within ourselves, therefore, is the way of truth.

(*d*) There is another doctrine, more ancient and deep-seeing than agnosticism, which almost since time began has bidden us seek the truth within.

(*c*) This is not an unreasonable doctrine, and, if names be anything, it possesses a philosophic name, it is the Doctrine of the Interior Life, or of the Life Within.

(*f*) It is said that in adopting the precepts of this doctrine it is possible to extend our knowledge beyond the limits of the phenomenal world, by bringing into exercise another instrument of knowledge.

(*g*) This instrument is placed in the noumenal part of our being.

(*h*) All knowledge is acquired hardly, and this which is the most recondite form of all knowledge is acquired more hardly than any other, but it can be attained. Here we shall do well to remember the words of Thomas Norton, the English "perfect-master," who affirms with melancholy precision,

> That of a million hardly three
> Were e'er ordained for Alchemy.

(*i*) It is fundamentally possible to all, but it is practically open to few because of the invalidating character of most human environment in respect of the search for it.

(*k*) There is no positive penalty attached to its neglect, but there is the indirect penalty of privation from a grand possible good.

(*l*) There is no essential danger in the quest, because "we exalt our souls in seeking," but there are possible dangers which accompany experiments in unknown regions, and these are of sufficient magnitude to justify the custodians of this knowledge from publishing the actual methods of the experiment—the *noumenal praxis,* which is Meurdrack's "Light of Chemistry," the "process of the stone," and the *practica operis magni.*

(*m*) At the same time, no effort would appear to have been spared to direct attention to the nature of the experiment, and the results which are obtained when it is conducted to a successful issue.

(*n*) From the inherent nature of the agnostic doctrine, it is *à priori* reasonable to regard the mystic doctrine as a possible source of light.

(*o*) The mystic doctrine is supported by facts in the phenomenal world which are unexplained by the theorems of physical science, as well as by the universal faith and the universal aspiration of humanity.

(*p*) It is at least an intellectual refuge, and as such is worthy to be compared with the art of Goethe—"Art still has truth; take refuge there!"

II.

Mysticism as a New Basis of Demonstrative Faith.

"THERE is a sublime sorrow of the ages as of the lone ocean." These are the words of a Mystic, and the sorrow to which reference is made can be none other than the desolation of the everlasting soul, grieving after its unfulfilled aspirations, after its unachieved prospects, after hopes which have not been realized, and after the truth which it has failed to attain.

> For what
> Can spirit, dissevered from the great one, God,
> Feel but a grievous longing to rejoin
> Its infinite, its author, and its end?

But there is also a divine joy of the ages, which is like the jubilation of that primeval morning, "the bridal of the earth and sky," when the morning stars sang together, and all the Sons of God uttered a joyful shout. This joy is the beatification of the everlasting soul, beatified in achieved aspiration, in fulfilled ends, in the crowning glory of attained truth. There is no aspiration, there is no ambition, there is no purpose to compare with the search after truth. It is the "wise man's crown," the way of the "temple of wisdom," and the "glory of the Rosy Cross." To some natures the necessity for truth is as imperative as the necessity for love. In some natures the passion for truth is more strong than any physical passion. Whatsoever the direction it may take, whatsoever the end in view, we may be sure that the search is noble because the truth is always good. "A familiar acquaintance with the different branches of knowledge has taught me," says the alchemist, Edward Kelly, "this one thing, that nothing is more ancient, excellent, or more desirable than truth, and whoever neglects it must pass his whole life in the shade." There are times and there are seasons which are more appropriate than others for the communication of certain truths, and knowledge out of season may be dangerous, but the truth is always good. There is not a branch of enquiry which can be legitimately included in the search after truth, that, when properly regarded, is not a holy thing. There is a sanctity of learning which is the splendour of the beauty of truth, and even the methods and processes of science by which we discover and learn, have that sacredness of sentiment which attaches to the vestments of a saint.

The pursuit of knowledge is, of course, undertaken with every variety of intention, and for ends innumerable. It is undertaken for gold and for glory, but it is never more illustriously prosecuted than when it is followed for its own sake. Next to the corporal and spiritual works of mercy, and equal perhaps with these because it partakes of the nature of them both, a single-minded and unselfish research into any unknown region is perhaps the noblest undertaking which is possible to intellectual man. It is the "grand key" of Artephius, the *clef majeure de sapience et de la science des secrets de la Nature.*

And yet within the limits of the phenomenal, which are the limits of all ordinary knowledge, and of all physical science, there is something unsatisfying in the pursuit. Could we purchase the world and all its treasures, the Mystics assure us, that, without God, the heart of man would still go hungering and unsatisfied. In like manner, the intellect may become saturated with knowledge, and yet find no rest from its craving, because all its investigations of phenomena have not brought it into contact with the absolute Truth and Reality, which underlie appearances; and as long as it falls short of the absolute, even when it denies the absolute, the truth-seeking intellect can find no peace. Moreover, there is a transitory nature about all earthly knowledge, and in the exaggerations of ascetic theology it has frequently been regarded as vanity precisely on this account. Whatsoever we learn in time, we, of course, hope is so much experience and so much inheritance for eternity, but from the philosophical standpoint, this pleasing conception may not be of higher value than the sentimental belief in the future reunion of friends who have been separated by life and death.

But there is one subject, or rather there is a class of subjects, which transcends the phenomenal world, which transcends the things of time, and, when judged from the highest standpoint, seems alone .worth investigating. The subjects to which we refer are the supernal questions connected with God and the Soul. And so the seeker after truth, if he be worthy of his high calling, and a lawful child of aspiration, turns almost instinctively from the transitory to that *apud quem non est transmutatio nec vicissitudinis obumbratio*—wherein there is no change or shadow of vicissitude—to the positive and the imperishable.

Now, as it is so ordained, the most important of all knowledge, as already hinted, is that precisely which is most difficult to reach. We are told that the seeker after God must believe that God is, and that He recompenses those who search Him out. At the same time, it is certain that to many persons who at the present day have undertaken this quest after the Absolute, there has been no way opened up. The *Liber Benedictus* remains a *Liber Mutus,* and a shell of adamant encloses the "sophic nucleus." The paths of faith are many, but the way of knowledge is one, and there is no open entrance to the closed Palace of the King.

Is there any need that we should speak more plainly? When the intellect turns from the phenomenal, and endeavours to know God and the Soul, it casts about it for an avenue of knowledge, and in most cases casts about it in vain. There are churches, creeds, and bibles; if anyone be prepared to believe, there are doctrines, and dogmas, and articles, which are ready to shape his faith, and he may take his choice among every variety of teaching. But if anyone desire to *know*, there is no church or creed that can help him, and, other resources failing, he is brought to a peremptory standstill at the threshold of his grand design. The fatal distinction between faith and knowledge paralyzes action; the materials for search are wanting; the edifice of aspiration collapses; the phenomenal has ceased to satisfy; to the reality there is no approach. The result in most cases is a blank agnosticism, which frequently becomes aggressive. In a few this same agnosticism is leavened, as we have seen, by a faint element of optimistic hope, which finds a certain forlorn consolation in the utter darkness and irretrievable uncertainty, because there is no test of the limits of possibility in the midst of our infinite ignorance. In others, less intellectually robust, the desire after positive truth, combining with an arrested activity which cannot even begin to seek it, begets a certain embittered morbidity concerning this "little brood" of earth, which is so impossibly ambitious of the sky. And others, yet again, become engaged in diseased self-analysis; they attribute their personal failure not so much to the desperation of the design as to their private unworthiness, and lament that their life and its level has fallen short of the elevation of their purpose, as if the highest table-land of human existence could approach the Himalayas of aspiration.

There are many earnest persons who believe themselves to have attained the consolation of positive truth in the message of modern spiritualism. In that revelation they believe the age of faith has been transfigured into the age of knowledge, and indeed it would be difficult to esteem at too high a rate the extent to which it has enlightened this century. It has proved to us that, outside of the visible world, there are other intellectual orders, and that the dead of earth are there. But, of necessity, it has its limitations. Like physical science it deals, for the most part, with the phenomenal alone; and though by the mediation of phenomena we may have evidence of the worlds beyond, we must transcend the phenomenal and the physical if we would really know those worlds.

The methods of this transcension are offered us by one science alone—and that is the science of the Mystics. It has come to heal our intellectual diseases, to open our spiritual eyes, to illuminate our interior darkness, like the parabolic "morning" of alchemy. It cries to the aspiration which has not escaped defilement, but has still been sincere and true: "Though ye have lien among the pots, yet shall ye be as the wings of a dove that is covered with silver wings, and her feathers like gold." And for him who, without finding rest or truth, has discovered that the search after the Absolute is, in the words of Eliphas Levi, "the death of the joys of earth, and of the pleasures of sensual life," and has suffered intellectually without much of moral lapse, for him it has also a message: "Oh, thou afflicted, tossed with tempest and not comforted, behold I will lay thy stones with fair colours, and lay thy foundations with sapphires, and I will make thy windows of agates, and thy gates of carbuncles, and all thy borders of precious stones." It is old and it is new—this Voice. There were prophets before John the Baptist, and the Spirit of Christ was present in the holy men of old before ever Christ came in flesh. So also there was spiritualism ages before the other world first knocked for admission at the doors of Rochester, and, in the same manner, mystic thought and action almost antedate history. The philosophy of the Mystics may or may not acquaint us with a solution of all problems, but it can provide us with such a measure of positive knowledge as will constitute a demonstrative faith, which is a faith that is founded on warrantable inference derived from certain fact, from fact that can always be verified, that does not belong to an irrecoverable past, does not depend upon the authenticity of ancient documents, is not of the historical order, and does not in itself require the gift of faith.

It is a matter of interior, intimate, and indubitable personal experience, which, if not within the reach of all, is, at least, possible to all who are intellectually in need thereof.

Mysticism, we may therefore affirm, is the one avenue of knowledge concerning the absolute of being; and in this claim there is nothing narrow, intolerant, or exclusive, from the simple fact that there are no other claimants. It is open to anyone to reject it on the ground that we cannot know; it is open to anyone to be indifferent about positive truth; but if that truth exist, and there be a known way of its attainment, then Mysticism is that way. It is the "metaphysical foundation" of the "hidden chemistry"; it is that art both ancient and infinite, to which those who would conceal it have "pinned the narrow name of *chemia;*" it is Nature's explication concerning the "sephirotic heaven" of Steebe, and Sidrach's "chief fountain of science." If indeed there be a *Hortulus Hermeticus*, may that marvellous virgin of Stolcius, that "lady the wonder of her kind," who "from morn to even" ministers in the parabolic garden, lead us with her white hands to the concealed flower, and instruct us in the "Romance of the Rose."

III.

MYSTICISM A PRACTICAL SCIENCE.

WE have seen that the search after positive truth can be pursued only in one direction. There is one only system, a sole philosophy, one single science which has ever claimed to possess or dispense it. That system, that philosophy, that science is Mysticism, which professes to endow its disciples with a method of direct intercourse with the spirit of God. It is no longer a question of astral bodies and of astral shells, of earth-bound spirits, or of unprogressed disembodied humanities. It is not even a question of the souls of just men made perfect, nor yet of creating correspondence with those exalted hierarchies of existence whose altitude of interior development transcends whatsoever can be imagined of the apex of human evolution. It is a question of the union of man's individual consciousness, of his immortal part, of his inalienable interior self-possession, in the universal consciousness of God.

To be qualified for a Mystic a man is not called on to make any sacrifice of his reason; he must exercise it to the fullest extent, must apply it to his personal improvement, and his progressive development. He is not required to profess any definite creed; the Mystic is concerned with the attainment of knowledge, not with the enunciation of dogma. But it is undeniably required of the candidate that he should be possessed of spiritual aspirations, and, above all, of that aspiration after immortality, which is a testimony of the interior man contributed to the truth of immortality, and is confirmed by a testimony without in the external facts of spiritual communion. Whosoever is acquainted with these facts has a certain and substantial knowledge on which to base his faith, and thus the mysteries which surround him are transfigured. Even in this life he may reasonably anticipate in the future a solution of many problems to which as yet we have found no key.

"There is not a people," says the grandest of the French mystics, Louis Claude de St. Martin, "and I may say there is not a man in possession of his true self, for whom the temporal universe is not a great allegory or parable which must give place to a grand morality." And the spiritual mind which has been illuminated even by purely external transcendental experience, and by such phenomenal testimony as can be obtained from the world of the departed, will incline to the dictum of the Mystic. Now, as the doctrine enunciated by St. Martin is a fundamental principle of that fundamental philosophy which is common to all the Mystics, its acceptance is the first step towards becoming a Mystic.

So far as our enquiry has proceeded it has endeavoured to establish certain chief points. There is first of all the reality and imminence of consciousness, an immediate testimony to ourselves which transcends all need of proof. There is next the phenomenal nature of all normal knowledge, as admitted by every thinker. There is thirdly the existence of an unseen world, with which many persons now living have been made acquainted by manifestations, also phenomenal, that are directly to be referred to that world. There is lastly the existence of an absolute reality behind all appearances. This is the *cœlum philosophorum* which is attained by the "anatomy of Mercury." The position of Mysticism in reference to all these points can be very clearly defined. It takes hold of the absolute actuality of the human EGO, on the one hand, and of the ETERNAL SUBSISTENT, on the other, and it seeks to join these two, setting aside, on the one hand, the phenomenal portion of psychology as unnecessary to its design, and ignoring altogether, in this connection, the existence of the normal world of appearances, on the principle that phantasmal existences can offer no real barrier to the correspondence of absolute realities which desire to unite. As to the methods of the Mystics, it is well known that they are in the main of an interior character. They consist in cutting off correspondence with inferior things, and in creating a new correspondence with things above.

We have it on the testimony of the Mystics that these processes can take place in this life, that it is not necessary for the soul to leave the body in order to see God, because the body when modified by Mysticism offers no insuperable obstacle. Finally, they tell us that the body can be visibly transfigured by the ecstasy of the interior experience. The historical evidence for these matters is to be found in the lives of the Mystics—among others, of Bonaventura, Tauler, Eckart, Böhme, St. Martin, and St. Theresa. The interior evidence must be sought by those who desire it.

It must be evident that Mysticism—if it can substantiate its claims—is a practical science. Its experiments are conducted upon the one subject about which we *know* anything—namely, our interior, conscious selves. It is not certainly a science for the crowd; it is in its highest aspect for the *élite* of humanity alone. At the same time, it has a message for the whole world, and a process for the gradual regeneration of the whole world, it has good tidings of great joy which it can publish to entire humanity, though it is a secret science. It is this message and these tidings which—in all humility—we shall endeavour to make plain in this little book on the coming spiritual reconstruction. May it prove to be *aditus facilis ad Hermetis artem*, and the tomb of intellectual poverty!

IV.

The Revival of Mysticism.

I N a work which is mainly addressed to the disciples of transcendental philosophy, and after all that we have now said, it may seem almost unnecessary to justify the revival of Mysticism. Yet it is well to keep defined in our mind not precisely the reasons for the faith that is in us, because fundamentally the transcendental philosophy is not of faith, but the practical purposes which inhere in the course we are taking when we advocate that revival. It is possible to summarize such an explanatory apologia in a very few words indeed. Mysticism constitutes, in the first place, a method which is superior to spiritualism for the attainment of phenomenal knowledge concerning the occult forces of Nature, and the invisible hierarchies of being, but these classes of investigation can be fitly abandoned to those who may deem it worth their while to pursue them. It includes, in the second place, an interior process for the attainment of positive knowledge concerning the realities which underlie phenomena. And it offers, finally, a key to the future progress of humanity, and a practical *modus operandi* for the evolution of the perfect man. These statements may be reduced within even narrower limits, and we may say: Mysticism comprises a physical demonstration concerning the unseen which is around us, whence it is the true alchemical *introitus in veram atque inauditam physicam*, and an interior illumination concerning the unseen which is within, together with a way to God, who is the end of all human development. It embodies also a system of education towards the perfect life, both physical and spiritual.

These, it is submitted, are sufficient reasons for the dissemination of its doctrines and principles. But we may advance beyond this initial standpoint, and we may affirm that a way to God, and a way to the perfect life are the essential elements required in that new religion towards which all the higher forces in humanity seem to be instinctively moving—in that new religion which shall realize the best aspirations, and constitute a transfigured synthesis of all previous creeds. Now, as existing religious systems are incommensurate to existing necessities; as faith is less than knowledge, and is therefore an inferior ground of conviction; as the Mystics offer knowledge; as knowledge is required by the age; as the development of humanity has not been perfectly accomplished by systems based on faith; as Mysticism is in harmony with the conclusions of modern science, and with the theorems of modern philosophy, in harmony with the best aspirations embodied in all religions, and is itself committed to no arbitrary doctrines—it is incumbent on those who receive it to spread the knowledge which they possess, to endeavour by personal experience to increase that knowledge, and undertake, so far as in them lies, to begin the education of humanity in the perfection promised by the Mystics—in the doctrine of "elective physics" and the science of spiritual election.

V.

Transcendental Science and Transcendental Religion.

W HILE the broad tendency of accredited philosophical opinion at the present time is directed towards the negation of intelligence outside the physical Cosmos, and would reject the conception of an immortal principle subsistent in human nature, the psychological facts of the day, imperfectly investigated as they are, seem to indicate in no uncertain manner that the age of spiritual speculation is passing, in the normal course of evolution, into an age of experimental knowledge concerning the things of the soul and the realities of the life beyond. The psychological experiments in question include the higher phenomena of mesmerism, hypnotism, clairvoyance, and that communication with disembodied intelligences which has been more or less certainly established by the agency of the spiritual circle. A portion of these phenomena are being to some extent seriously considered by the official representatives of physical science. Concerning all it may be affirmed that the overwhelming majority of persons who have sufficiently investigated the subjects have become convinced of their truth and reality. At the same time, there are distinct limitations to the knowledge which can be obtained from these departments of phenomenal psychology—limitations, in fact, which are well known to all advanced investigators. Under these circumstance, it is permissible to look in other quarters for an increased light, and with the desired illumination it is believed that the old Mystics were familiarized by other methods than those which are included under the term phenomenal psychology. From the standpoint of their philosophy, it is possible in this life and in this body to discern and know God in a spiritual but actually realizable manner, to partake of "the blessed manna of the philosophers," and to enter into a transcendental communion with the hierarchies of superior subsistence.

The methods and processes to which reference has just been made are practically identical in all ages and nations. At certain periods, and among certain peoples, the investigation of psychic possibilities has been pursued further, and more spiritual knowledge has been attained and accumulated. An extreme interest has been manifested within recent years in much that pertains to Oriental mystic thought, and there are many who imagine that *ex oriente lux* is the sole maxim by which a student of esoteric science should direct his researches. But it needs only a moderate acquaintance with esoteric Christian literature to be assured that there is a pure well of living water of divine truth, far more easily attainable in the writings of the Western Mystics. The revival of psychical research has, however, permitted this mine of wealth to remain practically untouched, though it is true that occasional papers on the Occidental doctrines of the life which is within life are scattered through the spiritual journals, that in France there is at least one periodical nominally devoted to Christian Theosophy, and that both here and in America there are many secluded students who seem to have attained to spiritual reconstruction, and to have beheld, in the words of Philalethes, Diana Unveiled.

It should be clear from the statements that have been already made that the subject of transcendentalism admits of a broad separation into two main sections, the phenomenal and the noumenal, the exterior and the interior, the objective and subjective; these two sections may be conveniently denominated Transcendental Science and Transcendental Religion. The first division, the domain of experiments, phenomena, manifestations, includes all that we understand under the names of practical magic in the past and practical psychology at the present time. The *Magnum Opus*, the highest point and pitch of Transcendental Science, was the establishment of a direct correspondence with the hierarchies of supramundane subsistence. It is true that it included alchemy, the mystery of the *sol chemicorum*, which was such an investigation of natural secrets as would elicit a practical method for the conversion of certain substances, generally metallic, into gold and silver. Transcendental Science included also the entire scope of transcendental medicine, the search for an Elixir of Life, for the Universal Medicine, and the Renewal of Youth—conceptions which were understood by the magicians in a more or less literal sense. There was, finally, the evocation of the souls of the departed, which must take rank among the most important and fascinating achievements of ceremonial magic.

The successful conduct of these experiments revealed to the operator not only the vastness, the depth, and the height of the great world, but the infinite possibilities of that which was usually distinguished as *Minutum Mundum*— the little world of humanity, microcosmic indeed upon the physical or phenomenal plane, but co-extensive with all time, with all space, in its interior or noumenal part. Under the light of this revelation, the Magus passed into the Mystic, the field of exterior experiment was abandoned for that of interior research, from Transcendental Science he entered into Transcendental Religion. The same process is taking place at the present day. Modern psychological phenomena are to a large extent parallel with the historic prodigies—*la belle et rouge Magie*—of the elder world. And with us, as with the old magician, these phenomena are but the threshold of the true science, "the greater illumination" of Flamel; they are but outward signs to indicate the realities that are within.

4

They are not the truth itself; they are finger-posts which point on the road, which point us one way, wherever they are situated, and that is into man's own soul, which is the only path to the Absolute that we call God, in whom is life and truth, and whereby we can attain truth—truth whole and undefiled—because he who wins an entrance into the sanctuary of his own soul can enter also into the enjoyment of all knowledge, and the participation in all reality through a consubstantial union with the Infinite.

There undoubtedly were many magicians in the past who never became Mystics, and fell short of truth and reality, though perhaps they could perform wonders, though they may have held converse with spirits, though some of them may have made gold, though they must have been well aware, by a close experimental knowledge, that they were immortal spiritual beings. Never for them did the "soul descend from the pyroplastic sphere"; never, like Elias, were they caught up to God. So also at the present epoch, in spite of prevailing indifference, in spite of enlightened unbelief, in spite of universal doubt and ever-multiplying difficulties in all matters of doctrine, there are many who, by entering upon another path, have come experimentally to know that there is another world, and that it is possible, under certain conditions, to have inter- course with the denizens thereof; many are acquainted with at least the ele- mentary phenomena of trance and ecstasy, and other psychological mysteries. Yet these are not Mystics; they have not penetrated into the interior man; they are contented with phenomenal results; they do not know truth—that truth and beauty "ever ancient and ever new," which is the "desired desire" and the whole "treasure of philosophy." To evoke Apollonius of Tyana is not to know God; to become convinced by undeniable experiment that genuine materializa- tions occasionally take place at séances is to be assured of a fact in science, pregnant with solemn significance, if you will, but still only a fact in science. Once more, it is a sign, or finger-post, which points in the right direction for those who have eyes to see. It is neither fitting nor possible that scientific facts should, as such, be erected into a religion. The evocation of Apollonius and the manifestation of John King may have occurred or not, but, even if they actually took place, they cannot constitute a religious truth. Therefore, neither spiri- tualism in the present nor magic in the past are in themselves a proper basis for a new departure in esoteric religion; and it is pertinent to draw attention to this, because there are tendencies in such a direction on the part of many earnest persons. No form of experimental psychology will directly lead us to the highest intelligence; none of them can plunge us in God. And if in our spiritual questings we fall short of God, then we fall short of the Absolute and the Perfect; we fall short of the end of Mysticism.

VI.

THE MYSTICAL PHILOSOPHY OF NATURE.

WE have seen that the agnostic philosophy is a preface or prolegomena to that of Mysticism; that the two systems have one basis,
and that they overlap each other. Mysticism steps in where
agnosticism finishes its mission. Mysticism expounds the noumenal, the
existence of which can only be indicated by agnosticism. But as, in a sense,
agnosticism demonstrates the noumenal, making its existence a necessary
assumption, so Mysticism interprets the phenomenal, and has thus a consan-
guineous affinity with another philosophy—that of poetry; for interpretation is
the keynote of the life of poetry, and there is the further fundamental connection
between poetry and Mysticism, that both deal with the formulation and realization of the ideal. In other words, poetry defines the scope of human aspiration
in the transcendental order; it gives form and expression to man's yearning
after that which is higher than himself and better than his environment. It is
in this sense, the divine melody of Hermes and the planetary music of the
adepts, once expounded by an inspired scrivener of Paris. Mysticism guarantees
to this aspiration a field of realization. For that which man would attain and
be, read poetry; for that which he can be and attain, learn of the Mystics; for
that which he is, see life and the world around us.

It is curious to note, at first sight, that the connection between poetry and
Mysticism again brings us róund to agnosticism. One essential element of
poetry is possessed by the agnostic philosophy, and that is mystery—even that
mystery which the vivid limelight of physical science, the progress of invention
and discovery, seem almost to have banished out of being. To that faculty
which is at the foundation of the poetic faculty does the agnostic philosophy
make a distinct appeal, and to that also it offers a new ministry. We speak of
the faculty of wonder. It restores mystery to the universe and wonder to the
mind of man. It effaces the limitations of sharp and clear outlines bounding
the intellectual horizon, and it substitutes the dim, prolonged, and shadowy
vistas of unknown possibilities. Under its touch the commonest objects of
knowledge are invested with a peculiar and subtle sanctity, and transfigured in
a weird dream light. There are not only sermons in stones and books in the
running brooks, but there is the ultimate of an infinite mystery behind every

stream and pebble. Science may explain to us the laws which regulate the manifestation of the moon over the deep sea, but to the agnostic philosopher the manifestation is no less a mysterious portent speaking from the heart of things —a sign and wonder from a world unknown, enveloped, like its own halo, in a luminous mist of mystery, projected upon the background of the unknown, as upon an impenetrable height of heaven, and with a profundity of the unconceived beneath it, as of a deep, unfathomed ocean.

> Across the altitude which spans that height
> The Bird of Hermes wings his flaming flight,
> And o'er the waters of the waste below
> Doth bright Aurelia flutter to and fro—
> That Golden Butterfly which sages know.

In a sense, the light of common knowledge may seem to have belittled all existence, but agnosticism has returned us a rare mystery in everything, full of signs and wonders which dilate and inspire the imagination.[1]

The Mystic regards the entire phenomenal universe as a grand parable or allegory which is destined one day, as we have seen, to give place to a grand reality. In the words of Emerson, the American seer, "The whole world is an omen and a sign." Thus, even in the natural order, the education of humanity is proceeding by type and by symbol; thus, God is the Great Symbolist, who teaches from behind the veil by signs which He writes upon the veil; the stars are secret ciphers with an interior and divine meaning; everything that exists is an outward sign of an inward thought of God; it is therefore a sacrament, an exterior index of an inner grace and virtue, and the worship of the beautiful in Nature is a homage paid to the perfection of the divine thinking.

When Christ came, He also taught in parables; He established symbolical ceremonies; His life and death are a great symbol which eternally preëxisted in the starry heavens. The most divine of all missions to man was fitly the most parabolic of all. The doctrines which have been developed in the churches that bear His name, if rightly understood, are also symbols—they are economies of divine things, and the Mystics, in common with the Grand Symbolist, in common with the Spirit of Nature, in common with the greatest of their Masters, have invariably taught by the eternal method of typology, have ever quickened and fertilized the minds of their disciples by the suggestions of parable and allegory, have ever promoted by these means the culture of the imagination, the education of the faculty of wonder. They have elaborated a tissue of many-sided symbolism—part obscure, part diaphanous—which is like the aureoles of dim gold round the heads of the canonized hierophants.

[1] See Appendix I.

All mystic symbolism, like that of Nature, has reference to the two interiors, the world which is within man, and that which is within, and veiled by, the visible universe. The Mystic knows that there is "a depth below the depth, and a height above the height," that "our hearing is not hearing, and our seeing is not sight." He knows also, could we scale those altitudes, could we sound those unmeasured profundities, could we once get behind the veil which is woven everywhere around us in the gorgeous panoply of the phenomenal universe, that there is an actuality we should arrive at, and that the "vision" is He, the King in His beauty, the absolute of the Mystics' imperative aspiration when he has ascended to the summits of his being, and high above all the splendours of the visible world, above all secondary causes, sends forth the clarion challenge of the soul into the timeless immensity, and cries—no longer as "an infant in the night," but with the whole strength of his nature—for the desired light, as the spirit in the dread and the stillness pauses before the closed eye of the Unknown Darkness. "Thou art emblazoned," says the *Crown of Flowers*, "on the everlasting banners, O thou eye of Sol! Thine eyelid is the night of Chaos, and thy glance is the universal harmony of evolved universes Thy pupil is the stone of the philosophers, even that stone which is beheld by the just man, *et sicut palma florebit.*"

It is said by the Mystics that the veil is dark, but that it is very thin. When we consider the many-folded mysteries with which we are on all sides surrounded, the veil is indeed dark, but if it be penetrable at a single point, it is sure that it is thin. They say also, "My veil hath no mortal ever lifted." And the mystic poets describe it, when they have regard to the beauty of the phenomenal universe, as a thing of light and stars. "In the beginning ere man grew, the veil was woven bright and blue. . . Over his features, wondrous, terrible, the beautiful Master drew the veil. . . And since the beginning no mortal vision, pure or sinning, hath seen the Face!" This also is true, for the Mystic remembers that the flesh cannot see God. If there be not something within us which transcends mortality, and unites us to all that is permanent in being, the quest after positive truth is a bitter folly. But the Mystic is aware by experience that there is a spiritual world both within and without him—that the other side of life is after all like the house of man—that more than one traveller has returned from that bourne whence it has been falsely said that no traveller returns. He is aware, therefore, that if the mystery is dark, the veil is bright, that it is thin because it is penetrable, and although what is mortal of man cannot lift it, or win entrance to the sanctuary that is behind, there is another and a higher man to whom this possibility is granted. "Herein is the *cœleste palmctum*," says the Little Office of the *Gift of God.*

It has been affirmed that analogy is the last word of science and the first of religion, and it is well known that the exoteric or casuistic part of the mystical body of doctrine is based wholly on the analogical doctrine that the visible is a measure of the invisible.

> Seven snowdrops
> Sister the Pleiads, the primrose is kin
> To Hesper, Hesper to the world to come.

Analogy also is the perfection of the poetic method, and the gift of discerning analogies is a part of the "seeing sense," which is termed otherwise poetic insight. There is a world of false but plausible analogies which is the happy hunting-ground of the inferior poet, and the world of merely sensible impressions is the only *terra cognita* for most of the children of men, but they are both a *terra damnata et maledicta* for pure inspiration and true genius. When once it is received as a truth that there are no realities whatsoever outside the sublime order of intelligence, that the spirit of man is placed in a world of purely illusory phenomena for the education of his genius and the regulation of his spiritual evolution, the mind is illumined by a new series of profound metaphysical sensations which are akin to direct revelation, and may well become the golden seed of a regenerated garden of song. In the splendid pageantry of the grand and holy sea, in the divine hush of moonless nights, in the glory of the stellar world, there will be perceived the ministration of a lofty and significant symbolism which exists for man alone, and develops its resources to infinity according to the measure of his investigations. All the discoveries of science, all the outreachings of acute speculation, become new fountains of suggestiveness in the place of new proofs of the realism of material things. The vistas revealed by astronomy, the interplanetary spaces, the star-depths, the overwhelming sense of the immeasurable, the discovery of new worlds quivering on the outposts of infinity, exist only for the nourishment of supreme imagination. By the glass of the astronomer man gazes deeper into himself, by the excursions of the mathematical mind into "the magical, measureless distance," he gauges and surveys himself. Nature widens in proportion as it is investigated, for the links in the silver chain of symbolism multiply as we follow them, and the divine dream of the universe deepens and intensifies about us the further we plunge therein. When the spirit sets forth on that mighty sea, it need never fear the desolating disillusion of a limit attained. There is no end to the sublime delusion. The mystical sequence of natural typology is a series without end, as it is without beginning, and the soul can sail for ever. This is the grandeur and the beauty and the glory, and the philosophic joy of idealism.

Gabriel de Castagne portrays it in his *Terrestrial Paradise* under the evasion of a miracle in medicine. The goal is for ever within us; the dream also is within; and the splendour, the meaning, the charm, the witchery, the enchantment, the depth, the height, the distance, are all in a sense within us; for the so-called material universe is only a stage of the soul's advancement in the development of her infinite self.

> It is no sea thou seest in the sea,
> 'Tis but a disguised humanity . . .
> All that interests a man *is* man.

At a higher stage, a higher symbolism, a wider universe, a deeper meaning, an increased joy, an intensified loveliness, till the supreme spirit in the full possession of itself, having achieved its own creation, shall enter the Summer Land of eternal maturity, the New Jerusalem, the beatific vision, the higher consciousness of Nirvana.

Now, in the order of idealism, beauty and harmony are the touchstone and the test of truth. It is for this reason that false analogies, false images, and deformed conceptions are detestable and revolting things—the perdition of the intellectual soul—for the mind of man creates the universe after its own likeness, and it is pursued by the phantoms it produces. An irregular and diseased imagination will imprison the soul in the Tophet of the false and the monstrous. To the priests and poets of the future be, therefore, all health, and the Christ of God within them for their nature's sublime exaltation! Theirs be "the scale of the sages," and the "philosophical garden of Love." We beseech you, sweet brethren, everlasting friends, by the Crown and the Chrism, by the stars in the eyes of Israfel, and by that chaste light—*lumen de lumine*—which is the jewelled glistening of Lucasta, to purge the world from darkness by the clarity of intelligence, and by the creation of a loftier symbolism to accomplish the evolution of a loftier Ministry of Song. To you, standing "in the foremost files of time," is committed the Cosmos, as a plastic matter, to be fashioned after your own imaginations for the Sons of Futurity, whose faith is in your hands. "The light that never was on land or sea" is within you. It is also in your power to project it over the visible universe, and to accomplish thus the complete transfiguration of the world. For the Cosmos is the inheritance of imagination, the potter's clay of the poet, to be shaped however he will. It is also an illimitable symbol to be interpreted by his genius.

Teach us no more that the world is dead, that the beasts perish, that the departed sleep. But preach unto us, O inspired apostles, commissioned from the Spiritual Parnassus, the evangel of everlasting life, of the permanence, beauty, joy, progress, triumph, and continual ascent of all that lives and is! Shew unto the Children of the Poets, the universal humanity, till "Sorga's stream ascends to Helicon," that all heights are possible to the spirit of man, who is called to the creation of himself, the redemption of others, and the adoration of the beautiful.   Prophesy unto us of "that far off, divine event towards which the whole creation moves."   That end of creation must be one of high-exalted destiny for all its intelligences.   What is matter but the support and footstool of spirit, the substance it adapts, and in no way its own end? The universe exists for its intelligences, and as for man, so far as he can use it, it exists for the use of man.   The poet is the magician of dreamland.   Let him accomplish the realization of the dream by the power of his magical art, and he will be the demiourgos of the life to come.

Who indeed is the demiourgos of the life to come, the *paradisus aureolus Hermeticus*, if it be not the prophet of many melodies, clothed with song as in a garment of multitudinous splendours, who has seen, who has proclaimed, who has foretasted and pre-realized, the good and joy to come, in the sublime pre-realization of the ideal? Who is the pontifex, who is the bridge-builder, who is the instrument of communication, between the seen and the unseen, between that which we are and that which hath not yet appeared in us, but which we shall and must be? It is the poet only, the priest of Nature, who is in touch with what is above Nature, who speaks from an ulterior standpoint. We do not exalt him beyond the scope of his vocation; his vocation it is impossible to exalt.   He is the instrument upon which the Æolian airs of futurity can alone play.   We do not affirm that he can give us the entire harmony; he is the glass of vision; it is, in some respects, a darkened glass, and we see through it darkly with the dim eyesight of an undeveloped intellectuality.   The scope of his seeing sense is the earnest—not the full measure—of our sight to come.   That which he has dreamed through the ages, it is that which is to be revealed to us and in us.   When we would shape in our thoughts the future of the human race, and the perfection which is to appear through evolution, the blossoming of Eden's bower, and the "reign of Saturn revived," he must be our guide.   He interprets ourselves to us, and he interprets the world to ourselves. He sees deeper than official philosophy into the heart of things, for his inmost nature is in contact with the great universal heart.

The supreme poet of the century, the Chief Interpreter, who is also, *par excellence*, the grand Mystic of this age, more grand because his Mysticism is of the unconscious order, not perhaps realized formally and philosophically by himself, much less by his literary critics, as the highest innocence is also unconscious—this excellent and wise master, to whose laurels we have added a

coronet instead of a tiara, has condensed the philosophy of the phenomenal
universe into a single versicle:—

> Flower in the crannied wall,
> I pick you out of the crannies, . . .
> Little flower, if I could understand
> What you are, and all in all,
> I should know what God and man is.

There is no object too insignificant to lead us into absolute truth, could we
only know it well. But no sage, no chemist can tell us what principles are at
work behind the outward appearance of the humblest lichen or fungus, and so
what we call science can reveal to us nothing of the noumenal world. "Rift
the hills and roll the waters, flash the lightnings, weigh the sun"—yes, it may
do all these, but it can say nothing of the true and the real. Who is there that
would impeach science? It has recognized its own limitations, it has affirmed
its own inadequacy, and has guaranteed to us, in so doing, the validity of its
credentials within its proper sphere. Honour to the way of knowledge, and to
the progress made therein! It has told us that the phenomenal world is the
veil of a grand reality. When the science of the West was in its manger in the
Bethlehem of the dark ages, the Mystics knew that, and they aspired to the
"truth and beauty ever ancient and ever new." They called it the *Mysterium
Magnum*. Now, the Mystic was a philosopher modified by poetry, and the true
poet is a Mystic, possessing the "accomplishment of verse."

But if the phenomenal universe be a veil in analogical language, it follows
from the analogy itself that it can suggest to us the outlines of the concealed
reality. It does hide and it does distort; it has its inherent defects, and these
are what we call evil, with its consequences of sin and misery; but, as veils will
have, it possesses its own grace, and it hints at the grace within. We must
interpret the unrealizable beauty of that which is behind the veil, by the
graciousness of the veil. In this matter the poets are our only interpreters—
that is, legitimately—because the problem is outside science, which is concerned
with the veil alone; and it is outside ordinary philosophy, because ordinary
philosophy has affirmed that the reality is unknowable; and the best conclusions
from analogy are to be learned of the masters of analogy, of the kings of interpretation, of those who see furthest, who possess that intuition which is the
deepest instrument of supersensual research, and is in fact that higher faculty,
that sixth sense, at which we have already hinted, which we now openly affirm
is *par excellence* the mystical instrument. Those only who are in touch with
poetry can have part in the life to come. It is therefore eminently, and before
all things necessary, that we should see after the manner of the poets, and the

mystical philosophy of Nature is to be found in them. In all things which concern man and his environment, the difference between that which is actual in life, and that which is conceived by them, is the measure of our falling short of excellence; it is the distance that we have to climb in the course of our evolution; and then beyond that point achieved, there will be a new poetry, a new idealism, a new measure of deficiency, and another grand ascent. The possession of the spirit of poetry is thus an indispensable condition of achievement; it is the agent of transfiguration; it is the philosophic stone which transmutes the world and man. How does poetry interpret Nature? What is its message from the future? These are the questions which we have to answer. It is a practical enquiry because it is a proposal for the realization of the ideal. If in another sense it be not practical, let us take that to our hearts and be comforted, because it offers to all who need it a refuge from the sordid motives of a mean environment.

VII.

EVOLUTION AND MYSTICISM.

HAVING discovered a connecting link, a common basis, and to some extent an identical mission, subsisting between systems so apparently, and in certain respects so truly, diverse as philosophic agnosticism, mystical philosophy, and what we have termed the philosophy of poetry, it remains for us now to delineate a final correspondence which for the purposes of this book is the most important of all—that, namely, which exists between mystic doctrine and the modern scientific doctrine of development or evolution. Long before the principle of evolution was formulated in its crudest shape by the author of *The Vestiges of Creation* the less instructed aspirations of humanity at the close of the eighteenth century had conceived the doctrine of perfectibility, and had recognized the operation of an arcane law which was continually ameliorating the condition of mankind. Under the influence of the poetic instrument which constituted the mind of Shelley, this pious faith was gradually exalted into a species of nebulous transcendentalism which, in the guise of its later developments, was held up to ridicule in the literary criticisms of Edgar Allan Poe. Imperfect as the formulation was, it proved to be the precursor of a coming revelation; it was the first contact of uninitiated consciousness with an undiscovered law of being; it was touched rather than grasped; it was sensed rather than conceived; it was felt rather than understood; it was believed rather than known. But in the fulness of time the revelation came, and the scientific doctrine of evolution, uttering its *fiat lux*, cast a flood of new illumination upon the mysteries of the phenomenal world.

The doctrine of evolution comprises these points as regards the development of humanity:—

a. The capacity for improvement.

b. The existence of undeveloped potencies.

c. Facility of correspondence with modified or improved environment.

d. The operation of energy mainly in the direction of improvement.

The Mystics may not have been acquainted with our alleged descent from apes; they may only have realized dimly the significance in Nature of that law which regulates the survival of the fittest, though they did not need science to teach them that the weakest go to the wall; but they were acquainted with the capacity for improvement in all substances and in all departments of

Nature; they believed in the existence of undeveloped potencies in every kingdom of being. They studied the mysteries of correspondence and the great law of conditions; they investigated the operations of energy in the direction of improvement. But they did what we do not; their great end was to assist Nature, to bring consciousness, reason, intelligence, to help in fulfilling the law; to begin work where Nature left off, or was arrested, to improve what was defective, to complete what was unfinished, to ameliorate the ill-conditioned, to refine the coarse, to remove the superfluous. "The work of Nature," says Trevisan, "is assisted by alchemy." They believed that a change might be effected in all substances, and they sought to work up to the archetypal idea which dominated in each department of Nature. In other words, they endeavoured to realize the ideal, to produce perfection in the given substance. Thus, the Physical Mystics, or alchemists, elaborated the potencies of metals in order to obtain gold. And then in regard to man, the Spiritual Mystics sought to produce his archetype, to realize the ideal humanity; and we find in their writings and their processes a clear proof of their acquaintance with a law of spiritual evolution which we can discern to be in rigorous analogy with that of the physical world. Modern science has concerned itself but little with the possible future of humanity as it is indicated by the law which it has discovered, but underlying the literature of Western Mysticism there is the consciousness of a grand future of both spiritual and physical transfiguration, perfection, beauty, and visible illumination—things outward being an index of things within— which is possible, perhaps inevitable for man, and this future can at any rate be achieved by the elect.

Whether contemplated from the merely scientific standpoint, or from that of the higher science of Mysticism, it may be affirmed that the object of physical evolution, working in the natural world, is to accomplish the transfiguration of the natural body of man, to develop what Freemasonry terms the Perfect Ashlar. The object of spiritual evolution is to accomplish the transfiguration of the interior man. The processes of Mysticism, in both departments, are true processes of development. There are, therefore, two evolutions and two transfigurations, both of which have man for their subject, and his perfection for the end in view. Therefore also Mysticism regards man from the standpoint of modern science, as a developing being, a phenomenal manifestation, having a hidden reality. In accordance with the doctrine of scientific evolution, and in accordance with mystical philosophy, it is the aim of this book to indicate and to foreshew a method for the development of the interior resources of physical, intellectual, and aspirational man, "by a natural process devoid of haste and violence." It is a book of the life present and a book of the life to come; the second part is devoted exclusively to a science of the interior, and to a way of entrance into the world of true light, founded on the wisdom of the ages, and constituting a guide from that which seems into the supersensual repose of the real. It deals with the prospective existence of the regenerated race here, and that of the individual hereafter. Its aim is fixed upon that far light which is beyond all stars and suns; upon the truth which is above fact, upon the dream which transcends life, upon the supereminent transcension of that altitude of the fruition of being which surpasses all known summits, upon the repose of that energy which is greater than all material activity, because it has another impulse; it is a message and a mission to every mystic thinker; it is a solemn remembrancer that our profession commits us here to the development of mystic action on the plane of the phenomenal, and must energize us for work amidst the homes and haunts of men. Ours is no illuminated idleness. If we are possessed of the Great Stone of the philoso-phers, it is not to hide it in a napkin, but to turn the world to gold. Let not therefore the cold severity of a calculating practical criticism condemn our wisdom as a dreamer's lore, gorgeous, perhaps, but still a light of dream; it is the gospel of a new work; it is the development of man the perfect. Ours is the prospective field of evolution; our domain is the Ascent of Humanity. Man's future in the physical order is a prospect which has been opened to us by science; that prospect has kindled the enthusiasm of a noble and ennobling aspiration; and that aspiration it is our work to exalt into religion. The last word of science is the initial message of the New Mysticism. Throughout the first division of this book, the method which will be suggested, as also the system which will one day incorporate that method, and the religion, or way of the life to come, which will, in effect, be that system in its evolved form, will for all practical purposes be confined to the elaboration of humanity here on earth. This division, and its method will, however, be but the gate of the sanctuary which will give entrance to the Holy of Holies of our most holy and chrism-consecrated aspiration, to be set forth in the second part and by the second method.

PART I.
THE OUTWARD MAN.

THE OUTWARD MAN.

CHAPTER THE FIRST.

THE HERMETIC DOCTRINE OF DEVELOPMENT.

I.

Evolution in the Light of Mysticism.

WHEN the profound consideration of the Law of physical evolution has convinced, as it must convince us, that it is a duty in our condition as conscious beings to devote the best qualities of our power towards the fulfilment of that law, the intelligence within us being gifted with sight to see, albeit dimly and in part, the direction and the drift of things, whence it is ethically an outrage against Nature, and a violation of the harmony of being, to go counter to that drift and direction—when this consideration has thus convinced us, and we would earnestly set ourselves to fulfil the law of our existence, we shall find that there are three sources to which we can look for assistance, and for a certain light and knowledge, as to the precise nature of our endeavour. Those sources are to be found in the universal aspiration of humanity, in the higher faculties of humanity, and in the processes by which man in all ages has endeavoured to produce in his actual condition the ideal of perfection and happiness. The history of such processes is, in effect, the history of civilization itself; there is no doubt that each of them enforces its own particular lesson, and that we, as Mystics, can be made wise by the experience of them all. The work of pioneers and reformers does not live only in the ameliorated or favourable environment which it has helped to make, and in the general improvement of the human race; it lives also in the lesson that it teaches to the pioneers and reformers to come, and in every possibility of fresh application which is contained within it.

Now, if we would be truly acquainted with the end of our evolution and the nature of our perfection, the law of our welfare, the goal of our happiness, and the source of real being, we must learn these things of the Mystics. For it is the prime postulate of this treatise on physical and spiritual sanctity that arcane science is the fountain of initiation into the mystery of fundamental truth. We address those who have accepted this postulate, about which we do not argue or endeavour to verify because those who know are already convinced, while those who have yet to learn can be instructed only by experience. If unto these Mystics have been committed the keys of spiritual knowledge, it follows that it is not unreasonable to suppose that the possessors of the one transcendental science should, if we question their oracles, prove qualified to instruct us in the secrets of physical transcendency. From the double stem of the Golden Rose of Hermes there issue two perfect, mature, and adorable blossoms. If these, in their first significance, are the Sol and Luna of alchemy, and in their second, philosophical meaning are the physical and spiritual sides of the *Magnum Opus*, they are also more profoundly, and at the same time in a more direct manner, the two branches of the Great Subject Man—differentiated in sex but one in essence, one in root, one in origin, one in the divine completeness of a perfection that is more than possible, because it is substantially guaranteed by law; and they are, moreover, the outward and the inward side of this same great, universal, and supernal subject.

Those who know God must know also the secret of all power and of all beauty in heaven and on earth, and it is the thesis of this book that the counsels of mystical perfection which constitute the rose-lined pathway of the Absolute, the way of light and fragrance, though directly they act in the soul, have action also in a reflex manner upon the outward body of man. It is the law of that reflexion, and the education of that indirect action into an outward and manifested potency which is the whole subject of our enquiry as regards the outward man. Thus in the light of the Hermetic philosophy, the path of perfection becomes the path of beauty, as it is that of peace and joy. There is an exterior complexion of the ripe and perfect peach which is an index of its sweetness and delight; so do the Seven Gifts of the Spirit beautify by radiation from within the casket in which they are enshrined, and the Twelve Paradisiacal Fruits have an outward bloom and glow. The attainment of the end of evolution in the external man, the Christo-Theosophical culture of the fair flower of Christ, the "double rose of love," can be secured only by the observation of ethical and spiritual laws. But the laws of the Spirit, the laws of God's love, and of the joy in God, are in their ultimate the Grand Secret of the Mystics. Once more, therefore, it is to them that we must have recourse.

If we assume for the moment that it is our object to ascertain the nature of physical perfection in humanity, and the end towards which evolution is working in respect of the body of man—which we shall speak of hereafter, in accordance with mystical terminology, as the Glory to Come, the Manifestation of the Dual Flower, the Blossoming of the Almond, the Realization of Venus-Apollo, the Flowering of the Garden of Eden, and by such other names as an informed enthusiasm may direct us in accordance with mystic usage—if we assume this, and if we elect further to have recourse to the Mystics for light and guidance, our first and most natural step will be to enquire whether in the literature of Mysticism there may be any trace of a doctrine of evolution or development.

Now, it is a matter of general knowledge, and in these days when the silver trumpet of the soul sounds clearly through the nations, it is by no means confined to the Mystics, that all Hermetic literature is written in a strange terminology, that its principles and secrets are generally disguised in allegories, and buried beneath an entire palace of symbolism. If, therefore, such a doctrine should not appear on the surface of mystical literature, from an acquaintance with the methods of all the grand initiates, that would by no means be proof positive that they were uninstructed in the workings of such a law. It would be legitimate to look for it behind the veil, and beneath the surface, for the precious gems which do shine not to the outward sight on the walls of the King's Palace, or do glisten on turret and cupola, might not improbably be stored all secretly in the subterranean treasure-house of the King. Indeed, if the jewels in question be the most prized of all jewels, it is perhaps reasonable to expect that they would be concealed, nor ought we by any means to despair of finding them, if we are convinced that the King is exceeding rich, that indeed he has the secret of all wealth, and that he is the possessor of all things that are high in value, provided only that, in his grace and his mercy, he permits to us the key of his coffers. Thus, it is *prima facie* exceedingly likely that in order to discover the principle of development in mystical literature, we shall have to undertake an analysis of mystical symbolism, and he who is a lover of the Mystics should not be deterred from the enquiry by any common difficulty of research. It is, in fact, from a study of the typology of the physical Mystics that we shall expect later on to receive some assurance as to the nature of our Coming Glory.

So far, however, from the doctrine of evolution in Nature lying *perdu* among the tenebræ of symbolism, it is, perhaps, the one principle of arcane procedure that the Mystics have paraded everywhere, and the first thing that must strike a modern reader of the old books is that every true alchemist—taking alchemical literature for the moment as the palmary branch of the written tradition of the Hermetists—was, in fact, an undisguised evolutionist.

The doctrine of development was the open secret of the Mystics, as it was subsequently that of the Freemasons, who through the whole period of their history have been less or more attached to the tradition of Hermes.

But we are seeking not only for traces of the existence of an evolutionary doctrine; we are in need of an application of the law by which intelligent and conscious man can bring his own faculties to assist the law of his nature, and this also we shall learn from the Mystics, for such an application is indeed the end of Mysticism, while it is also ostensibly, as it was once in sincerity, the chief object of research among the illuminated brethren of the square and compass. But *redit Saturnia regna*, and, in the time to come, there may yet be a regeneration of Masonry.[1]

II.

Spiritual and Physical Alchemy.

Simplicity or plainness has been said by a Hermetic writer to be "the seal of truth," and if it were needful to define the whole scope of transcendental wisdom in the plainness and simplicity of one unadorned phrase, we should say, in the language of Sendivogius, that it is "to make that which is occult manifest." It is thus the eduction of powers and the elaboration of latencies. The definition covers all and includes all, from the parabolic mystification of Paracelsus concerning that "mineral water" by which gold can be made to grow, and the "imbibitions" and "distillations" of alchemy, even to those high altitudes of mystic action by which the lost memory of the soul's anterior states can be recovered. Now, we have affirmed that there is a doctrine of development which is not merely discernible, but is present beyond all possibility of misconception in mystical literature. The transcendental theology of Christendom deals wholly with the evolution of man's spiritual potencies in the direction of perfect life in Christ. But the physical perfection of humanity is forgotten or ignored therein. Side by side, however, with transcendental theology, there flourished the Hermetic school of science in the West, nominally deriving its arcana from the theurgic philosophical traditions of the Græco-Alexandrian period. The disciples of this college present themselves before us under two aspects—as Magi and Alchemists. They both operated in the region of phenomena, and the magicians represent the connecting link between transcendental

[1] See Appendix II.

evolutionary Mysticism and what may be called the physical Mysticism of the transmutatory process. The theurgic wisdom of which they were inheritors gave them in each case an illumination which transcended their mission. The evokers of spirits aspired to Deific union; many alchemists, while they exploited the capacities of metals, dreamed of the soul's evolution. Some of these forgot their physical purpose, and surrendered their search after wealth for the purely spiritual research, led on by the resources of their terminology and the suggestions of their profound symbolism, which possessed, as we shall see, a dual field of application—in man and in the mineral world. This application was not arbitrary, and it was not forced. There is a parity and parallel between all mystical processes, because all are evolutionary. The transcendental illumination of the illuminated Christian Mystic is the application of evolutionary law to the soul of man. The physical Mysticism of the alchemists applied the same principle in the metallic kingdom, while the magician was concerned with the creation of an environment which acted as a species of forcing-house for the external eduction of the transcendental faculties of the inner man.

But the experimental foundation had also a philosophical basis in the great dogma of Hermes. It was in virtue of this central analogical theorem of Hermetic science—to which we shall again have occasion to refer—that the process in all mystic action was identical in nature and principle, but applied with due regard to formal difference. The seven states of the Stone in alchemy are intimately related to the seven stages in the castle of the interior man. Both are allied to the Mysteries—that is to say, to the sequence of hierarchic pageantry by which, in the penetralia of the so-called pagan temples, the elect of those ages were inducted to the methods of supreme illumination. God alone knoweth after what precise manner the Mysteries were connected with that Holy Assembly, the existence of which we shall have occasion to affirm later on, but we do know, and are convinced beyond the possibility of indecision, that they produced a royal issue to the line of Mysticism, and that even in the light and joy of Christ, wherein, as children of the transcendental, we ourselves believe that we can experience all joy, and be enlightened with all light, there is neither peace, nor joy, nor clarity of perfect spiritual seeing, to surpass that which was experienced by such vessels of election as Plotinus.

We may, therefore, enlarging on our previous classification, divide Mysticism and its dependencies into three chief sections—that of Transcendental Religion, as professed by the higher Mystics; that of Transcendental Science, which includes all ceremonial magic, and wherein there is no real interest, and that of the physical Mysticism of Alchemy. The rise of alchemical literature is coincident with the collapse of Theurgic Neo-Platonism, the downfall of

Gnosticism, the proscription of the pagan cultus, when the extinction, or loss, of all knowledge of the inner meaning of Greek and Latin mythology—a knowledge vested in the priests of the cultus—was very likely to ensue, and indeed might seem almost inevitable. It was coincident also with the degradation of the Mysteries, and with the materialization of the Christian Church. From all these vanishing theosophies it inherited light, leading, and authority; it is founded on all, it appeals to all, and its character is exceedingly composite. It is not to be judged from a single standpoint, or interpreted after an individual method, and it is full of difficulties and pitfalls. In attempting to penetrate its mysteries, our investigations lead us, it may seem, into strange and perhaps uninviting regions. But we are erecting a house beautiful of eternal hope, and we must seek in many quarries for our onyx, amethyst, and chalcedony.

No student of Mysticism, historical or philosophical, can afford to ignore alchemy. There is a solidarity, if we take only the lowest standpoint, and as we have elsewhere and often iterated, between the physical processes of occult chemistry and the spiritual processes of the Mystics. Now, in so far as this solidarity was known to the *Turba Philosophorum*, so far were all alchemists themselves Mystics, and alchemy—that is, the physical part of the process—was a Mystic work. We regard alchemy, as we regard the larger philosophy of which it was a part, and a mode of expression or of presentations, under a dual aspect. As in the one case Mysticism is capable, as we have seen, of division into Transcendental Science and Transcendental Religion, so in the other alchemy is to be regarded as a spiritual and physical work. We do neither doubt nor question that many alchemists sought only the transmutation of metals, and applied the principles of arcane law only among mineral genera; of this fact their lives are the evidence. But our researches have also convinced us that their labours were overshadowed by the portents of a higher achievement—that even as their works read obviously in two ways, literally and trans-literally, so also their operations had two objects, and that both these objects were pursued from the first beginnings of the science, and are contained in its earliest literature. The spiritual interpretation was not an afterthought; the spiritual search was not an aftergrowth; the testimony to these matters is not less strong in Geber than it is in Khunrath. The arcane knowledge in both cases preceded the arcane literature. The secrets of the ancient sanctuaries and of the Holy Assemblies embraced both the physical and transcendental. It was known that one law variously applied obtained in all departments of Nature as regards the development of species and of the potential energies in all things. Their acquaintance with that law enabled the adepts to develop the latent possibilities of the mineral world, which possibilities resided not in the differentiated species but in the common elements. Their acquaintance with the same law also enabled them to elaborate the transcendental potencies of man. Thus, in vulgar parlance, they could transmute metals, and they could transfigure humanity. Alchemical literature enshrined both processes, which accounts for its composite character, like a skein of silk in which two colours, distinct, though almost inextricable, are confusedly tangled and braided. The evolutionary doctrine of alchemy is scarcely a subject for formal quotation from the sequence of alchemical literature, for it is the foundation and sum of that literature. There is, of course, the hackneyed maxim everywhere cited by the champions of the "spoliated past," that maxim which puts tersely, after the manner of the wisdom of old, the whole theory of the development of species into a nutshell. "The stone becomes a plant, the plant an animal, the animal a man, man a God." But that is not the evolution with which we are now dealing; we are not here concerned with the mode in the manifestation of the law which differentiated species, but rather with a fundamental principle, and a philosophical reason for the principle, which all Mysticism applied in practice. The principle briefly was this: All natures, however diversified, have a common origin; there is but one substance in the universe; the latent powers which subsist in any species are the capacities of the First Matter; it is impossible to ameliorate or to improve species except by having recourse to the fontal substance and source, whence all multiplication, all generation, all energy of development proceed. By recourse to this storehouse of universal potency every species can be ameliorated and developed. Development proceeds under the providence of Nature up to a certain point, beyond which it can be carried by art, and to the highest point and pitch of this evolutionary art the Hermetic adepts apply the name of alchemy. No recognized initiate and no intelligent disciple who has followed in the footsteps of a master have ever attempted to confine the scope of alchemy to the mere conversion of metals. Paracelsus defines it as artificial generation or production, of what kind soever, and it includes the eduction of the potencies in plants, animals and men, as much as the "augmentation of Sol." Referring to the transmutation of metals, Alexander Seton testifies that there are "further and higher secrets." And Sendivogius, his inheritor, states that "the Philosophers propounded to themselves that they would make trial of the possibility of Nature in the mineral kingdom; which, being discovered, they saw that there were innumerable other arcana, of which, as of divine secrets, they wrote sparingly." It is also in this sense that we must understand the explicit information of Thomas Vaughan, already cited, who assures us that *Chemia* is a narrow name which ought not to be applied to the science, as the latter is ancient and infinite.

III.

Alchemy as a Supernatural Science.

Supposing that Alchemy was either not concerned with the transmutation of metals, except as with a veil and an evasion, or that it was concerned with it actually, but only as an inferior or collateral branch of experiment, there is one mark which we ought to find in its literature to distinguish it from an operation of merely physical science, and that is the Mark of the Supernatural. Now, Alchemy comes actually before us in every case, and under all its forms of presentation, even as in each century of its practice, as an essentially sacred science. It is sacred in its fabulous pedigree, sacred in its end and intention, sacred in its concealed methods, and classes among the *Magnalia Dei et Naturæ* as a special gift communicated from on high.

"Most happy is the son of that man," says the author of the *Golden Calf,* "who, by his prayers, obtains this art of arts, unto the glory of God. For it is most certain that this Mystery can be known no other way, unless it be drawn and imbibed from God, the Fountain of Fountains. Therefore, let every serious lover of this inestimable Art judge that the whole work of him required is that he constantly, with the prayer of true faith, in all his labour implore and solicit the Divine Grace of the Holy Spirit. For the solemn manner of God alone is, candidly and liberally, either mediately or immediately, to communicate His gifts and benefits, but unto none unless to candid and liberal minds. In this holy way of practical piety, all inquisitors of profound Arts find what they seek, when they in their work exercise themselves theosophically by solitary colloquies with Jehovah, religiously, with a pure heart and mouth. For the Heavenly Sophia indeed willingly embraces our friendship, presenting and offering to us her inexhaustible rivulets, most full of gracious goodness and benevolence. But happy is he to whom the Royal Way in which he is to walk shall be shown by some one expert in this Arcanum."

So also the *New Light of Alchymy* assures us that the "commendable art" is "the gift of God, and truly it is not to be attained to but by the alone favour of God." The *Hermetical Triumph* describes it as "a divine science" which is communicated from God, and that only "to those who will make a good use of it." The mode in which it is imparted is like that of all revelation, an "illumination of Mind," for "the knowledge of our Magistery," says the *Key of the Secret Philosophy*, comes by "the inspiration of Heaven," and "this truth is acknowledged by all Philosophers." It is acknowledged by Geber when he forbids his disciples to meddle with sophistical operations, "because our art is reserved in the divine will of God, and is given to or withheld from whom He will, who is glorious, sublime, and full of all justice and goodness." It is not therefore to be degraded or misused, and those who pervert it should be "blasphemed to eternity, because they have left to their posterity blasphemies, a curse by their error, and a diabolical instigation instead of the invention of verity." It is equally acknowledged by the initiates of the French school, and by the mediæval German adepts. "Let no one expect to be enlightened on the mysteries of the Stone of the Philosophers who is blind in the mysteries of faith," and the spirit of Christ is an indispensable element of the more composite spirit of philosophy, for Christ, says Benedictus Figulus, is "the true theosopher, Christ the true astronomer, Christ the universal physician, and to Him alone is the glory." It is acknowledged by the English alchemists, for whom, as for Elias Ashmole, the physical work was but the lowest achievement of the great work of philosophy.

"The Mineral Stone is wrought up to one degree only, and hath the power of transmuting any imperfect matter into its utmost perfection. But as to make gold was the chiefest intent of the Alchemists, so was it scarce any intent of the ancient philosophers, and the lowest use the adepts made of the *Materia*. For they, being lovers of wisdom more than of material wealth, drove at higher and more excellent operations. And certainly he to whom the whole course of Nature lies open rejoiceth not so much that he can make gold and silver, or the devils become subject to him, as that he sees the Heavens open, the Angels of God ascending and descending, and that his own name is fairly written in the Book of Life."

For others, like Helvetius, all Heaven enters into the composition of the Grand Catholicon, and the initiation begun on earth is completed *in aula cœlestium*. "Thus have I described what I myself have seen and done, and have caused the same to be printed for you, Candid Reader, out of mere liberality, gratis communicating it, according to that of Seneca: I desire in this to know somewhat that I may teach others. But if any man doubt of the real truth of the matter, let him only with a lively faith believe in his crucified Jesus, that in Him, by the strict way of Regeneration, he may become a new creature, and may hence, through the watery ocean of this tempestuous and rocky world, arrive in safety at the most blessed port of Eternal Rest, and sing the New Song with the Triumphing Philosophers of the Heavenly Jerusalem."

The pedigree of the science is supernatural, like the science itself; it is true, as we have already hinted, that it is a fabulous pedigree, its history has an inner meaning, and is not to be literally understood; the inner meaning connects it with the Holy Assemblies and the initiation of all the ages, even as all initiation connects with the soul's history in the state which preceded generation, in the higher consciousness of the first subjective being, which is also the last interior state, the end and summit of philosophy. "Know then," says *Gloria Mundi*, "that Almighty God first delivered this Art to our father Adam in Paradise, for as soon as He had created and set him in the Garden of Eden, He imparted its arcana to him." The secret knowledge is represented as descending from Adam to Abel, who established its first principles; it was imparted by Abel to Seth, and thence, as the most precious inheritance of the primeval world, to the chief college of Hermetic initiation, the *Turba Philosophorum*.

IV.

The Importance of Man in the Art.

Assuming once more that alchemical literature deals primarily at least with the conscious intelligence of man, and with the unevolved possibilities of the body and mind of humanity, there is another mark which, through all veils and appearances, ought to be distinguishable therein, and that is the importance of man in the Art. It is to be remembered that symbolism, though it is meant to act as a veil, is also designed to be understood, if we are to regard its creation as occurring under the law of right reason. It is intended to raise a difficulty, but not an insuperable barrier. The alchemists must have had some object in writing and circulating their innumerable books, and we may take it that they served as decoys which attracted the wonder of a concourse of curious enquirers, and out of the *Turba Vulgorum* the elect were picked and preserved by a kind of intellectual selection. Alchemical symbolism was thus designed to be *caviare* to the crowd, but not impenetrable to the prepared. And it is satisfactory for our purpose to note that the sequence of typology was so adapted to the purpose of these profound researchers, that the key to the process—or, rather, to the nature of the mystery of the process—was held out without any evasion or subterfuge, and in many cases was almost as much paraded as the sacredness of the Art, while, at the same time, it was of such a kind that it was likely to be discovered only by those who deserved to possess it. It was adapted to the quality of the mind that the Mystics desired to attract; it would be passed over by those who were devoid of that quality. The "bellows-blowing alchemist," or *souffleur*, whose ambitions were limited to the merely physical experiment, was the least likely among all possible disciples of Hermes to attain the Grand Secret. The slave of the literal meaning, he had no eyes to see, no mind to interpret, beyond it; in many cases, with a truly pitiable earnestness, he may have devoted his life to the quest, but, through a natural incapacity, he became the victim of the veil and symbol, and not without cause might accuse the Hermetic method which misled him. But ever does science demand and obtain her victims, and law of itself has no mercy to an inadequate faculty or an incomplete instrument.

We may conclude, then, that alchemical symbolism was not of the nature of a cryptogram which might surrender to the sharpness of a good guesser. The few persons who in these days have accepted its literature in any serious manner have been apt to regard it as a puzzle, which was to be arranged and rearranged till the right answer was reached. But it is clear that the adepts of a true, and above all of a divine, science would not inclose their mysteries in cryptograms, which exercise only the ingenuity of the seeker, and give no guarantee whatever of his moral or spiritual qualifications. Now, the key which we refer to is precisely that which, on our assumption, we ought to have found in alchemical literature, and it is actually the importance of man in the Art. He, says St. Chrysostom, is "the most resplendent and glorious image, and the most exquisite portal and epitome of the unseen world." This is the key-note of spiritual Mysticism, and it is the key-note of practical alchemy. "If that which thou seekest thou findest not within thee, thou wilt never find it without thee," says Alipili. Among the strange, archaic treatises comprised in the *Turba Philosophorum*, there is one which, by a characteristic Hermetic evasion, is ascribed to the patriarch Abel. If it be possible to speak with more force on this point than was done by the Arabian alchemist, then the words of Pseudo-Abel may perhaps be even more direct and convincing. "Man is the mountain of mountains, the stone of stones, the tree of trees, the root of roots, the earth of earths. All these things he includes within himself, and God has given to him to be the preserver of all things." It is, therefore, in man himself that we are directed to seek for the solution of that chief crux of alchemy, the nature and locality of the First Matter of the Philosophers. Even as all magical power is in the inward man, so is the *Magnum Opus* defined to be before all things the creation of man by himself, and that perfect emancipation of his will which ensures his universal dominion over Azoth and the domain of Magnesia. "In us is the power of all wonderful things, which the Supreme Creator has, of His infinite mercy, implanted in our Soul; out of her is to be extracted the First Matter, the true *Argent Vive*, the ☿ of the Philosophers, the veritable *Ens* of *Sol*, namely, a spiritual, living Gold, which will endure fire, test, and coppel. Our soul has the power, when the body is free of any pollution, the heart void of malice and offence, spiritually and magically to act upon any matter whatsoever. Therefore have I said that the First Matter is in the soul, and the extracting thereof is to bring the dominant power of the pure, living, breathing spirit and eternal soul into act." So also Geber, perhaps the most ancient of the adepts who are historically traceable, declares that "the universal orb of the earth contains not so great mysteries and excellencies as man reformed by God in His image."

V.

The Spiritual Interpretation of Alchemy.

It is necessary to state at the outset that the spiritual interpretation of the literature of the physical Mystics is not a new interpretation. It began openly with Jacob Böhme, but it was first systematically developed in the *Suggestive Inquiry into the Hermetic Mystery and Alchemy.* However, both in the writings of the Teutonic Theosophist, and in the wonderful elaboration by the daughter of Mr. South, or again in the hundred and one successors in the "spiritual hermeneutics" of transmutation literature—from Hitchcock to Hartmann, from Eliphas Levi to the "adept" Papus—the system has dealt only with the department of Hermetic psychology. It has never been discerned that the principles which work mystically in the soul can be applied outwardly in the body of man—that if alchemy in its higher significance can inform us of the soul's development, and of the end of the soul therein, it has something also to tell us of the mystery of our physical evolution, and of a coming glory in the manifest even as in the withdrawn order. But the adornment of the vessel of philosophy is of high importance in our holy art. The redemption of the body must be accomplished along with "the salvation of the soul." We must not underrate the importance of the vehicle of interior perfection, for we are incarnate here to no purpose if we neglect our bodies. The law of evolution must fulfil its course both in the outward and the inward man. The exclusively spiritual interpretation is, we think, an error of enthusiasm which has operated on suggestive texts and ignored the context, and has forgotten that the lives of the alchemists were in many cases those of laborious investigators into natural secrets, distinct from arch-natural experience. There is no doubt, at the same time, that the texts to which we refer are sufficient in number and gravity to excuse, if they do not warrant, the conclusion, while there are many individual cases which possess a peculiar force. "As soon as any one discerns the intention of the philosophers from the seeming sense of the letter, the dark night of ignorance will fly away and a glorious morning of light and knowledge will break forth." Here, as in a multitude of similar cases, there is stronger language than could be reasonably used in connection with a physical secret, and it derives a fresh significance when it is compared with the dark hints that are found in writers like Norton, who refer to an operation that is not of metals or minerals, but belongs to a high order, is comprehended by few, and is truly philosophical in character. This is that work which begins with a heavenly Mercury and an imperfect body purified, while the white glory of its triumphing conclusion is the whole end, as it is also the one ecstacy of the illuminated and the wise.

The investigators of old, being unacquainted with the doctrine of continuity, and not having defined that limit of scientific possibility beyond which facts are forbidden to stray except at their own peril, conducted their experiments into the scope of unknown forces with an almost exuberant licence. Thanks now to the doctrine of continuity, the philosophy of the unknowable, and other salutary provisions which have been proclaimed as immutable law, a matronly character, an almost rotund respectability, and a solid and general sobriety, have been infused into physical science. She has forgotten the follies of her youth, her multitudinous initial extravagances. She has forgotten that she believed once in God and the angels, in Paradise and Heaven, in immortality and beatitude, and the law of the world to come. She has forgotten, above all, that she once believed in miracles, in the transmutation of metals, in the elixir of rejuvenated life, in the magical resurrection of the dead, in sorcery, spells, and witchcraft. If there be any who have faith in these now, they are a perishing remnant of benighted votaries, and she counsels her confessors and disciples not so much as to speak with them. Yet this vagrant old world science instructed the men of Eld in the mysteries of their own constitution, on its interior side, and in the depths of Nature's heart. To modern knowledge, as to Peter Bell, a primrose is a yellow primrose, and nothing more; the mesmeric trance is an abnormal sleep, and hypnotism is a pathological condition. But the primrose was more than a primrose to the past masters of Mysticism; it was a little world which contained the great as in a miniature. That was the position of the Mystics, and the difference between them and the luminous expositors of modern botanical physics was the difference between Peter Bell and his poet—

> To whom the meanest flower that blows can give
> Thoughts that do often lie too deep for tears.

For them, consequently, trance and the hypnotic state were not simply conditions to be observed, but possibilities which were to be developed, and just as

Professor Max Müller has discovered a religion which is behind all religions, so is it affirmed that the Mystics attained to the abiding and permanent wonder which is behind the common flux of all magical marvels, to the evolution which is within evolution, to the subsistent spirituality which is behind all souls, to the life which is beyond life. A fact in the sphere of the abnormal was fertilized by their vivid perceptions and pursued in all its ramifications as far as experiment could extend. If a patient in a certain stage of a malady developed the sense of sight at the pit of the stomach, or at the extremities of the hands and feet, the Mystics recognized that the house of life had more than seven windows, and to them the opening of a new window, for however brief a period, suggested the possibility that new views could be obtained from the new standpoint, and they conducted their experiments accordingly. And the alchemists in particular proceeded after precisely this manner, with the same eager scrutiny, the same keen eye, the same open mind; in the continual presence of the unexplored possibility of Nature they may be said to have worked and lived. No matter what the operation in hand, for them always there was a higher achievement in the same or an analogical order. The breadth of their view was in consequence of the scope of their theory, which comprised all being within a single principle, having a special mode of application, which was the inheritance of their initiation. They applied it in the mineral kingdom, and they evolved perfect metals, "better than those of the mines"; they applied it in the kingdom of humanity—the result was their crowned Dian and the supernatural Son of the Sun.

We have spoken already of the identity in both evolutions, and we shall speak of it more fully hereafter. For the moment it will be sufficient to say that as throughout their literature the alchemists treat of things physical in the terminology of the spiritual world, so also their chemical processes possess a pneumatic side and admit without distortion a spiritual transliteration.

Let us take as a typical example the alchemical significance of ANIMA, and let us have recourse to the *Dictionarium Alchemiæ* of Rulandus, not because it will best serve for our purpose, but rather because, with its tedious metallurgical and mineralogical catalogues, it is in appearance the least promising of its species. Martinus Rulandus was a chemist and a physician of his period, and all that is of chemistry and medicine in his ponderous quarto is dull, laborious, and German. The more sprightly Langlet du Fresnoy, though he also compiled catalogues, dismisses it in a single sentence, *C'est peu de chose.* But Rulandus was also an alchemist, and that which is alchemical in his treatise runs through its tedious pages with a certain flash and coruscation which vitalizes the inanimate mass, and at times the veritable Rose of Hermes blossoms in the barren desert. Accepting him at his best for the moment, let us read in the book of Rulandus with an interpretation, and give the sense so that we can see the meaning. "As the Philosophers conceive three principles, Salt, Sulphur, and Mercury, so also they conceive three other divisions"—that is to say, divisions on another, higher, interior, and intelligent plane—"Soul, Spirit, and Body; not that the Soul and the Spirit are to be distinguished as cattle from men, but by way of similitude. The Soul is nothing else but a living, formed body, which is turned into Mercury"—here we must remember that, according to a proverbial Hermetic maxim, there is concealed in the philosophical Mercury the thing which is desired by the Wise—"and when this is done to the dead Body and Spirit, then the whole is made living Elixir." Now, the ancient alchemical theory supposes that the inferior metals are smitten by a leprosy, or by some complaint or disease, of which they may be healed by Art, and when the Artist has thus healed them, they will become and will attain to the stature of perfect metals. This can only be effected by the confection of the mysterious Medicine of Metals, or the Metallic Elixir, and this Elixir, regarded in another aspect, or in its applied state, is itself the one absolute and perfect triumph of the mineral kingdom. And when the Great Subject, Man, has been elaborated by arcane evolution till the Soul and the Body, hitherto spiritually dead, have been transformed by the Mercury of the Spirit, then is the whole man made also a "living Elixir." He has become a part of the force of evolution, of the law which "makes for righteousness." There is no action and there is no thought which is, traceably or not, without its effect on the universe, and the accomplishment of the grand Iliaster by one individual makes the mystic passage more easy to all others. When the crown of evolution has been reached, the whole race will itself be a living Elixir for the transmutation of the generations to come. In another sense, the passage which we have been interpreting deals with a dual regeneration—namely, spirit-quickening, and the development of the arch-natural body. "Therefore, make no mistake," says Rulandus, "when the Philosophers speak of one Soul instead of two Souls"—that is to say, when they make use of the generic and popular division of man into a material and spiritual being—"for it is all one thing." In other words, we are not to be misled by terminology; there is but ultimately one real Man; isolated from the impulse of God, divorced from the divine, there is only dead body or dwindling astral shell; true individuality, constituting true Man, is impossible when we are apart from the Absolute. Whatever the best of us may exhibit of individuality here is but the result of an electric contact with the eternal *verve* of God. "The Mercury has in itself the Soul, and is called our Mercury, which is the House and dwelling of the Soul"; in like manner the arch-natural body contains the eternal essence, as a medicine is enclosed in a capsule. The eternal essence is the one and true Medicine both for body and mind; it is the spiritual all-healer and the transmuting agent. But in the passage just quoted it will be seen that the Soul is referred to as if it were the highest part of Man. In his next sentence Rulandus explains his mode. "Also the Soul is called Spirit, and the Spirit is called Soul." As a fact, this arises in two ways: (i) By the common confusions of an uninstructed terminology which prevails through much Christian theology. (ii) By the instructed confusion of Hermetic writers, who, justifiably or not, seem often to have misled their readers. "The Spirit produces the Soul from the Body, and returns it when it is white." Note well this point, and the arcane mystery that is here alluded to—the material world contributing to the substance of the Soul, the Soul in this life still in course of formation, present environment operated upon by the resident divinity in man, its quintessence extracted for the basis of a future environment. "Therefore it is called the Life of the Soul," *Vita Animæ*, the theological *Anima Animæ*. "Should the Spirit depart from the Soul, it would not give the Life." The Spirit is thus the seat of life; the overshadowing of the Spirit—always psychologically at a distance from the objective organism—produces, as it were, the exterior life of man. When it is withdrawn the phenomenal man perishes. "The Soul unites and conjoins the married, body and spirit." Here is the true philosophy of the nuptial state, and, as Vaughan hath it, "how one should use a wife." There is an intercourse of the interior body as well as of external sex, and this is called commonly a communion of souls; but note that there is another marriage, that of spirits, which is higher than any psychal union, and note also that the Soul partakes of the sensual nature, and in the transcendental order there is a joy of the sense of Soul. "So the Spirit unites the Soul with the Body till it is all one thing. There are two Souls—one of gold, one of silver. The Soul of the gold must remain, and cannot do so without the Spirit, nor yet the Spirit remain without the Soul." Thus the presence of the divine essence preserves the union of Soul and Body, and, as all esoteric philosophy indifferently teaches, both depart together. "There must be fixed, abiding, undying Souls. At first the Soul lies hidden under the Spirit, finally the Soul and Spirit remain hidden under the Body." At this point there is actually no interpretation needed, for the sense is transparently spiritual. It is a plain statement, spiritually accepted, that the first subjective, or psychic (paradisiacal) state, is originally potential in the Spirit, as the Spirit itself was potential once in the timeless and the God-consciousness; afterwards the First Man, or first objective, immaterial, psychic state, and that which indwells or broods over, which, in fact, in a certain sense, may be said to overlap the psychic man, were, as they now are, both hidden in the physical, exterior man, whom we all desire to be dissolved that we may be with Christ, albeit that without dying we may all see God. "Then dost thou first behold pure Mercury." It is in man only that pure and eternal intelligence first became manifested on this material earth. We now—that is, normally, at least—only behold pure Mercury imprisoned in a body; but there will come a day, and then indeed the Morning Stars shall sing together, when we all shall behold it, and that without a body —namely, the body of our death—a pure, fixed, intelligible, constant fire of ungenerable Spirit. Then without flesh shall we see God; then also in God shall we see and possess all things, and be united to all desirable subjects with a completeness and intimacy of essential union, which, as we shall learn hereafter, it is impossible to experience when we are separated from those subjects by any form of environment. "Through the crude Spirit is the pure Mercury taken away from the released body." That is to say, the psychic principle, as appears from what has preceded, when separated at death from the physical environment, departs, still enclosing the eternal man, the form and font of our humanity. "This is a fixed ash, remaining behind to be dissolved further," as indeed occurs physically to the abandoned exterior form. But there is also a death of the body which is only esoterically known, and it is "out of this," as Rulandus continues, that there "is extracted a petrine incombustible Olitet, or germ, which vivifies, unites, and welds the natures together; and as they separated the natures through the Spirit, accordingly through the Soul they unite them again." Now, the separation which takes place after regeneration between the desires of the body and the desires of the mind, which has been made pure, occasions a species of impermanent division between the individual and personal man, which occurs through the Spirit; in other words, the action of the Spirit within us draws us away from our lower part, and it is in this sense that Christ came not to bring peace but a sword, to set father against son and wife against husband. But when our aspirations and desires have been caught up through the power of the approximating Spirit into the region of the Soul, a compensating action follows, and the influence of the Spirit is extended into the phenomenal man, who is strengthened, purified, and transfigured, until, by a more complete and harmonious interaction and rhythmic correspondence between the triadic natures, the complete man is manifested, whole and one. "This Olitet preserves the colour of the Spirit, even to thickening," and so the physical body of the regenerate man has a tinge, a colouring of his Spirit; contemplated in his wholeness as a triad, he exhibits at the apex of his being the eternal presidence of pure essential mind, and at the base, as it were, thickened spirit, that which is above made manifest below in a concrete form, but still

6

preserving a colouring or permeation of the splendour of the summit. "Then is it fit for the production of royal weapons and metallic figures." That is to say, the adept has control over the energies of the universe, and he shapes these forces to his purpose; he can possess the power of the king, symbolized by weapons of warfare, or the power of the pontiff, represented by the figures or images, which are also said to be of metal, because both forces are in their ultimate of the same nature. "It manifests itself as golden in gold and as argentine in silver," because there is but one substance infinitely differentiated in the universe. "The Soul's ascent is when the Body becomes white, clear, and fluid," that is, the inner man is exalted in the purification of the outer man. The state of whiteness signifies the clarity or molecular refulgence of physical purity; the transparency is the atomic exaltation which follows the process of regeneration; the fluidic state is the dissolution of the hardness of the material condition, and signifies that the possession of a physical environment is no longer an invincible obstacle to an interior progress, but that the body itself passes on with the other principles, even as a stream flows, from ascension to ascension. "Immediately they are one and living." When the Body has been thus operated upon, there is a consanguinity of life subsisting throughout the triad. "Then is there danger. If the Soul should escape or burn, it is lost." The universal voice of occultism bears witness to the dangerous period which must inevitably follow the first plunge into the mysteries of the Inner Way. All initiation symbolizes it; all allegories depict it. "So is the Soul quickly given to the Body, and takes shape;" here the necessity of the phenomenal manifestation of the Body is shadowed forth. "The Soul proceeds out of the unified Body; she is herself the living Body." Here the reference includes two Mysteries. When the physical body has become atomically unified with the higher principles, its quintessence, or subtlest and purest part, is made use of for the constitution of the inner or spiritual body, which is the envelope of disembodied humanity. Thus, one of its uses is to provide an environment for the next stage of subsistence, and the evolution of the arch-natural man, by another compensating action, creates a more perfect correspondence between the psychal and the physical man, and will actually, with the progress of the race, manifest the Soul as a transfiguration of the atomic body, and then, in a sense, the Soul will be actually the living body. To this conception the alchemists gave the names—Rebis, Animal Stone, Blood, Sulphur, Olitet, etc.

VI.

The Subject or Matter of the Philosophers.

No alchemical book has ever revealed the materials on which alchemy operated for the transmutation of the metallic natures. This is not because the materials have never been named, but because they have never been really described. Every new writer has given them a new name, and everyone in assigning their qualities has contradicted one, more than one, or all of his predecessors. We have stated this plainly before, and we again state it plainly so that there may be no possibility of misconception, and that no person may be so distraught as to undertake at our instance the discovery of the physical Stone of the Philosophers. The exoteric chemistry of to-day, were it brought to believe that transmutation has occurred in the past, would consider the secrecy of the adepts as a foolish and culpable thing, but it will be seen from foregoing remarks that the veritable initiates, in our conception, did well to conceal, even in announcing, their discovery. They had found in their process the complete vanity and worthlessness of material riches; the desire for wealth and its amenities had melted under fire in their crucibles; the ambition which henceforth seems to have ruled in their lives was to subsist without ostentation, and to keep the "Grand Secret." To them the conception of a rich alchemist was more mad than an "undevout astronomer." Let us hear Eirenæus Phila-lethes appraising the gold which he pretended to manufacture. "I wish gold and silver were as mean in esteem as earth. . . . I disdain, loathe, and detest the idolizing of silver and gold, by which the pomps and vanities of the world are celebrated. Ah, filthy evil! Ah, vain nothingness! . . . I do hope and expect that within a few years money will be as dross; and that prop of the anti-Christian beast will be dashed to pieces. The people are mad, the nations rave, an unprofitable wight is set up in the place of God." Nor is "the true Philalethes" alone in the violence of his disdain.

Thus even for the physical alchemists, who never pretended to work otherwise than in metals, the chief end of attainment was that they might "enjoy this gift of God secretly." The annals of the science contain no record of an adept who has amassed wealth, a fact which is explicable on two hypotheses only—that which regards the enquiry as a delusion or an imposture, but with this we are in nowise concerned; and that which regards transmutation as the lowest achievement of the arcane knowledge, the veil chosen by the Wise as a cloak to their ulterior designs. This is our own standpoint, and regarded in this light, initiation into the lesser mystery involved at least a theoretical acquaintance with the possibilities beyond, while that acquaintance inevitably destroyed the desire for material wealth.

But the larger proportion of genuine alchemical literature is concerned, in our opinion, with a spiritual as well as a physical work, and the true adepts were Mystics in the pneumatic sense before they became alchemists. Their knowledge was perpetuated by inheritance from a certain Holy Assembly, or resulted from contact therewith, and their operations, like their works, are to be understood in two senses. It is easy to distinguish these Masters among the *Turba Philosophorum*, for they invariably say that the achievement of alchemy is philosophical gold, and not gold of the mines, whereas the physical school of adeptship worked upon common gold, and is not backward in assuring us of the fact. To this class belonged George Starkey, and the *Marrow of Alchemy* is a typical work within its own division. From writers of the higher degree we may select an initial definition:

"The gold of the Philosophers is a heavenly substance; it is heaven, and the rays of the sun. It is the most eminent medicine. It has in itself all the stars of heaven and all the fruits of earth." These are words borrowed from the higher alchemists. We may compare them with a passage from the interior philosopher, Jacob Böhme: "He in whom this spring of divine power flows carries within himself the divine image and the celestial substantiality. In him is Jesus born of the Virgin, and he shall not die in eternity." (*Six Points*, vii. 33.) "Heaven and earth with all their inhabitants, and, moreover, God Himself is in man." (*Tilk.*, ii. 297.) From the correspondences between these passages, it is easy to reach a conclusion as to the nature of the Gold of the Philosophers regarded from the standpoint of Basil Valentine, Eugenius Philalethes, Khunrath, and Alexander Seton.

VII.

The Nature of the Physical Achievement.

We propose to refer briefly to the nature of the physical achievement. The aim or object of occult chemistry was then to perform the *Magnum Opus*, to accomplish the confection of the shining and wondrous Stone of the Philosophers, which again has a dual aspect, for in one of its applications it serves for the transmutation of all metals into the ideal metal Gold, and in another it constitutes the "pearly drink of bright Phœbus," in other words, the veritable elixir of life and of philosophy. To the confection of this Stone, thousands, no doubt, in past ages must have devoted the energies of long lives in which laborious research ultimated but too frequently in the bitterness of complete failure. The physical alchemists may be therefore divided into:—(*a*) Those who discovered, or believed themselves to have discovered, the secret of metallic transmutation. (*b*) Those who attempted the experiment and did not succeed in their design. (*c*) A vast crowd of later pretenders who neither found nor sought, but exploited the credulity of their period by proclaiming that they possessed chemical secrets. Representatives of each of these divisions betook themselves to writing books—the first to announce their achievements, the second to register for the guidance of future experiment what matters of moment they had discovered by the way, the third to support their imposture, as well as to reap further spoils from publications which sold readily. The representatives of the middle division wrote little, as a rule, but they had the merit of speaking plainly, having no motive for concealment. The actual discoverers veiled their revelations in a symbolic language and in pictorial symbols; in a word, they did everything to confuse their readers, and to make their own attainment impossible to their successors. The impostors, whose name became legion, were more secret and mysterious than their antitypes. To distinguish a true adept and a genuine process among the chaos of failure and simulation requires infinite pains and wide reading in alchemical literature. Even then the result will provide us with the process only, and not with the materials. It is useless for anyone to undertake the study of alchemy in the hope that he will be able, as a result, to transmute metals. That arcanum can be learnt only in two ways—by communication from the Holy Assembly which we believe to be still possible, but the knowledge would be entailed as a consequence of attainment in the transcendental order, and would not be otherwise derived—or by some future revelation of analytical chemistry, independently of all arcane knowledge, and from that we anticipate disaster.

Shall we ever manufacture gold by science, is at first sight a tempting question, and the enquiry—in advance of any answer—cannot fail to bring a pactolian water into the mouth of the average man and woman. Theoretically, of course, all right thinking persons are supposed to despise money, and we know that it is generally regarded as a moral act to speak of it in an impolite manner. The philosopher terms it vain nothingness, filthy lucre, the root of all evil, and claims high authority for doing so. Those who are not philosophers are depreciatory after their own fashion. It is the correct thing to describe gold by its opposites, and in compliance with this sentiment, it is known vulgarly as brass, tin, dross, and it has also other titles which would indicate its worthless character. All this is exceedingly satisfactory; it is a good thing to be superior to our necessities; but the thing is after all a necessity, and most persons, perforce, spend their lives mainly in ministration to their need of it. Now it is commonly so hard to make money that it might well seem more easy to manufacture gold itself. And then—if we only could! Ah!—in however small a quantity—however little at a time—it would be like possessing the purse of Fortunatus. The purse of Fortunatus was a very narrow one, but it always had one coin in it. Its owner lived respectably in a quiet way, and had no fear of his creditors.

"Shall we manufacture gold?" would appear to be a reasonable question. There are persons of some consideration who regard the achievement as possible. M. Louis Figuier, the French scientist—and a very exact gentleman —thinks so and says it. Mr. Edward Pinter, the last of the alchemists, may not think so, but he also says it, and was prepared, on a memorable occasion, to transmute metals in the presence of learned counsel, and under the auspices of a court of law. It is only a short time since that we heard of a Paris philosopher, who had studied mineralogy in Mexico and found out how the whole process was managed by Nature herself. And he says it. But he despises the purse of Fortunatus and its one inexhaustible dime. Give him the necessary plant— for he is a poor man—and then watch for a change in the Bank rate, a panic on the Bourse, and chaos in all securities. The most sober of all sciences is chemistry, because, *par excellence*, it is the experimental science. And chemistry, though it does not say actually that we *shall* manufacture gold, because it never forecasts the future, does practically admit that there are, so to speak, shadows around it which may be cast by some coming event of the kind. It is yearly discovering new elements. Within a recent period, it has presented us with "Damaria"—the lightest of known substances—and with the grey metal, Germania, which is similar to antimony in character, and becomes volatile at red heat. But, what is more to the purpose, this same science is no less persistent, and quite as successful, in decomposing those substance which have been hitherto supposed to be elements, and not capable of decomposition. Thus a chemist of Munich is said to have separated the constituent principles of cobalt and nickel.

These are technological matters which are of little moment to the ordinary reader, but it will be interesting to any one to learn the direction in which they point. They substantiate the theory that our supposed elementary substances— of which gold is one—are mere compounds and alloys, in which case it would be possible to manufacture gold, as we now manufacture rubies, by a chemical process.

Of course, it is natural to suppose that the result of such a discovery would be something approaching a metallic millennium, in which there would be

Gold! and gold! and gold without end!

Gold to lay by and gold to spend,
    And reversions of gold *in futuro!*

We should realize the dream of the alchemists, and the precious metal would become a kitchen ornament and the material for stewpans. But, as a fact, nothing of the kind would result. Gold, or its equivalent in paper currency, is the *summum bonum* from a commercial standpoint. The Moonstone (of Mr. Wilkie Collins), the Koh-i-Nor, and the Idol's Eye, or, for that matter, certain black pearls which may be seen occasionally in the Palais Royal, may be intrinsically more valuable, but to ascertain or express their preciousness we must refer to gold as a standard. It is like the "milk-white hind" of Dryden; it is, so to speak, "immortal and unchanged." It is alone genuine, alone immutable, alone a legal tender. He who owns it in a solid and collective sense possesses all Mammon potentially therein. Now, every attempt to depreciate the value of gold is certain to be regarded as high treason against the absolute of finance, and of all such attempts, that of manufacturing the precious metal on a large scale by a cheap process would be at once the most vicious and insane. It would be vicious, because it would strike almost at the roots of society, making our system of exchange worthless, and annihilating our legal tender. It would be foolish, because it would make paltry that which is precious and give us nothing precious in return; it must, in fact, impoverish the whole world without enriching any one.

Should, therefore, a process for the inexpensive production of gold be at any time discovered by science, it is obvious that its unlicensed manufacture must be at once made penal, and that to a degree of penality which would be barbarous in minor matters, like that of the illicit whisky-still. Otherwise, the chemical crucible which first transmutes metals will decompose more than a scientific element, for it will contain the materials of a financial and social cataclysm. Whosoever may discover such a process had better remember that silence is more precious than any metal or any ore. Let him be content to become the billionaire of the future, whom we have descried upon the financial horizon, and, above all, if it be possible, may he permit his secret to die with him! By so doing he will deserve well of society, which he will have saved from the most disastrous of revolutions.

But the prophetic foresight and the claimed achievements of the old workers have been so frequently fulfilled independently by the experiments of modern research that we must face the possibility at least of success in this instance, and for any consequences that it may entail. The denial of such a possibility will not help matters any more than we can reasonably expect to elucidate the mysteries of spiritual chemistry by denying that there was a physical end in alchemy, or that the transmutation of metals was sought with as much earnestness as the elixir of life. For the elixir of life was sought in all earnestness, though here, as in the process on metals, there is no uncommon insight required to discern that this also had two fields of application.

There was a spiritual and a physical Medicine, there was a dual recon- struction of humanity, the grand restitution included both body and soul, the processes were intimately united, and in a sense they were almost one; the com- position of the physical elixir was analogous to that of the spiritual; regenera- tion within was the divine complement of renewal without, nor could the lesser achievement be truly and permanently achieved till the larger work had been accomplished. As in alchemy, so also in the Universal Medicine. Physical transmutation we regard as having literally taken place; the youth of the body can, we believe, be renewed, but even were these lesser dreams spurious from the external standpoint, yet for the inner, the true and real man, they cannot be either fond or foolish. They are the consciousness of operating potencies whose ultimate evolution we can only distinguish in prophecy, but they are there and they do act. Let the faculty of interpretation distinguish by all means between the less and the great, but do not let it ignore the less, or absorb one into another. Concerning the physical perpetuation of youth, we repeat that it was sought, even as the achievement of conversion in metallic alchemy. That is a short-sighted criticism which is content with the showiness of merely suggestive interpretations, such as that of Eliphas Levi, which is set forth in the ensuing citation: "The Great Master has said: My flesh is meat indeed, and my blood is drink indeed. He that eateth my flesh and drinketh my blood hath everlasting life. And when the crowd murmured, He added: Here the flesh profiteth nothing, the words which I speak unto you are spirit and life. There- fore He meant to say: Drink of my spirit and live by my life. And when He was about to die, He attached the memory of His life to the sign of bread, and that of His spirit to the sign of wine, and instituted thus the communion of faith, hope, and charity. In the same manner the Hermetic Masters say: Make gold potable, and you will have the Universal Medicine. That is, appro- priate truth to your use; let it be the spring from which you daily drink, and then will you possess within you the immortality of the Sages."

Such interpretations eliminate the entire *raison d'être* of Hermetic termin- ology. The aphorisms of a commonplace morality neither deserve nor require the elaboration of a conventional language, nor a vast sequence of allegorical symbols. It is an insult to the intellect of the Hermetic ages to suppose that the labours of all the philosophers were confined to the enclosure of meta-physical truisms in the many splèndours of a pompous typology. The *aperçus* which have already been allowed to the students of modern psychology are sufficient to warrant them in concluding that the masquerade of the Mystics was the first act of the Grand Mysteries, and a prelude to the "unheard of curiosities" which are stored in the penetralia of the soul.

Now, physical alchemy, according to Eliphas Levi, was a species of metallic culture; the alchemists everywhere recognize that their theory could be applied also in the vegetable and animal kingdoms, and the science in the hands of Paracelsus was as much the artificial generation of fruit as it was the ripening of minerals. He taught the incubation of eggs into living birds after the same manner as we now perform it, and with as much gravity as the generation of gold or silver. The process in all cases was concerned with the application of a certain arcane heat. Alchemical experiments in the vegetable world which were not concerned with the manufacture of an elixir of life do not seem to have been pursued in the past, but the possibilities then indicated have become actualities in the present. Let us take an illustration at random from a recent achievement in that electrical world which is the true fairyland of science, an enchanted ground where all things seem possible, and where every explorer is sure to meet with great adventures and to discover hidden treasures. It is said that the development of vegetable seeds may be rendered far more rapid by submitting them to the action of an electric current. The influence of this treatment is shown by a larger crop, and by the growth of vegetables of enormous dimensions. The monster mangel, the colossal carrot, and the herculean haricot will be a godsend to vegetarian societies at the dawn of the twentieth century. The epicure of that day will also revel in the titanic tomato and the mammoth mushroom, for the amiable "force of the future" will doubtless preserve delicacy of flavour, while, at the same time, it magnifies size. Experiments extending over a period of five years have been tried with satisfactory results at Kief in Russia, upon the seeds of beans, sunflowers, and spring and winter rye, as also upon pot-herbs and flowering plants. In fact, we may shortly expect in our gardens a flora that would do honour to the vaster orbs of Neptune or Saturn. Rapidity of development and increase in dimensions are not, it may be objected, everything. Is it not possible that gigantic vegetables may be attacked by titanic diseases and Brobdingnagian parasites? It is possible, no doubt, but electricity is equal to the occasion; it is said to be the human cure-all, and it is the cure-all of the vegetable kingdom. Manipulate the seed with electricity, and the potato, it has already been discovered, shall know no blight. Subject the seed of the grape vine to the gentle and vitalizing shock of the

continuous current, and the vine shall have immunity from phylloxera. We
are practically in possession of new weapons with which to do battle against
the enemies of vegetable growth.

What a prospect is here opened to agriculture! Will the process stop short
at the vegetable kingdom? It is impossible to expect too much of a science
from which anything may be expected. If electricity can be usefully applied to
any germ of life, it is reasonable to conclude that it may ultimately, and with as
much profit, be extended to all. We shall then have an improved process of
horse-breeding by the application of the electric current, the natural selection
which perpetuates favourable variations, and has been assisted by the selection of
humanity, being still further supplemented by the all-potent force. To go a
step further, who among modern scientists can affirm at the moment that some
one, greatest among the physiologists of the future, may not succeed in elaborating the perfect man—the dream of all idealists, and the ideal of all Utopias—by
a judicious adaptation of the mysterious force of electricity to incipient human
life? It is at least certain that, should a material golden age ever be restored it
will be by the assistance of electricity; should a time ever come when, in the
words of Philalethes, "all currencies shall be destroyed," it will be when
electricity has accomplished the *Magnum Opus* of manufacturing the precious
metals. We conclude that evolved man, subsisting independently of currencies
in a world renovated by electricity, having electrically accomplished the navigation of the air, the colonization of the sea, and the secret of universal fecundity,
is as good an illustration of a material age of gold as can be supplied by the
imagination of the most inspired prophet of any physical science.

The sequence of processes in the evolution of the metallic natures has been
variously classified by the alchemists. Purgation, Dissolution, Separation,
Conjunction, Cibation, Fermentation, Exaltation, and the Magical Marriage,
are designations applied to the various stages of the work; and when we treat, in
our second part, of Mysticism as a practical Science, we shall make use of this
chain of development to indicate the analogical stages in the operation of
spiritual evolution. It is set before us in other presentations under the guise of
the Keys of Philosophy. There is that which opens the dark prisons, that which
dissolves the compound, that which perfectionizes Mercury, that which reduces
philosophical water into philosophical earth, that which produces the fermentation of the Stone with the perfect body, "to make thereof the Medicine of the
Third Order," and that which gives entrance to the secret of the Multiplication
of the Stone. It would be easy to elaborate the pneumatic significance which
abides in this sequence; it would be easy to provide others, and to explain them
all, for all proceed after the same mode and make for the same end. That end is

the "Supernatural Generation of the Son of the Sun," and it is accomplished in each case amidst a manifestation of light and a coruscation of glory, a radiance and ravishment of the eye, which has won for the perfect achievement that name, at once most dear and most familiar to all true philosophers, the Work of the Light. No matter how the process was accomplished, with what tinctures or medicines, with whatsoever sulphurs or mercuries, and however assisted by the salts of life and the Protean spirits of the worlds philosophical, its end was the development of a perfection which was brought forth after much labour amidst a great glory.

VIII.

The Doctrine of Correspondence.

Such was the process by which the alchemists of old endeavoured to elaborate into the perfection of full activity the arcane potentialities which reside in metallic substances, and such also, on the same Hermetic theory, was the operative sequence which obtained for a similar achievement in all kingdoms of Nature. This is the practical or experimental side of the great doctrine of correspondences. How does evolution proceed in the development of a life-bearing globe? Answer this question, and you indicate the process in the development of a man from the formless chaos of the fœtus to the complete stature of the mature humanity. Such also is the process in the development of mind in man, and of soul, and of spirit. The speculative side of the same doctrine creates by analogy a conception of the worlds unseen by an argument from the known to the unknown. It may appear to be an arbitrary dogma, but it is enforced by our entire inability to conceive the invisible order except upon the supposition that it is analogically like unto the visible. We have no other ground to go upon. Man is inevitably anthropomorphic. It is impossible to understand him subsisting in a disembodied state without preserving the formal outlines of his embodied mode; it is impossible to conceive him subsisting without an environment; and it is equally impossible to imagine that environment except as a sublimated and exalted prototype of the present world. If the experience of time is to be stultified utterly in the timeless, our present life is devoid of an assignable *raison d'être*. As long as man remains man he must be at least analogically like unto himself, and there must be a ground for comparison, that is, a feature of likeness, a similitude, between his future and actual surroundings. Otherwise, he will not be man. The practical side of correspondences must stand or fall by the test of experiment. It is possible, however, to indicate a rigorous analogy between Hermetic operations in chemistry, the avowed process of metallic elaboration, and the development of the arcane potencies which reside in the subject man. Were we asked to state why in the abstract twice two are four, it would be mathematically pertinent to answer, because there is no reason that they should not be so. It is thus also with the Hermetic dogma. It may be taken as true theoretically, because nothing can be assigned against it, and just as everything, in fact, irresistibly points to the figure 4 as the sum of multiplication between two and two, so everything in experience points to the application of analogy towards things unseen, because it is impossible to conceive the unseen otherwise than by the help of analogy.

The nature of the analogy between the chemical development of metals and of man, once admitted as true, in the sense that the Mystics conducted both operations along lines that were analogically similar, casts a flood of light upon the problems of esoteric evolution. Taken in its most obvious and initial aspects, we shall find our aspiration towards a condition of visible and illuminated glory for the perfect, developed man abundantly foreshadowed, nor is the source and reason of this physical illustration concealed. The process of sublimation reveals that the body is spiritualized and the spirit is made corporeal, the result being a glittering whiteness. In other words, there is such an interchange of activity established between the inner and outer man as conduces towards a unification of elements. The analogy has a deeper meaning than the development of the physical man, for soul is necessary to illustration, and it is really the profounder operation upon which the surface work follows. The analogical chemistry of Spirit is the Grand Work of evolution, and its principles have been elaborated by a writer who has preceded us. The anonymous lady who was the first to discern in the processes of alchemy the history of the Soul's evolution deserves to be distinguished by a title which will commend itself to the Hermetic student, and to be called the modern Pernelle, fitting helpmeet for a new Nicholas Flamel! We refer to that epoch-making book which was published in 1850, under the title, *A Suggestive Inquiry into the Hermetic Mystery and Alchemy*. Without being committed to the entire scope of its doctrine, we gratefully acknowledge that it has been a source of help and leading, and has chiefly impelled our researches into the transcendental activities of Azoth, and the supreme mystery of spiritual evolution.

IX.

The Alchemical Transfiguration of Humanity.

We may search the literature of alchemy, and we may search the world itself, for the supposed First Matter of the physical *Magnum Opus*, and, as we have seen, our trouble will be in vain.   Modern chemistry continues to elaborate after its own fashion the innate potentialities of metals without having recourse to the alchemists.   The books of those old workers might still teach us something, even in chemistry, could we find scientists to read them.   But they will not teach us the grand metallic secret; and if Seton and Lascaris, or any other initiated Celt, or any other Greek Archimandrite, have their veritable descendants to-day, there are apparently no Helvetius, no Delisle, and no goldsmiths' apprentices, to whom they will impart their arcanum.   But the processes psycho-alchemical, and the processes organo-alchemical whereby the interior possibilities which abide in the souls and bodies of men may be developed into active operation are not impracticable for want of a material to work upon.   In metallic alchemy we know that it was not mercury and it was not sulphur of which the *Turba Philosophorum* availed themselves as the foundation of their procedures in esoteric decoction.   In this other alchemy, we know that the subject is man, that the end is his transmutation, that his body is the vase, and that his inner latencies are the energies to be educed.   There is no foreign substance to apply.   The work is exclusively one of purgation, eduction, and exaltation.   We have to purge the impurities, to unfold the virtues, and to raise the elements.   Thus, the work, in the main, that is to say, after the preliminary cleansings, is wholly one of unfoldment from within. Even in its grand finale, the union of the individual with the Universal Spirit, it is the individual which must seek the Universal, the Soul God, the steel filing the powerful magnet; it is the spark divine, the "vital spark of heavenly flame," which must return into the ocean of light.   Grand is the destiny, and the way after all is facile, for it is not the maceration of flesh; it is not eternal war with environment; it is not renunciation—at least, in its hard and common significance—by which we shall gain our end, becoming "a star amid the stars of mortal night."   It is by the perfectionizing and beautifying of the flesh; it is by adjustment with higher environment, and by civilizing what is savage in our surroundings; it is, in a word, by acquisition that our "cycle" will "move ascending"; and doubtless these things are easier than the old way of asceticism.   They are the way of poesy and pleasantness, of joy and gladness, of divine delight in Nature and all her beauty, of felicity and humanity, leading up to communion with the Divine, and to permanent immersion in beatitude.   And how therefore, not easy, when it is possible to ascend into Heaven on the wings of a woman's voice, singing in the spring of the year, and in the spring of being?   And how therefore not possible when it is easy to enter Paradise through the open gladness and light of loving eyes?

Now, before proceeding to a work of concoction either in chemistry or cooking, it is necessary to cleanse the vessels, and in a work of approximation towards the perfect life we have to deal first with the vase, which is the body of humanity. Let us take a suggestive lesson thereon from the devotion of the Church Catholic. Let us regard the jewelled chalice of silver and gold into which the symbolic God of the Christians is invited to descend. We also have to offer a habitation in our human tabernacle to Eternal Deity, and we must prepare our shrine—bright as the altar lights, precious as chalice and monstrance, sweet-scented with spiritual incense and flowers from the garden of the soul as was ever an Altar of Repose during the solemn hush of a Maundy Thursday night. It is no little thing to which we devote ourselves in the pages of this division—the adornment and illustration of the body of man. There is no part of it that should be called trivial; it should be approached in earnestness and reverence. A great and sacred thing is the beauty of humanity, which abides in the body of humanity; great also and very noble is the intention to adorn that beauty, and under the perfect adjustment of an enlightened law to take all joy fully, freely, without stint, and above all common measure, in all its felicities and delights.

It remains for us now that we should state in a few words the outcome of the prolonged consideration which we have given to the Hermetic philosophy, and it is also the highest point and keynote of our informed enquiry into the operation of the Hermetic Azoth in the Outward Man. Seeing then that all esoteric procedure is regulated in accordance with one fundamental working principle, that all esoteric aspiration is parallel within the lines of that principle; seeing also that alchemy claims to be derived from the fountain of supreme initiation, and does according to our interpretation include the manifestation of the perfect man as well as of the perfect metal, we affirm that there is a Glory to Come, that the Supernatural Generation of the Human Son of the Central Philosophical Sun is a Generation unto Divine Light; that even as alchemy conceals a pneumatic and a material meaning, and is concerned with the elaboration of a potency in both orders, so the mystical elaboration of the interior man is also dual, is concerned with an illumination within and a radiation from the centre to the circumference which is the outward man; in other words, we affirm that the transfiguration by light of the Body of Humanity will accompany his interior evolution, and that the unmanifest perfection in the withdrawn order of his spiritual loveliness will, when evolution has carried its point and has achieved its end, show forth visibly in the order of physical beauty.

CHAPTER THE SECOND.

THE PERFECTION OF HUMANITY IN THE LIGHT OF ASPIRATION AND LEGEND, AND IN THE LIGHT OF THE ACTUAL MAN.

I.

The Testimony of Aspiration.

W E may admit that the processes of Mysticism are those of a spiritual development; we may allow that the procedure of alchemy is one of physical evolution in a given department of Nature, but both these admissions notwithstanding, it is no less grotesque in appearance to infer that the transfiguration of outward humanity will take place amidst a splendour of material light because a similar manifestation accompanied, or was supposed to accompany, artificial transfiguration in the kingdom of metals and minerals. The arcane doctrine of correspondence supposes a parallel method and a kindred mode in all departments of Nature, but even here there is apparently only an inadequate justification. To become identified with the Hermetic standpoint, we must realize that development in the spiritual order is the opening of our nature into light after its own kind; it is the antitype of physical evolution in the body of man; while the system of metallic development is the shadow of both. The Mystic does not look for the manifestation of a splendour of light in the perfect humanity to come because that achievement has been compassed in a department of esoteric mineralogy, but because it is a consequence of the operation of an arcane law which has a varied field of operation, and is founded in the things of the spirit. Even in the metallic region it is not a merely chemical process, for it is the application of a principle to matter which is known only to the Masters of Soul. Spiritual hierophants alone have been true adepts in alchemy. But it is possible to approach the subject from a side which is not esoteric, and it is our purpose in this chapter to show forth after what manner all visions and aspirations after the perfection of humanity in the matter of the outward man are inseparably connected with light. Our chief and most powerful appeal is to every mythology of the past, to the entire cycle of intellectual outreaching after a conception of the higher forms of subsistence in the unseen

order.   The method of all these transfigurations has been the investment of
actual humanity with the glory of manifest light.   But if we turn to the region
of poetry, or to the supernatural of romantic fiction, we shall find the same law of
conception prevailing, and, in fact, even as beauty is inseparable from the idea
of our physical perfection, so is light inseparable from the perfection of physical
beauty.   Now, that which is indispensable to the ideal notion must at any rate
possess its correspondence in the concrete realization, and we submit therefore
that independently of alchemical parallels, and independently of the analogies
of spiritual evolution, an evolved and perfect human body must be sublimed
after some manner in the substance of light.   The synthesis of aspiration will
indicate after what manner, and there are facts in life as it is which will
expound the direction of any operation for the accomplishment of such a
development.   In the first division of our thesis, appeal will be made to universal mythological conceptions upon the forms of supramundane subsistence,
to the legends of the subjective state, and to that which after any manner has
descended to us concerning the aboriginal perfection of objective man.   In the
second division we shall advert to the drift of certain forces which have always
been at work in humanity, and have elevated it to its present standard, as well
as to the significance of accepted psychological facts.   Concerning all, as a needful prestatement, it is only wise to say that we are indicating lines of reflection
over a momentous theme, we are not attempting an exhaustive enquiry.

Is there anything in the humanity around us, or in its past history, which
can in any sense encourage us to regard the Hermetic vision of transfigured
glory as within the possibility of man?   If we enter into the gentle and
benign world of illuminated meditation, we shall discover that a pure light of
physical perfection is not only possible in law, but would seem to be guaranteed
by aspiration, promised by tradition, discerned in the poetic rapture, supposed
in the typological history of the term light, realized in part already by the
outward manifestation of mentality, and demonstrated by psychological phenomena.   From all these sources, and by the assistance of the instrument of the
imagination, which must be regarded as a chief or prime factor in the coming
transfiguration of humanity, we must seek briefly for guidance.   They are as
seven mystical component colours in the celestial bow of promise, whereby we
shall be able to realize something of the hue and tissue in the outward vestment
of the elected vessel and the supreme subject, and shall approach towards an
adequate conception of the end of evolution in humanity, the finality of the
perfect man.   The philosophic, religious, prophetic, and poetic dreams of the
glorification and regeneration of the race shall thus be constructed into a synthesis of essential vision, which shall be unto us such a light as may inhere in

a grand, universal revelation. We are proposing unto ourselves a lofty and desirable end, though our hearts are fixed upon a time that is distant, a land that is very far away, and what may seem unto us a strange people. We are speaking of the world's end and of the millennial age. Our eyes are looking for the remote manifestation of "the exquisite and celestial Rose of Beauty, joined on to the prolific stem," for the realization of "Venus-Urania, or Heavenly Beauty," whose every look and thought shall be "hallowed in the hallowing light of the Supreme Lord"; for her who has been transfused by the "electric or magnetic flame which is the Life diffused throughout the Universe," for the Virgin, the Bride, and the Mother, the true Woman of the Future, of whom every Idealist in his confession of the life to come shall aver, with the seer of old: "I preferred her before sceptres and thrones, and esteemed riches nothing in comparison of her; neither compared I unto her any precious stone, because all gold in respect of her is as a little sand, and silver shall be counted as clay before her. . . . . In her is an understanding spirit, holy, one only, mani-fold, subtle, lively, clear, undefiled, plain, not subject to hurt, loving the thing that is good, quick, which cannot be letted, ready to do good, kind to man, steadfast, sure, free from care, ... a pure influence flowing from the glory of the Almighty, ... more beautiful than the sun, and above all the order of the stars." Her archetype has been fabled in heaven by the mytholo-gists of the whole world, as "a virgin-spirit of most ineffable loveliness." She was "the Astrean Maid of purest light, clothed in the Sun, and mantled in the shining stars. The moon and silver spheres of Heaven were beneath her feet; she was crowned with all the brightness, majesty, and knowledge that her celestial essence merited or required. She was the Minokhired and Mayo-Khrati, or Divine Intelligence of the Zoroastrian and the Zend. She was the Shekinah of the Jews, in whose shining, central, circumambient, flame-like glory, God was wont to manifest His presence when He created: she was the Eros or Divine Love which, impregnated by Heaven, produces all things." For the translucent symbol which the mythology of the past has erected in the heaven of mind must return to earth, because there is the field of its realization. What we have borrowed from the beauty of womanhood must revert again to womanhood, and invest her with all its glory. The perfection which we have fabled in the sky must be actualized here on earth. The Celestial Virgin indeed must bear a child, and that child is indeed the Woman of the Future.

And next in regard to Man. We have fashioned God in man's likeness. Now we must re-create man after the image of our Ideal God. And he comes before us in the archetypal or mythological world as an emanation from God, the Prince of Heaven, "the long-expected Parasu-Rama and Mahidi of Indian

7

and Arabian" prophecy. He is the So-Shiôsh, or Saviour King, and Baggava-
Matteio of the Boodh, or "Wisdom-Born Religion." Do not the Hottentots,
even as do we Mystics, the last born of time, the head and crown of philosophy,
the culminating point in the development of an all-benign and Catholic religion—do not they also expect the manifestation of this "man of men"? Yes,
in their Goonja Ticquoa, their god of gods, who occasionally becomes visible to
humanity, and is "in appearance, shape and dress the finest among mortals."
For the ideal Man is the Lord of Fire, the Child of the Sun; he has a divine
mission from above. He is Apollo, he is Hermes, the son of Maia; his heroic
spirit mingles with the stars. He is the most eloquent of speakers; chains of
gold flow from his mouth; he is a sweet-voiced musician. "In a word, all
religions have him, and confess his universality." When he manifests, or
develops, "the universal globe shall enjoy the blessings of peace, secure under
the mild sway of its new and divine sovereign." He is "a young man of high
stature, taller than the rest."

The testimony of aspiration towards the physical beauty of humanity as
the result of interior development is thus chiefly derived from the ideals of
universal religion, but the evidence might be easily extended into conceptions
of another order. In this respect, however, we have sufficiently indicated the
line of research, and whether from religion or from poetry, as fruitful in ideality
as religion, or from what store soever in the great treasury of aspiration, we
may be left each one of us to construct his own synthesis; for the same result
will be reached in every case, namely, that the external manifestation of
advancing interior perfection will take shape in the form of an illuminating
beauty. In a word, our ideal faculty conceives the divine by an evolution of
human loveliness, and in all divinity we realize our own image transfigured in
light. Beauty manifesting amidst glory is our highest notion of physical perfection, and the illustration of humanity is inseparable from the dream of its
perfection.

II.

The Ministry of Light.

Having spoken somewhat already of the physical and intellectual light, it
remains that in order to arrive at a clearer conception of the probable condition
of the perfect man, being in the enjoyment of an arch-natural body and of a
transfigured environment, we should pursue a little further our enquiry into this

connection of man with light. All legend and all religion have ever supposed that glorified spirits are ablaze with actual light—are luminiferous, though not burning—shining not with the reflected radiance of the material world, but with a glory manifested from within. The most transcendental and supreme mode of subsistence with which we are acquainted even in our imaginings is therefore intimately bound up with the phenomenon of light. The messengers of God shine with many splendours; the Psalmist sings of these many splendours of the Holy Ones; God Himself dwells in light inaccessible; the distinction between light and darkness indicates to most minds the gulf between good and evil. And it is the same in the intellectual order; the gifts of mind appear to us under the aspect of lights; the ignorant and uninstructed intelligence is dark, dense and obscure, while enlightenment is the ascribed characteristic of the cultured mind. In things inward as in things outward, light, therefore, is the desirable and the good. It is, of course, the *summum bonum* of the physical universe. In the Mysteries, the Epopt was supposed to be illuminated by the rays of divinity; God manifests to seers as the Central Sun; the Home of the Blessed is sphered in *Campos Liquentes;* the Spirit of God is an everlasting splendour. His word is a lamp unto the feet, and a light going before the eyes. ·Etymologists say that *Lux* is a primitive radical both for Light and Truth. Again, the Sanskrit cosmologists tell us of a light not perceptible to the elementary sense, but extracted from the all-comprehensive essence of the divine perfection which was the first emanating substance from the eternal, sole, and self-existent Spirit, after which manner we may interpret the interior light of mind, which is not less true light, real glory, and substantial splendour because it manifests only from mind to mind, and is latent to physical sense. Out of the Apocalyptic sea of hyaline, bright and clear as a pure crystal, there rose the luminous rainbow, the covenant of God with man, the pledge of illumination and splendour. According to Robert Fludd, the Soul of the World is a pure Spirit of Universal Nature, formed and vivified by rays of Divine Light, emanating directly from the Eternal Monad, and reduced with these by the union of holy love into a living and spiritual nature:

> Love is warmth, and wisdom light—
> These are God's interpreters.

So also in the arcane revelations, the Divine Mind appears out of the profound deeps, replete with glory and serenity. After the first wanderings of the Mysteries, the coruscation of a sudden splendour displays itself before the eyes of the Mystæ, and shining plains open on all sides before them. Light is the Key of Knowledge; it is everywhere identified with life; it produces life and motion; it is the Archa, or Rainbow Arch of Beauty. The Golden Egg out of which Brahma was produced blazed like a thousand suns.

For the typology of sunset clouds, for the splendours of celestial incandescence, for the poetry of light in Nature, we must have recourse to the poets themselves. If we turn to the Mystics, we shall see that light figures as the First Matter of the *Magnum Opus*. It is the Ignited Stone, and the Fiery Chariot of alchemical symbolism; it is the substance of the Philosophical Stone. In religion, in ritual, and in folk-lore, it has ever played a part of the first importance. We shall find it figuring suggestively in dream and legend. The imagination itself is a light. Light is essential to all operations of magic. It is the one thing needful. It is, in particular, inseparably connected with every conception of the future glory, beauty, and perfection of humanity; and it may be reasonably submitted that this universal reaching out of aspiration indicates a truth to come, is the sign of a fact which will be realized, namely, that the hope of the Hermetists is a possible and desirable thing, and that we may look for the physical bloom and garment of light, for a coming radiance in humanity, for the evolution of the Lords of Glory. The expectation is at once symbolical and literal; and just as the exterior light would be an unsubstantial ravishment if there were no life within, so is the interior light, so is the interior beauty, the fountain and source of the external. Any ideal system of education towards the perfect life must foster both—the evolution of physical radiance and beauty, the evolution of interior charms, for the production of that which shall be the desire of all eyes, the perfect phenomenal expression of a perfect intrinsic truth. It is a process of the eternal ages. Mysticism can offer no transfiguration which shall take place in a moment, in the twinkling of an eye. It is a far off and divine event, but all creation is moving towards it; and if we will, each successive generation may be a step further on the road, till at length we shall in truth behold

> The spiritual city and all her spires
> And gateways in a glory like one pearl,

and all "four spaces clothed in living beams," when man is at one with his environment, and the world dissolved with man in a common glory. It is not too hard a task; it is not too long a strife; it is not too severe an education. It is a long beatification of endeavour closing in a splendour of fulfilment. Our method is contained in a short phrase—to beautify; to beautify mind and form; to beautify soul and body; to beautify thought, and word, and deed; to beautify dream and aspiration; to beautify imagination and fancy; to beautify philosophy and religion; to beautify birth, bridal and burial; to beautify life in all its relations, all man, and all his circumstance. Then shall there be nothing common and unclean, nothing mean, nothing ignoble, nothing hideous or cruel. Then truly shall God wipe away all tears from our eyes; no mourning or sorrow shall be any more; for the former things shall have passed away. We shall dwell in the "new city of intelligence and love."

As then in the intellectual order illumination would seem to be the highest pitch of our perfection, so in the physical we may be confirmed, by the considerations we have mentioned, in our belief that the illustration of humanity is inseparable from the conception of its perfection.

III.

The Testimony of Spiritual Tradition.

There is a testimony of all ages and nations to a lost knowledge and a lost perfection of humanity. This testimony is dual in its nature; it is interior and objective. There is the mythic cycle which is concerned with the spiritual condition of the primordial man, and there is the cycle which is concerned with the Garden of Paradise and of God. Now, the perfection of humanity is also dual—interior and objective—and the nature of the divine operation which it is our task to indicate is dual, and is described dually in this book of the divine light of Mysticism and of Azoth. The legends of the first interior, or primordial condition of ante-natal and unmanifest perfection in which the essential man abode in the sphere of the timeless, will illustrate to us the nature of the interior absorption or rapture in which evolved man will attain to the positive knowledge of God, to immediate correspondence with the Eternal Consciousness, to the immersion of individual in universal being. The pre-existing soul of man, as these legends tell us, was punished for pre-natal transgression by union with matter in the body, whence we may conclude that the exaltation into perfection and glory of this vehicle will end the punishment, and the whole man will be swallowed up in light and immortality.

Before they were associated with the body, the Souls of men, according to the Platonists, existed in God, they were emanations of the Great Soul, the fellows and members of the chief Deity, and even now, though enveloped by the body, they may participate in divine contemplation through the subjection of the passions, and through a life of interior absorption. It is to this belief in the doctrine of pre-existence that there has been referred the opinion of many ancient peoples concerning their descent from the gods; who also affirmed that they had been once in Heaven, but were now changed into another form, having suffered a lapse. The place of this pre-existence is described as a Realm of Light, and the spirit of man, though prisoned in the flesh, and to some extent darkened by the Lethean draught, nevertheless retains its primitive ante-natal powers, which need only opportunity and development. "We may regard God through our Soul," says Plato, and Iamblichus illustrates the beatitude of this contemplation in the terms of the physical senses. "The theorems of religion are to be enjoyed as much as possible, as if they were Ambrosia and Nectar, for the pleasure arising from them is genuine, incorruptible, and divine." Porphyry is unanimous with the rest of the sublime seers of the great mystic wisdom. "Man may unite his soul to God. To this end there requires no sacrifice except a perfectly pure mind. Through the highest purity and chastity we shall approach nearer to God, and receive, in the contemplation of Him, the true knowledge and insight." Macrobius affirms that the Soul, until purified by philosophy, suffers death through its union with the body, whence we may conclude that the Soul, purified in the light of the positive knowledge, may ultimately illustrate the body by its own essential light. The doctrine of the deplumation of the Soul will be found in the commentary of Hierocles. He says that the Soul, stripped of her plumage, is precipitated into an earthly body, and deprived of her former happy estate. Once it had communion with God, and enjoyed that intercourse in pure light. In the Mysteries, the soul was exhorted "to hasten to the luminous abode of the Great Father, from whom it emanated, and to seek for Paradise." What is this Paradise? It is the parabolic Mountain of Syon, which by some is said to signify repose in its Sanskrit analogue. It is, therefore, the Mountain of Ecstacy or Paradisiac absorption into the Eicton of Iamblichus, the First Occult Power, who is worshipped only in silence, and attained in "the mystical union of God with the Spirit of God, and of the Spirit of God herself with all souls." What is that portion of man which is to attain this union? It is not the red earth which is the matrix of the diamond. That indeed is capable of illumination and transfiguration. It is not the Adamic earth, but the jewel within it. What is the quality of life which alone will insure this union? The *Bhakta Mala* can tell us. "Retirement from the world is desirable, because the passions and desires, the hopes and fears, which the social state engenders, are all hostile to tranquillity of spirit and purity of soul, and prevent that undisturbed meditation on man and God which is necessary to their comprehension." And we can interpret the dicta of ancient philosophy in the light of new doctrine. "The souls of men," says Plato, "will never see the end of their sufferings until the revolution of the world shall have brought them back to their primitive state, and they shall become cleansed from the stains produced by the contact of the four elements." What does this mean in its ultimate but that evolution must modify environment till the soul attains a more fitting vehicle for communication with the manifest universe? Nor is the retirement from the world to be interpreted in an ascetical sense; it means simply the establishment of correspondence with things superior by the cessation of active correspondence with inferior things. Thus, we shall "learn to do good" when we "cease to do evil," and though we dwell in the midst of evil we shall not have part or communication therewith.

We see, therefore, that aspiration is confirmed by tradition, which in all mythologies has connected the first state of emanant existence with an environment and an individual participation in the glory of spiritual light.

IV.

The Garden of Paradise and of God.

What is the work to be achieved? It is the union of the first interior with the first objective. Then once again shall the Morning Stars sing together, and the visible splendours of the quiet waters of eternity shall wash upon the sands of time, shall overflow them and involve and permeate, each individual particle shall be held in crystalline solution, and that which is individual shall enjoy the isolation of a complete self-possession in the all-embracing communion of the universal substance in which it is immersed and is deified. In the peaceful and beatific contemplations to which we have recently referred, we have possessed our minds with the condition of the first interior, and the instrument of abstract thought, plunged in the profundity of its subject, has been withdrawn keen and clear and burnished. In the contemplation of Venus-Urania and of Hermes-Apollo, of the exaltation of Israfel and of the jewelled glistening of Lucasta, the many splendours wherewith the man and woman of the future have been clothed upon seem already to invest our minds. The day seems nearer, the joy brighter, the hope stronger; faith enters into certainty, and we know that some time, in the good and grand time of ripeness, mellowness, and harvesting, God's own good time which never is too late, the world shall behold this source of all perfection, this fulness of complete consolation, and in our tears of delight and gladness we taste already of the gladness and delight of that time when the heart of man shall radiate with the white heat of emotion having God for its impulse.

And now we are concerned with the Garden of Paradise and of God, with the Terrestrial Paradise of Humanity. We have to learn again from legend and poetic lore of that fabled period when man came perfect from his Creator's fashioning hands, and when the Elohim walked with the Adamic nature in the cool of the evening. Did ever this fabled time have a place in fact is a barren enquiry. It at least has a place in the future; we must either work up to it or back to it; the desire of all the world spurs us on to achieve perfection. We may, or not, have possessed it in the past, but at least in the past we have dreamed it, and, God willing, who is indeed willing, we must, we will possess it in the coming time, and all the infinite possibilities which are involved in the divine and luminous meshes of the great futurity must be appropriated and shaped for our achievement. Is the gate of the mythical Eden indeed "built up with a final cloud of sunset"? No, for the purpose of God "overflows the firmamental walls with Deity," and all barriers will melt away. It *is* possible for man to re-enter Paradise. If the swords of the Cherubim guard it, it is with those swords that we must pierce the intervening barriers. We need chiefly a new impulse and a new purpose, and then we shall be one with the drift of our being which "makes for righteousness"—with the high law of evolution. When Darwin discovered evolution he discovered God's intention towards man; he opened out before the view of all the pathway which leads to the "divine event." All creation is said to move towards it, and yet it is within possibility that creation moves blindly, mechanically, and unconsciously. But when the mind of man sets itself consciously, reasonfully, seeingly, to fulfil the law of evolution, the man will no longer move, he will run, and for each generation that divine event will loom larger, nearer, grander. What is the keynote of true progress along this path? The *Imitation of Christ* will tell us: *Ista est summa sapientia, per contemptum mundi tendere ad regna cœlestia.* What does that mean? That we must despise, as we have seen, and cast behind us the evil environment, all things dull, common, and unclean, all that is tame and arid and commonplace, and set ourselves to enter into that other and divine environment, illuminated by the purple flower of love, wherein all is poetry and romance, wherein all is dream and vision, and where the amber light of the ideal, and the dead gold and the old rose of the enchantment of a moderated aspiration involve all land and all sea in the permanent vestment of a subdued incandescent glory. Not as the apostle of an acrid and gloomy asceticism do we appear in our mystic ministry. We preach the contempt of that world wherein Christ has not anything, but it is the world of the sordid and soulless, not the magnificent pageant of tender and luminous parable which is this starry Nature around us, not the celestial host of bewildering loveliness which for ever deploys about us in the high, pre-sanctified mass of our holy humanity. These are of the *regna cælestia.* The so-called reality passes; the ideal remains. The prose dies and festers; but the things of poesy are permanent. The coarse sensualism of fact pastures briefly in the pen of its own corruption, but the archetypal loveliness of romance does not fade or grow old. Therefore, *Vanitas est diligere, quod cum omni celeritate transit: et illic non festinare, ubi sempiternum gaudium manet.* God is not fact, but truth; God is not prose, but poetry; God is the ideal; and at the culminating and apex point of all high dream, vision, aspiration and romance, there only will the soul find God. For God is that which is furthest removed from commonplace and the rags of realism. We must eliminate realism and the commonplace if in life we would realize God.

But the mode of Edenic existence, the first objective state, was illuminated and arch-natural as all legend testifies. We may consult the theology of the Latin Church or the *Paradise* of Milton. Once more then, it is impossible now, and impossible has it ever been, to conceive the perfection of beauty apart from the illustration of beauty; and all legend, like all aspiration, points in the same direction. In particular, the tradition of the Earthly Paradise, and of man's first objective condition, must be included among the transcendental mysteries of Light.

V.

The Testimony of the Transcendental.

The phenomena of mesmerism, esoteric clairvoyance, magic, and even spiritism, are full of supreme significance as witnesses of the occult energies which exist in the soul of man. Those who by the teachings of the higher philosophy have become theoretically acquainted with the infinite energies or potencies which lie latent, and, as it were, lost in our interior being, and those who have become by contemplation and introspection aware, however dimly, that ordinary consciousness does by no means embrace the whole man, but only a small portion of his nature, are already prepared by their knowledge to accept these mysterious phenomena whenever they are presented within the circle of their experience. On the other hand, those who in the absence of such knowledge have had these phenomena introduced into the field of their cognizance, are invariably conducted thereby to the threshold of the Sanctuary of the Soul, and to the recognition of the inevitable postulates of the higher philosophy. The development of our latent faculties is the great work of Mysticism, and this development may be expressed after another manner as the extension of the field of consciousness over the entire scope of our possibilities. We have all heard of the distinction which was made by the old philosophers between the Macrocosm and the Microcosm, the great and the little world; but the doctrine which was a part of it—namely, that the *Minutum Mundum* of man was an exact copy in miniature of the *Magnum Mundum* of the universe—is not very generally understood, in so far, at least, as the *raison d'être* of the alleged correspondence. But if we regard the Microcosmos as that world which is presided over by the consciousness of the phenomenal man, and the Macrocosmos as that vast realm which lies behind consciousness, and is man's latent, undeveloped nature, the mystery will be largely cleared up, and we shall be consoled by the assurance that whatever the extent of our introspection, and whatever the breadth of our development, we shall never get outside our humanity. Under the light of this learning we shall read a new meaning in the old theological exhortations, as, for example, the circumscription of our interests and affections within the narrow sphere of phenomenal life: *Stude ergo cor tuum ab amore visibilium abstrahere, et ad invisibilia te transferre.* Strive to detach thyself from the littleness of thy lesser being, and fix thy desires upon the spiritual magnificences of the grander man. Turn aside from the beaten track of mundane existence, and seek the interior path, at some point or bend of which is "the sudden illustration," of which we read in Thomas Vaughan, *Eritque in te cum Lumine Ignis, cum Igne Ventus, cum Vento Potestas, cum Potestate Scientia, cum Scientia sane mentis integritas.* And again, in the words of Aquinas: *Disce exteriora contemnere, et ad interiora te dare, et videbis regnum Dei in te venire.* For the unassisted exterior man is mean, sordid, selfish; he is the sport of destiny, he is poor, ignorant, and dependent; but the arch-natural man within hath in him the seed of all the stars, the scheme of all creation, the *summa totius perfectionis.* "Our souls are so boundless that the more we explore them the more we shall find worlds spreading upon worlds into infinities, and among the worlds is Fairyland." There is nothing tame or prosaic in the interior man, nothing flat, or stale, or unprofitable.

The nature of the mystical possibilities and undeveloped potencies of humanity which we have already found indicated by legend and by poesy are exemplified, illustrated, and explained by transcendental phenomena. The physical and philosophical importance of the term light has prompted us to regard the evolution of humanity as very intimately connected with an increased polarization of visible splendour about the body of humanity, and transcendental phenomena amply verify what we have conceived under this head. Mesmerism and hypnotism offer the first steps towards the magical transfiguration of the body of man. The mind in clairvoyance is immersed in spiritual light as in a new atmosphere. The illuminations of trance and ecstasy are visible upon the countenance of the enthralled subject. At truly spiritual séances, the nimbus has often been manifested. And those who have attempted .the higher exaltations of practical magic can speak, if they will, upon the light there manifested, upon the new vestment that enswathes the body of the Magus, upon the interior lucidity. Reverently, from fields afar, we can fix our eyes upon Horeb, and whisper to our own souls that the Great Work of the Light which was there accomplished, was a sign and a pre-realization of the glory which is to appear in man when evolution shall have done its work, and when it hath appeared what we shall be.

From the analogies of Hermetic processes to the idealities of aspiration, from ideal conceptions to the actualized imagining of old-world lore and legend, and from all these to the testimony of fact in the phenomenal of transcendency, we conduct therefore the great argument of the Light, full of beauty and of grandeur, full of majesty and poetry. Already the nimbus of the hierophant seems to circle round us, and inspiration clothes us like a mantle as we proclaim the mystery of illumination.

VI.

The Testimony of the Natural Man.

. But it is in no sense required to have recourse to the world of transcendental phenomena for the evidence of our philosophical doctrine; we can have recourse for our argument to facts in the natural world, and to those which are the best, highest, and most affecting in daily human life. Love, chastity, with the modesty which is part of chastity, and intelligence which is the crown of our being, have at all times, and visibly, made beautiful, and have refined the human countenance. Here are actualities which can be developed. We have only to love more, to protect the virginity of thought and act, to develop intelligence; we shall then become more beautiful, and our nature will refine itself continually. We are already in plenary possession of the true beautifying principles. Again, the intellectual nature has its moments of rarer strength, of keener perception, of more comprehensive grasp. Under their influence the face enlightens, and that which is normally plain becomes beautiful for an instant, being suffused by a radiance from within. A permanent aspiration towards the source of this power and perception will be registered upon the countenance by an abiding radiance of its own kind, and thus again we shall work up towards beauty, and shall fix its fleeting brilliance. Once more, the inspirations of poetry visibly and vividly exalt the fitted being who is their subject; and if we shape our lives under the sun of song, then assuredly it will transfigure us all; we all shall reflect its light, till it enlighteneth every face that is born into this world.

Physical beauty is a prophecy of the transfiguration which is to come, and an index of the glorious possibilities which lie *perdus* in the soul of man. It is one of the few objects of desire in phenomenal life which are not vain and worthless. The search after beauty is the search after real good. It is not the truth, but it is a reflection and penumbra of all that is absolute and true; it is the music of eternity penetrating the closed door of the material; it is the parable which conceals the truth; it is the first and open meaning which enshrines the inner significance. It is a light of body and a light of mind; a consolation and a real joy, a rest to eyes and soul, a continual feast. We have heard that all charms are fleeting and that "beauty passes like a breath," just as we have heard that "love is lost in loathing." But to say so is bad in poetry and false in fact. True love is so universal and absolute in its nature that it leaves no room for aversion. · It fills all the heights and depths of limitless immensity; it is so full of "the splendours and eternal consolations of the sovereign reason" that there is no space for the unreason of its contrary. Truly, there are many things which pass under the name of love that wear only its outward likeness and are without its inward heart, just as there are many things and many systems which wear the outward habit of religion and are only its spurious substitutes. So also much which passes for beautiful goes by unchallenged only because it is beheld under a false light. But there is a satisfaction, and there is a joy, and there is a depth and significance in physical beauty, which no one should miss unless he would miss the significance of life. If we admit that the world is full of symbols and parables, then beauty is that portion of parable and symbol which is most touched with the divine light and meaning. If we say that the phenomenal universe is the veil of a grand reality, then at the points where beauty manifests, there the veil is thinnest. The physical beauty of humanity may be interpreted as an attempt of Nature to manifest the loveliness of the inner man. It may also be accepted that this manifestation is made wherever the environment will permit, and often independently of the interior development or disposition of the individual soul. As a general rule, outward beauty may, however, be regarded as an index of spiritual loveliness, either positive or potential in the person. It may certainly and absolutely be regarded as a faint expression in form of the undreamed and unapproachable ravishment which abides in the interior of humanity. Some of us have been horror-struck by thinking that all beauty would be annihilated were the range of our vision less limited. Could we look below the surface, it is said, and see that "every face however full, padded round with flesh and fat, is but modelled on a skull;" did we behold the serpentine circulation of the blood in veins and arteries, the mechanism of lungs and heart, the convolutions of intestines, all desire and love would die of sickness within us. And in a sense it is truly said, yet that were not a true penetration. Could we look within, that is, into the true interior, there is a world of unrevealed beauty; there is God, and Christ, and Heaven, and all the splendours and grandeurs of the Terrestrial Paradise.

We have, therefore, no need to pass outside ourselves, or to introduce any foreign substance into our natures in order that we may achieve perfection and enter into the full fruition of the evolved state. There is that within us which is all-sufficient to the work that is in hand. Our position, after all, is one that is extremely simple, that has been never denied, that is true at all times and in all places, for it is this, namely, that as there is a splendour of truth, so also there is a beauty of goodness, an outward lustre which manifests an inward virtue. It is impossible to be truly good, and yet not to appear good, and the appearance of goodness is beauty, for it could not manifest otherwise in the eternal economy which governs the relations between the seen and the unseen. Our study and intention also are extremely simple—we are concerned in nothing more than the eduction of an unerring tendency—in the intensification of that current which sets outwardly of itself towards beauty as it does inwardly towards truth. Virtue is the whetstone on which the instrument of intellect is sharpened to the needle's point of that consummate keenness by which alone it can penetrate into the noumenal. But the phenomenon—as already indicated—corresponds ideologically to its noumen, for the simple reason that every noumen must manifest according to the law of its nature, and the law of virtue is beauty. It is, of course, true in a high degree that such manifestation may be hindered by environment, and it is true also that the peculiar environment which constitutes the modern world, and is governed by the Prince of this world, which is the actuating spirit thereof, is one that is unfavourable to virtue. Moreover, that which hinders the interior cultus will prevent the outward ritual. Virtue cannot light candles on her altar when the reservation of the Sacrament has become impossible. But there is an exposition which is to come, and an adoration of forty days, when the altar shall blaze with lights, the music peal in the aisles, when there shall be the radiance and fragrance of a thousand flowers:—

> The violet damask-tinted,
> In scent all flowers above,
> The milk-white vestal lily,
> And the purple flower of love.

Then shall the spirit of the world become regenerate in the Spirit of Christ, and after the Resurrection and the Life of those mystical forty days shall humanity ascend into Heaven. The symbolical life of Christ is the synthesis of the law of our life, and the *résumé* of the history of evolution.

Thus, it will be seen, from the considerations of the present chapter, that everything which has been believed of the perfection of man in the past, and everything that is hoped for the elaboration of his perfection in the future, is inseparably connected with the idea of Light—a light within and a light without —the truth within and the beauty without as its form. We shall do well to refrain from forecasting the actual nature of the physical splendour of evolved loveliness; we should rather content ourselves with the central fact and outcome of this enquiry—that the harmonious evolution of the whole and perfect man will produce an arch-natural body—a physical vehicle analogical to his interior nature—that it will be full of grace, and illustrated by a special and peculiar glory. In all things, therefore, let us act and think with reference to the standard of the beautiful. A perfect correspondence with the law of beauty is life perfect, life sanctified, life glorious; it is life in Christ and God.

CHAPTER THE THIRD.

STEPS IN THE WAY OF ATTAINMENT.

I.

The Construction of Humanity.

WHATEVER be the extent of our illumination in the noble order of the mind, whatever be the scope of our resources, whatever the quality of our environment, we can all of us do something to help on the great day of evolution, something to speed the law, and the purpose of this chapter is to shape our thoughts in the lineal way of attainment. We can touch but the fringe of the subject, but there may be a certain light and guidance in the imperfections of fragmentary notes till a true teacher shall arise with a perfect plan.

That which we should propose to elaborate is a system for the education of humanity towards the perfect life, which is the end of evolution. Before we can attempt to devise such a system, we must be in possession of a still more clear idea of the kind of perfection in view. It may be briefly set down as that life in which man's best and most ennobled aspirations have become actual. When we speak of man's best aspirations, it is obvious that the reference is exclusively to those which admit of realization, which include nothing extravagant or absurd. Extravagant or absurd aspirations are neither good nor ennobling. To have the wings of the eagle is undoubtedly desirable in itself, but with our present physical constitution the ambition is impossible, and it cannot be rational or elevating to cherish it. When things which are desirable in themselves are beyond a literal fulfilment, we must be content with an approximate substitute. Evolution will never provide us with wings, but science by the motion of plane surfaces may yet equip us with machinery for the navigation of the air. The aspirations which admit of fulfilment, which must indeed be realized before the evolution of humanity into the ideal state can become an accomplished fact, are of three kinds—physical, intellectual, and religious or spiritual. Physical aspirations are concerned with the health and perfection of the body of man, intellectual aspirations with the extension of knowledge into new and unknown regions, while in the sphere of religious aspiration is included the cultivation of the moral and spiritual faculties. The classes are not independent. A healthy body is indispensable to a healthy intelligence—*mens sana in corpore sano*—and the advancement of man in morality is in strict correspondence with that improved environment which is the result of social progress.

The construction of man upon the lines of his highest aspirations may be philosophically described as the development of his interior potencies and as the adjustment of activities evolved from within in correspondence with a renovated social envelope. Poetically, it is the realization of the dream, and here it may be affirmed that man's best dreams are God's actualities, and they are the environment of the man of the future. Man is called to the creation of himself, the construction of others, and the adoration of the ideal.

In the physical order, we are in search of a perfect method of daily life, and of an adequate incentive to follow it; in the intellectual order, we are in search of a criterion of judgment on the great problems of being; in the religious order, we are in search of a new motive for the pursuit of the good, the beautiful, and the true.

Now, as it is by the development of the potentialities of the imperfect subject, Man, that the end of evolution is to be fulfilled, it is possible to synthe size the entire operation projected in a single term—the REGENERATION OF HUMANITY, the NEW BIRTH OF MAN, the new creature under a new Heaven and on a new earth. These are familiar terms—so familiar indeed that, as we shall see hereafter, they have been well-nigh emptied of their significance, and they are phrases which have been used in the interests of most of the *vieux cultes evanouis*, for, as a modern poet has asked,

> Which has not taught weak wills how much they can?
> Which has not fallen on the dry heart like rain?
> Which has not cried to sunk, self-weary man,
>   Thou must be born again?

But in the terms are involved a conception which is in an eminent degree the keynote of the Christian message, which, however, through a fatal misinterpretation, has been made void to humanity at large, the New Birth being supposed to be effected by a principle of arbitrary fertilization from without unassisted by any principle of development from within. The true Mystic knows nothing of such doctrine, but he is aware of the resources of the race which evolution has but partially developed; he is aware that the inner man, being the undeveloped side of humanity, is larger, grander, better than the outward man, which is the side till now in manifestation. He is also aware that the principle of regeneration by a seed unto spirit, which is deposited without a traceable principle of sowing, has had over eighteen centuries to accomplish the reconstruction of the race, and that it has not succeeded. So is it reasonable and legitimate to attempt reconstruction on another basis. At the same time it must ever be borne in mind that it is to Christianity eminently that we owe the formulation of the theory of the New Birth, and on this, as on other accounts, there is a debt of gratitude due to it, however much it has deflected in the practice.

The aspiration of humanity towards the regenerated condition is the fundamental aspiration which a system of philosophic evolution has to realize for humanity at large. The literature of Regeneration is to be found in the writings of the Mystics, and it is to them that one must turn for illumination on this subject. Their statements admit of presentation in the terminology of the modern philosophy.

Deep in the nature of every man there is the consciousness of powers which remain latent because there is nothing in his external sphere to give a field to their activity. Deep in the heart of every man, there is the consciousness of a better nature, to the development of which his physical environment is unfavourable. The most sluggish and unspiritual of persons will confess to the possession of aspirations which they would be glad to pursue if it were possible. There is something within them which responds to the great and the noble. There are times when the perfect life seems more eminently beautiful than any of the transient pleasures of a selfish and sensuous existence, however much the tinsel of extrinsic attraction may invest such existence with the ornate adornments of earthly joy. We are aware of the stirring within us of what seems to be a new faculty, a new power, a new purpose, even a new being. In moments of a rare penetration, the outer crust of our ordinary personality appears to dissolve for a little, and the radiance of an inner man transfigures the exterior nature. Something within us is attempting to burst through the hard and material sheath of our actual form of subsistence, and it seems to us that it would be possible, and well if we could, to subsist after another manner.

This, say the Mystics, is the motion of the new being within the old Adam, as within a womb, and it is only by a moral ordeal, which is akin to the pangs of parturition, that the strong child of the new life can be brought forth. This child is conceived, by the individual being, of the universal Spirit of Life— which is equivalent to saying that its generation is not of this world. It is not of this world in the sense that it is begotten of a spirit which is in antagonism to the spirit of the world. "The prince of this world cometh, and in me he hath not anything," says the Christus of the symbolic gospel, speaking in the person of the new age; and the pains of the spiritual parturition consist in the forcible severance of the bonds which bind the individual to the limitations and imperfections of the old order; these it is torture to tear asunder because they are the growth of centuries, the strong parasites of environment, and the tendrils of hereditary instincts which have entered into the fibres of our nature. The conception of the new man takes place in mystery because the consciousness of the life which is within our life has usually no traceable genesis, whence it is said: "The wind bloweth where it listeth, and none can say whence it cometh or whither it goeth: even so is every one who is born of the Spirit." On the other hand, the nourishment of the germ is a conscious process, and the bursting of the strings, and the breaking of the waters which give passage to the new humanity is accomplished by the individual force of will. It is in this sense that the Kingdom of Heaven suffereth violence, and that the violent bear it away, for the expression is unintelligible when it is applied to the spiritual world which has been conceived by Christianity, but in its application to the New Life it is appropriate and reasonable.

We must not, however, be deceived by analogies. The new man is that sub-surface and interior nature which is the synthesis of our superior and latent possibilities. The elements which constitute the germ of the new being exist in all men indifferently, and are not absent from the most depraved of our species. The gestation is the method of life which nourishes the potentialities into activity. The birth is that opening of the old nature which constitutes a severance from its present environment and the creation of a new personal environment which shall give to the new forces a proper sphere of activity. The new being comes not to destroy but to fulfil; the old correspondences are cut away, a new sequence is formed; the old personality transfigures into the new individual. It is truly a process of unfoldment and of development.

Coincident with the transfiguration of humanity must be the modification of environment, which consists, in the first instance, in the contemplation of life from a new standpoint. Here it is needful above all to remember that

> We receive but what we give,
> And in our life alone does Nature live;
> Ours is her wedding-garment, ours her shroud.
> And *would we aught perceive of higher worth*
> Than this inanimate, cold world allow'd
> To the poor loveless, ever-anxious crowd,
> Oh, from the soul itself must issue forth
> A light, a glory, a fair, luminous cloud,

Enveloping the earth,
And from the soul itself there must be sent
A sweet and potent voice of its own birth,
Of all sweet sounds the life and element!

What is this light which must "issue forth" from within us to transfigure that which is without us? It is "the light which never was on land or sea," but with which the mind of the poet can illuminate the world around us. It is an emanation from that concentrated centre of Nature, which is the inmost of the best of humanity, where the sun shines at midnight, as the Mystics term it. It is the "glory and the freshness of a dream," but of what dream? Of that dream which, in the language of the German seer of Fairyland, life is as yet not, but which it ought to become, "and perhaps will." It is the glass in which "the fairy-gifted poet perceives the same thing everywhere." What is this one thing? Ultimately, it is man, and the reason is to be found in another poet, whose words we have already cited—"All that interests a man is man," for it is modified in the light that he views it, and is ennobled in proportion as he rises. Here is the true key to the transfiguration of the Cosmos which surrounds us. The universe is fashioned in strict correspondence with the moral and intellectual status of the mind which perceives it. It is blank to the man who is personally devoid of soul; it is cold to him who is deficient in "the fire within"; it is dead to him who is himself without life. To the savage it is, in the main, dark, arbitrary, forbidding, remorseless, fearful; to the blood-guilty, it is "red in tooth and claw," and "with ravine shrieks against the creed" of long-suffering, patience, and mercy; to the pessimist, it is hopeless and evil; to the selfish it is the reign of might, and its law is *sauve qui peut*. To the peacemaker, it is a continual Sabbath, in which he "possesses the land," and his reward is with him. To the just, it is the ultimate triumph of law and order, and to this extent it is already "the Kingdom of Heaven" which is promised him. To the poet, it is the source and the field of his inspiration, and the fountain of his thirst for the good, the beautiful, and the true. It is rendered to every man according to his nature, nor can it be said of this or of that view that it is alone the true one, for the view is in the beholder, and the standpoint is the prerogative of the person who is in possession of it. We are in need of a new focus to obtain an improved view, of a new elevation to enlarge the field of vision, of a new mind to evolve a new medium wherein to view it. This is neither the creation of a romantic delusion, nor of an arbitrary and partial attitude. The development of the powers and prerogatives of the interior man will constitute an instrument by which he will be placed in correspondence with the higher laws of the universe, and this will be the

beginning of a new heaven and a new earth, because the "former things" will
have passed away.   The difference which subsists between Nature and humanity
as they are presented in actual life, and as they are presented in the light of the
poet, comprises the whole range of the difference between the present imperfect
correspondence of man with the universe, and that adjustment which constitutes the perfect life.   An instance may be legitimately taken from one of the
humbler walks of poetry to which we shall have occasion for another reference
at a later stage.   Let us recall one of the innumerable rhymes and roundelays
which have been written in praise of a country lffe, and of one of its special
features, as, for instance, the time of harvesting, and let us analyze the elements
which compose it.   What is the chief feature of this or that description?   It
is the elevation of the actual into the ideal, and its transfiguration in the glass
of vision and ecstasy.   It does not correspond to reality because it has
worked upon reality the transmutation of the light which is AZOTH in the
terminology of the alchemists.   The transformation has been accomplished
by a process of refinement which has left the dregs and the sediments at the
bottom of the chalice of life.   Once more, and also in the language of the
alchemists, the gross has been separated from the subtle, and the work has been
completed simply by the rejection of something "superfluous," which is the
littleness, the common-place, the baseness, and the meanness that narrow and
distort our present form of subsistence.   In poetry the sense of enchantment
is lent by distance.   If we advance nearer into the field of the toilers, we shall
see and hear that which will break the spell, and the dreamer will be cruelly
disillusioned.   When we can advance nearer without disenchantment, and take
part in the vintage, we may look to drink new wine in the Kingdom of the
Father.   When we can share in "the reaping and the mowing" without en-
dangering the poetry of life, we may look to walk with God among the sheaves
in the cool of the evening, and to make merry and rejoice with exceeding great
joy in the harvest home of the Golden Age.

The discrepancy between anticipation and realization is the measure of our
falling short in achievement, and it is the measure of the deflection of our
motive from ideal excellence.

If from these considerations we proceed to an enquiry into the powers of
the interior man, and what it is that we are seeking to develop, a little thought
will assure us that we are not in search of unknown qualities.   There is a strict
correspondence between that which is within and that which is without.   The
subsistent entity is one and the same; it is the form of the manifestation which
alone requires to be altered, and that by no radical change but by a possible and
natural transfigurement.   It is the splendour of intelligence directed to attain-

able truth and disengaged from the pursuits of delusion; it is the capacity of love enlarged in its direction to deserving subjects; it is the nobility of achievement directed to great and ennobling objects; it is the developed possibility of purpose; it is the strength of the fortified will, purged from the futilities of desire; it is ambition elevated by aspiration; it is the Seven Gifts and the Twelve Fruits of the Eternal Spirit of God, which are the Principle of the Higher Life and the law of permanent reality; it is the enlargement of the entire nature by its separation from what is trivial and transitory. Here we must admit that the ideal perfection which religion from its beginning has endeavoured to realize in man is the perfection which is the end of the new system; it does not endeavour to create a new object, but to realize it—other systems having obviously failed therein.

At the same time it is true that the further evolution of humanity will confer powers of a new kind, or, rather, it will so extend the germs of the potencies which humanity now possesses that the man of the future may be said to be in the enjoyment of new faculties, but this will take place after a rigorously natural manner, and not by any sudden transition. The child is father of the man. The potencies of the man are the potencies of the child developed to the point of manhood, but at a certain stage of the physical evolution of the individual a new sense germinates; he enters into the possession of a capacity which was hitherto undreamed of.

The analogy can be applied to the race, which, in spite of its comparative antiquity, must be still in its tender youth, because as yet it has not attained to the full development of any of its inherent forces. As long as we are conscious of a disparity between ideal excellence and the actual status of man, so long we may be sure that the race is short of its maturity. If it be still in its youth; if the puberty of the mind be not yet reached; we may look that its further evolution will develop a new power which shall be an instrument for the satisfaction of intellectual desire. By such an instrument of the mind, we may expect to be introduced into a world hitherto invisible, inexistent, unknown, which is that of supersensuous aspiration in the inmost of the growing mind. For the life of the interior man is the mind's life; the development of the mind is the development of the interior man, the mind being the synthesis of those qualities, capacities and forces which separately are will, understanding, the rational principle, the soul, the spirit. The "devotion to something afar" is, in the intellectual order, the index of a faculty to come. The analogy teaches that there is a world now unknown to which the mind will attain in the course of its evolution. This is the unseen world which has been desired from the dawn of evolution.

Here it is well to observe that we are concerned with an analogy alone, and the erection of analogy into dogma is a danger which has seldom been avoided by those whose ingenuity has been exercised in the creation of similar parallels. The intellectual craving after another world is regarded by some developments of modern philosophy as a sign of intellectual weakness; it is more accurately a sign of transition which indicates the accession of a new strength. This faculty to come we believe to be intimately connected with a development of the gift of intuition, as we have already hinted, and may again more at large express. Now, we freely surrender to "philosophy" the fertile field of pleasantry with which the admission will provide them; for there is little doubt that they will be equipped with a new text for the exposition of the hypothesis of weakness. But the true apostle of the Mystics has dredged the deeps as he has also plumbed the shallows of all prevailing philosophy, and he is acquainted with the limits of its canons. He does not deride or despise it, for he contemns nothing in the legitimate excursions of the thinking mind. So far as they are of value he simply claims that he has passed them all, even as he has gauged and appreciated all. The Monist of to-day derides the Dualism of yesterday, which he believes is for ever exploded, and that he has uttered the final culminating message of attainable wisdom. Let it pass; it is an incident of evolution. But the Mystic knows that there is another and a higher Monism which is undreamed by the Ethical school, advanced as it undoubtedly is, and that there is a law of interpretation which will harmonize what is divergent in both systems. All that we are required to keep in view is the existence in man of a strong desire after another world, and until that desire is gratified by the evolution of an instinct, intellectually speaking he will not be a mature and complete man. For the rest, we are concerned with capacities which in a degree we already possess, we are concerned with endowing them with a field, a motive, and a proper stimulus, and if it were needful to synthesize our purpose in a single phrase, it would be—the evolution of nobility of life.

II.

The Culture of Beauty.

It is, then, our intention to indicate after what manner the *Vas Philoso-phorum*, which is the *Vas insigne electionis*, may be adorned and prepared for the work. The perfection of the body of humanity can in nowise be conceived independently of physical beauty. That is the *Summum Bonum*, the thing desirable and the thing desired, in the exterior and presented nature of woman and man. It is not all that is needed for the perfection of physical humanity, but it is the path of promise, the earnest and the foretaste of the glory and the vision to come. But beauty at the present time is fortuitous. There is no traceable law which regulates its occurrence. It manifests spontaneously; it springs up anywhere; it is confined to no class; it can be predicated of no special environment that it is conducive to the production of physical beauty. It may be possessed in all plenitude by either or both parents, yet it may not be transmitted to the children; it may be possessed by the children in the absence of any presumptive inheritance. There is *à priori* no doubt that its manifestation could be controlled by careful breeding, as we develop the physical perfection of a horse, or the latent capacities of a rose. If we can trust ourselves to the attractive though precarious conclusions which are to be drawn from the analogies that are afforded us by these departments of Nature, there are many strange flowers of human loveliness which an advanced science of breeding might develop from the humble type of actual humanity. At the present time, with all our literature of heredity, natural and sexual selection, environment, and the influence of climate on the modification of human species, we do not possess even the elements of such a science, and we may add that our social condition precludes almost the possibility of experiment, without which the science can have no chance of making progress, so that the culture of human beauty depends upon the art of cosmetics, and the charlatanic recipes of a Cagliostro and a Rachel. If we are to have confidence in the operation of natural law, we must believe that evolution is very slowly improving the race in the direction of physical beauty, because in spite of society, in spite of *convenance* and utilitarian views of marriage, in spite of dowries and the detestabilities of "prudence," sexual desire is mainly energized by the beautiful, and there must be therefore a gradual elimination of what is plain and repulsive in appearance. Above this point natural and selective law cannot at present reach, so we must have recourse to a higher path, another method of elaboration. We must have recourse to the interior man. The influence of the world of mind upon external beauty can be made greater than any law of selection, and greater also than any influence of environment. It is strong even now in the result of its ungoverned action, for it is an old knowledge that the face is a register of the mental character. Who shall value too highly the influence of lofty thought upon the countenance? the influence of aspiration? the influence of the refining,' culturing, educating love of Nature? It is these we must seek to elevate; it is to these we must give free room for action. Let us think for a moment only of the sea's ministry to humanity in this respect, how "beauty born of murmuring sound" passes into the face of man. Let us think for another moment of the ministry of flowers and birds, of the sweet incenses of Nature and of the songs of her messengers—

Ambassadors of God, with ample powers.

Let us think once again of the immeasurable influence of an adequate philosophy of Nature, and of the deteriorating effect of a poor, ineffectual, material philosophy. There can be no doubt that three generations of an universal materialism would endow all humanity with the heavy jowl, the square jaw and the flaccid melancholia which are common to the sad experience of the new philosophical pontificate. But the perfection of human beauty demands the eyes of Keats and the face of Shelley. Let us think yet of the ministry of pure emotion at the white heat of pure love, how it will illuminate the countenance of Lily and regenerate the humour of Kenelm Chillingly. Let us think finally of the ministry of imagination, to which romance and poetry minister, which gives birth in return to more poetry and more romance, and will make of all life romance and all life poetry, when it is free to rule the whole man, as it is free in us who write, and as it is free in those who read, if they be indeed Mystics. For the life of the Mystic is the life of imagination supreme and imagination regnant.

III.

The Ministry of Intelligence.

What has been said in the foregoing pages will sufficiently prepare the reader to accept what we must now say concerning the ministry of intelligence in the evolution of the body of man, in the elaboration of the perfect dual flower of physical humanity, the true *Vas Philosophorum.* What is it which separates man from the animal? It is the possession of that intelligence which is the distinctive characteristic of humanity. What distinguishes sage from fool? The quality of intelligence. What enlightens, what illuminates, what illustrates, the countenance? Is it not the flash of intelligence? Intelligence refines, intelligence softens, intelligence makes strong, intelligence clarifies, intelligence beautifies; it is *par excellence* the beautifying principle. And how does it manifest? It manifests upon the face as a light. Let us develop intelligence, and then we shall intensify that light. And how shall we so develop it? By extending the field of knowlege in the direction of the beautiful and the true; by unlearning the science of evil—of that which is base, ignoble, small. It is in this sense that we must interpret the arcane maxim—*Summa scientia nihil scire—*

which was inscribed by the first Rosicrucian in the mystic register of the mystic palace of the king. And what is it then that we must learn? It is the majesties of intellectual thought; it is the altitudes of aspiration; it is the depths of feeling; it is the new birth of poetry; it is the secret meaning of Nature's parables. What saith the voice of many waters? What songs sing the stars in their courses? What signifies that speech which day utters unto day? What is that knowledge which night showeth forth unto night? We return, therefore, as we must return always, to our old standpoint—that in the poets we have all things, for to them we must look for an answer. Physical science cannot teach us. It is good and holy, but it is a register of dead facts which will not move until poetry has breathed upon the dry bones. We can learn only of the gospel of interpretation, and thereof the evangelists are all poets, though all may not write in rhyme. The poets are the kings of intelligence; by their insights, by their language, all life is beautiful and turned into a deep significance. It is therefore an arch-secret of beauty to understand well after the manner of the poets, and to contemplate all things, to feel in all things, to act in all things, from the apex summit of an intelligence which we have purged in the fires of poesy, which we have illuminated with the solar splendour of the poetic sun. If we conform in all things to the understanding of the poets, we shall attain to the ideal life, and all imagination, and all romance, will be the domain of joy and gladness in which we shall possess our consciousness. There can be no doubt that this is the true light and the true life, the way of all exterior perfection and of all internal beauty. It is the way of that Art which is above Nature, and of that joy which is within God. We must therefore aspire towards the "understanding spirit" of the Psalmist, towards the true criterion of poetic judgment which is the instrument of poetic interpretation. We must beautify our life in all things, our thoughts in all things, our dreams, our ambitions, our objects, our environment, and that which we do unto ourselves, we must do likewise, and in the same measure, unto others, for it is only by reciprocity—by harmonious interaction at all points with all humanity—that we can attain the ideal for ourselves. A false ideal only is possible to the selfish man, cultured and refined though he may be. Therefore, O friends and fellow Mystics, let us concentrate ourselves in the splendour of intelligence, and in all its beautifying power; let us believe that it will reign more and more, that it will put all enemies under its feet, and of its kingdom there shall be no end; for it will permeate, penetrate, and leaven until it transfigures ultimately the body of man, and completes the illustration of our true Philosophical Vase. Let us ever salute, revere, and worship the high-erected lustre and serenity of unfettered understanding, free from all prejudice, pure, unmixed, simple, intuitive, throned and regnant. Let us enlarge it in ourselves and in our children, that all, small and great, shall be informed therewith, till there be no longer a distinction of great and small, till that which is without shall be as that which is within, the actual humanity realizing the archetypal man; and, in respect of the grand patrimony of intelligence, till there shall be neither male nor female, but one uplifted, regenerated, all-ruling mind, accomplishing in peace and pre-eminence the reign of Messiah on earth, and the millennial joy and pleasure of a perfect world.

IV.

The Ministry of Imagination.

If we briefly recur to the connection of imagination with light, we shall see that, assuming the physical and metaphysical transfiguration of humanity to be possible at all, imagination must be a supreme acting factor therein. It is at the basis of all aspiration, because all aspiration is concerned with things that are conceived but not attained. In all things we aspire to the ideal; even in illicit desire, it is an ideal that is in view, though in the category of downward egression. All ambitions, all motives are concerned with the ideal, and the energy which directs us to achievement in every department of activity has its source in the imagination. In the youthful "yearning for the large excitement which the coming years will yield," in the struggle after the beatitudes of wealth and place, of power and fame, it is imagination which creates, conceives, defines, which gilds the prospect, which blows upon the smouldering fires of longing, and causes the steady tongues of flame to leap up towards the end in view. In the common round of daily life and circumstance, the field of imagination is circumscribed within a circle which, if not actually sordid, is, at least, narrow, not infrequently mean, and sometimes base. From little motives to high motives, from small ends to great ones, from things ignoble to the nobility of achievement—would we thus exalt the world, would we enlarge the scope of action, we must extend the range of motive, and to perform this we must expand imagination. If we can expand what is the source of all strength, all ambition, all aspiration, all desire: if we can endow it with a new vitality, a higher object, a grander reach, we shall have succeeded in one of the most important achievements towards the life of perfection on earth, because we shall have transformed the fountain and source of all progress. It is possible to accomplish the transfiguration of the universal world by the psycho-chemical instrument of an illuminated imagination. We do not overstate the case.

· The world is much as we conceive it; transform the received conception, and
we transform the world; it is a process which has been many times accomplished during the course of the world's history.   In Alexander and Napoleon
a colossal dream of conquest may be said to have changed the world.   In
Christ and Buddha, the milder dream of a benignant religion read life anew to
believers through long ages for untold millions.   The dream of Plato has
governed and directed all that is highest in philosophy.   And what here shall
we say of those poets in whose praise already we have said so much?   He saw
deeply into the springs which control human action, who said: "I care not
what man shall make laws for the country, so I make the songs of its people."
For though laws regulate action, song touches its source.   Thus the Third
Empire did well to abolish the Marseillaise, and when the Empire was over-
thrown at Sedan, and the Marseillaise burst once more from the lips of a revo-
lutionized nation, the imagination of France was electrified, the Republic was a
fait accompli, and the Empire was for evermore impossible.

     In all parts and spheres of the life of humanity imagination is equally
potent.   Is it religion?   Then the deepest and primal mystery of all vital
religion is the process which we call Conversion, and that is a radical change of
ideas, resulting in a new bent of mind, a fresh direction of activity, a deflection
of entire life.   All Theosophy, all Kabbalism, all Mysticism, have recognized
the power of imagination, of the Diaphane or Translucid.   It is the Great
Magic Agent of Eliphas Levi.   It is the *raison d'être* of the sensuous in all
hierarchic ritualism, and the development of imagination is the true object of
celestial magic and spiritual alchemy.   Imagination is to fantasy what the
aureoline side of the *Magnum Opus* was to the argentine phase.   The fancy
plays and pleases; the imagination commands, compels.   Imagination creates,
fancy combines only.   We are charmed by a tale of the fairies; we are enthralled
by a romance of magic.   The Countess D'Aulnoy is delightful, but we are overwhelmed by Tieck.   Fancy changes for a moment the withered leaf into the
precious metal; imagination institutes a permanent alchemical conversion.   So
also, what is fantastic in religious departures may shortly divert the soul, but
it requires the deep things of consecrated imagining to accomplish a real regeneration.   Fancy changes the manner; imagination transfigures the motive.
Imagination is then everything; in its own order it is supreme.   And in the
recognition of this fact we find another reason for an appeal to the poets, for
they are the hierophants of imagination.   The facts, principles, and theorems
of occult or Hermetic science are barren till they are vivified by the power of
intelligence.   Magical arts have exoteric actuality on the historical plane, but
they become factors in the soul's progress, and are spiritually illuminating only

on the purified plane of intense and supreme imagination. The true plane of magic is the psychic and translucid. What mystical science teaches is how to realize the dream. What are called the facts of magic offer in a certain sense a pabulum to aspiration, and are a plastic matter for the mind's creative faculty to interpret and adapt as it will. Here it is no question of romantic historical theories or brilliant but unreliable presentations of historical occurrences; on the plane of history these things are intolerable. It is a question of psychological interpretation, and the psycho-chemical transmutation of the commonplace for the arcane ends of the soul. It is a process which has taken place in all ages, which works at this day more powerfully then ever. It is that natural process by which the bitterness and trivialities of the past are unconsciously eliminated by the mind in retrospection, which illuminates the vistas of memory with the softened and beautifying radiance of the uncreated light. In sublimity and significance the most high-erected prodigies of magic fall short of the undefined grandeur which their first and far-away impression creates in an imagination that is at touch with the wild and the wonderful—which impression, on a nearer acquaintance, we perceive to

die away,
And fade into the light of common day.

This is the true secret of the vividness of fancy and the consequent proximity and realism of Fairyland for every impressionable childhood—the commonizing influence of close acquaintance has not had time to work. The Rosicrucian Mystery is full of grace and terror to the childhood of transcendental enquiry till the exoteric history of the Rosicrucians becomes known, when the amaranthine crown of those far-famed Teutons crumbles into ashes in the hand, and the Golden Apples of their alchemical Hesperides turn into Dead Sea fruit. At times, however, the stage of enquiry and study is followed by that of initiation, and then the Rose-Cross Mystery may assume a new aspect, with a light towards its solution.[1] We ourselves have investigated these subjects on the plane of history, and have plunged into the path of disillusion, but we have followed subsequently on a higher call, and by stretching forth our hand to place in the side of the Master, we are permitted to learn that which heretofore we believed not. However this may be, as a refuge from permanent disillusion and a revelation of heights undreamed, this book testifies with no uncertain note to the true Gospel of the Imagination, showing that the disparity which exists between imagination and reality measures the superior height of the human soul. Old legends read in this new light reveal new vistas; old facts, reconsidered from this new standpoint, proclaim new possibilities; old dreams are rapidly passing into

[1] See Appendix III.

realities. The domain of the Mystic is an unexplored dreamland, an illimitable wonder-world, the synthesis of the beautiful and the true; and the magical moon whose golden orb illuminates it is "the shaping spirit of imagination."

V.

Man and his Environment.

It is within a comparatively recent time that we have elaborated a philosophy of environment, that we have investigated its influence on variation and the adjustment of organism to new conditions; it is within a still more recent period that writers have attempted to "continue the investigation of the modifying action of environment into the moral and spiritual spheres." That man is shaped by his surroundings, and is therefore very largely the creature of circumstance, is a piece of proverbial wisdom which is older than many hills, while all Christian theology has ever insisted upon the choice of a suitable condition by any person who would make progress in the law of spiritual perfection. It has recognized that, spiritually speaking, the sole suitable environment is God. In Him we must consciously, as we do all unconsciously, live and move and have our being. He must stand round His people as the hills round Jerusalem. There is no need to elaborate further the philosophy of normal conditioning. We are in search of an arch-natural environment, that we may enter into the arch-natural life. We are in search of an ideal environment, that we may lead the ideal life. We know that there is a disparity between the things of poetry and the things of fact, and we are in search of an environment that will identify them, that will permanently invest both land and sea with the "light" which is said to have been never on either sea or land, and that will make distance no longer an inseparable condition of enchantment. We are aware that the tendency of evolution in humanity is to eliminate the coarseness of original nature, and to transmute it by continual refinement. We are aware that Love, Chastity, and Intelligence are supreme factors in the evolution of the Higher Life. And we seek to transfigure our environment, or to escape therefrom. If we follow our line of thought to its ultimate, we shall see that the transfiguration is to be accomplished, in the first instance, by the exaltation of small and commonizing things, so as to establish the weaknesses and humiliations of life on a basis above themselves, till we shall gradually eliminate all weakness and all humiliation. There are certain transcendental conditions of the physical body which seem to indicate the actual accomplishment of such an elimination. It is an old dictum of Magian art that the operator can force, if it please him, even Nature to make him free. The processes of physical generation can be abandoned for the felicities of spiritual fertility; for there is a spiritual as well as a physical generation. Again, man lives not by bread alone; he can be sustained by a spiritual sustenance. So also we can generate spiritually in others.

It is not, however, more true that the individual is shaped by his environment than that the environment is modified by the individual. As he develops, so it changes. It is a circumambient atmosphere rather than an inflexible armour. A marvellous evolution of psychic faculties, including clairvoyance and all extra-normal attributes on the super-celestial plane, would be a necessary consequence of the true spiritual development, the principles of which are laid down in this book. The aspect, the meaning, the lesson, the morality of the whole universe depends absolutely upon the point of view of the observer, and it is by virtue of this eternal principle that it is possible to poeticize life, and to transform earth into Eden. The modification of religious belief, after the same manner, can create a heaven of mind. And as the environment transfigures, is subdued, elevated, illustrated, informed, its gentle and celestial lustre, its ripe mellowness of meridian loveliness, will fall upon the face of the observer, and again we are led up to the manifestation and centralization of light about the man and woman of the future. And the light without, as the light within, the reflection and the radiation, all phases of arch-natural glory manifested within and about the human form, will, as we conceive, be regulated by the arcane laws governing the energies of the pure imagination and exalted will of the perfect, evolved humanity. So may we picture the head of the immaculate neophyte as crowned with seven stars, and that of the supreme adept as with a single flower of light. Perhaps the one thing chiefly needful for this dream to become an actuality is to find the link between imagination and reality. That link, we submit, can be supplied by Mysticism, because it is acquainted with the abyss and the altitude of our inner being, and it is there the force resides which can, as it does daily, develop all aspiration in the order of things possible into active fulfilment. The omnipotence of imagination has been said to belong exclusively to the domain of transcendental science, and the illuminated imagination is said also to endow the will with power over a universal agent. For imagination is "the eye of the soul"; it is the poetic instrument; by it we can make life poetry, life paradise, life dream, life joy and beatitude; by it we can therefore most assuredly, most really, and permanently, transform the world.

VI.

The Ministry of Gladness.

Let us realize for a moment the change which takes place in a person whose interior condition has been modified by the love of God. There is first and most evidently, that which occurs in his own nature, for the same is transmuted from, as it were, dull earth which cleaves ever to the surface, into a burning fire that ascends, and by an influence which seems to act from the region of the starry heavens, leaps and is drawn upwards, tending still higher and ever giving off into the empyrean. Something immortal and impassible seems to have entered into his whole being. There has been a readjustment of the centre of activity, of which the controlling motive is no longer derived from without, but from the energy of an interior purpose, whereby his life is illustrated henceforth. The immediate result is that he is no longer governed by environment, which, in its dominant aspect is the prince of the kingdom of this world, but he himself rules it, and it becomes henceforth for him the realized Kingdom of Heaven. He is no longer the subject of temptation on the part of the external sphere, for he has entered into the reign of law. He now acts rightly, thinks well, and aspires to perfection by a fiery necessity of his nature. He is not dead to pleasure, nor emptied of all desire; he is more eminently *l'homme de désir*, but he no longer seeks satisfaction on the plane of illusion and among the things of sense, where the real necessity of being is never satisfied. His rectified nature becomes itself a rectifying agent for all around him; unlike the just man, he does not fall seven times, nor is he merely negative, like the innocent; he is an instrument of positive righteousness, which not only does no evil but affects all things unto good, and draws all things after his own order in the lineal way.

Along such lines we propose the development of the perfect woman and the perfect man. At our back is the wisdom of the ages. We are the lawful descendants of Magi, Gymnosophists, Platonists, Theurgists; Egypt, Greece, and Chaldea, æonian India and far Cathay—of all these we are the heirs. We have their literature to help us in the grand construction, which may after all be a reconstruction. We have the processes of alchemy to help us. We have all dream and all legend and all poetry in harmony with the mystic dream, the mystic legend, and the poetry of Mysticism. We have also all religion, because whether it be Mysticism, legend, dream, poetry, or religion, the universal subject is still man. And it is man in alchemy—man the distiller, man the thing distilled, man the vessel and the alembic. The vision expands before us. All forces of imagination and aspiration collected from all these quarters centre for the elaboration of the man and woman of the future. The Christus stands for the archetype, but we do not ignore Buddha. We have Hermes and Apollo, the celestial Son of the Sun, Chrishna and Osiris. We have the Virgin Mother, the first-begotten Maid of Majesty and Wisdom, Isis and Urania, Aphrodite, the higher Venus, the Lady Lucifera, the Regina Cœli, Pallas, and Diana the Unveiled. Let us pause for a moment on the prospect. We look to see the manifested glory, majesty, intelligence, beauty, and royal apex of perfection outlined and adored in all these symbols walking this green earth. And that prospect can be actualized by the processes of Mysticism. Were such a splendid and many-tinted Iris of supreme promise—were this "floral arch of Paradise"— but a romantic lie, or merely the heroism of a dream, the world's good would be achieved by working towards it. But it is not a lie—by the love of Jesus and the bond of the brotherhood in Buddha, all aspiration, all poetry, all religion assert it. The resurrection of the righteous asserts it, the promise of the millennium includes it, the transfiguration of Christ pre-realized it; modern psychology proves it with the possibilities it has opened up in the higher phenomena of mesmerism, clairvoyance, and spiritism. Magic also proves it— that dread, unfathomed mystery of past achievements in arcane experiments. And as there is a light of the physical world, but also a light of mind; a light of physical beauty and a supreme illumination of intelligence; so is it in the ultimate ends of these dual splendours that we shall look for the accomplishment of the two sides of the *Magnum Opus*, the great work of the Light, the illumination of the New Age, the incandescent splendour of perfection, the brightness of the true, intimate life in the deep heart of Nature in touch with the heart of God.

We submit that imbued by such a hope we have cause for gratulation and a sufficient reason to be glad for ever. Now, this gladness, inasmuch as it is reasonable, and seeing also that it is eminently pure in quality, must be counted itself a factor in that sequence of activity by which the hope will pass into fulfilment. Whenever we review our aspiration and take joy therein, we shall speed the day of reconstruction, if only by rekindling our private zeal and enthusiasm, whereby we shall work better, having had recourse to a spring of strength and fortitude. So is the Ministry of Gladness a true and real ministry, and the enjoyment of our aspiration at once delight and help. We place Enjoyment definitely and finally before us as the true end of being. There is no real life apart from delight and joy. Suffering and self-denial may be necessary but they are only means to an end. There is nothing beautiful in suffering or noble in restriction, if we consider them simply in themselves; they are hard, hideous, and terrible. There is no sublimity about them which is derived from their own essence; they are sublimed by an essence from without, and that by which they are sublimed is their end. Now, the end of all action is that divine state which is *ter quaterque beatus*, and it is fitting that, as evolutionary Mystics, we should be glad now because of the gladness which we do look to attain hereafter, and for this also that between things physical and things spiritual there must be a certain parity and correspondence, and we know that, spiritually speaking, the Mystic is seeking the eternal joy which is in God; we know that Nirvana in Christ is the sum of all bliss, that the electric and magnetic contact between God and the soul is not only a pleasure which passes all words, but all possibilities of thinking. It is the sublimation of that enviable state which constitutes the *mens sana*, but, in another sense, it is beyond measure and above reason; it is the absolute, perfect, supernal bliss, limited by neither time nor space; it is the divine complacency of eternity. In the second part of this work we shall endeavour to indicate some attainable conditions of being which will provide a faint foretaste of this state, in which the well-spring of the *Fons Deitatis*, flowing through the infinite of our manhood, are no longer confined by the narrow limits of terrestrial personality. Here, in this first part, we must endeavour to enumerate as best we can some other conditions by which the felicities of the outward man can be intensified and developed—the evolution of the perfect man by the harmonies of joy.

VII.

The Circle of Necessity.

We have been absorbed heretofore in considerations which, realizable as they are, have an aspect of dream-splendour; it is requisite now that we should descend into the lower sphere of detail, and consider how in the things of daily life we can assist towards the development of the perfect man. To produce a perfect body, it is certain, for example, that we must have a suitable regimen. This is as essential as environment. The life of aspiration and desire, the life towards the ideal goodness, beauty, and perfection, requires a daily diet regulated in accordance with the ethical high-water mark at which we propose to aim. A fanatical adherence to any fixed form of diet is evil, because, before all things, and in all things, we are to be regulated by free reason and enlightened tolerance, and it is clear from the immense variety of educated opinion which

exists upon the subject of food and its laws, that we are not as yet in possession
of a perfect way in diet. Normally, we are guided by custom and appetite,
checked by the occasional control of an imperfect medical science, which is in
no branch of its practice more imperfect and limited than in those problems
that are connected with the ministry of food. From the empirical standpoint, it
is not, therefore, reasonable to dogmatize; but if we approach the question of
diet from the ethical and ideal standpoint, we shall obtain, à priori, certain rules
to guide us. And first and foremost, it is ethically and spiritually certain that
the veritably ideal life is closed in all its superior pathways to those who partake
of flesh. Here there is no question of a wholesome or strengthening food. On
that point opinions may differ, as they differ upon the subject of cereals. At
the same time, it may not unreasonably be considered that a food which is
ethically detrimental cannot be physically serviceable. Concerning the ethical
standpoint, there can, however, be no doubt. Viewed therefrom, the slaughter
of beasts for our sustenance and a repast on the carcase, however transcendental
be the triumph of the culinary art, is only removed in degree, and is not at all
removed in kind, from the dietary delights of the cannibal. In this doctrine
there is no fanaticism and no arbitrary dogma founded upon partial experiment.
Philosophy calmly and reasonably distinguishes the existence of an immutable
law in the region of ideal excellence. It supports the fundamental contention
of the so-called vegetarian, while discountenancing his aberration and mania.
At the same time philosophy revolts with equal good reason from that supple-
mentary contention which seems to bind up irrevocably what is termed total
abstinence with the abstinence from refection upon flesh. There is no law in
the ideal world which prohibits the use of wine; it has, in fact, an ideal excellence and a symbolic value; it is rich, free, and generous. There is, of course,
a law in ideality which absolutely prohibits the misuse of any food or drink, and
to be gorged with vegetarian stews is no less depraving than to get unreasonably drunk on Tokay. But wheresoever there is no fixed principle involved,
the supreme liberty of idealism will mark out no hard and fast lines in food, but
will make the laws of nourishment a subject of systematic investigation with a
view to elaborating an absolute science in the ministry of diet to health. In the
meantime, and while such a science is developing, we shall look as before to the
poets for assistance, and from them we shall gain our lights. We shall devote
ourselves also to the question of the ministry of cleanliness in the preparation
of the Vas Philosophorum, and therein whatsoever may assist us towards the
perfect life in physics will for us be a religious practice efficacious in the sanctification of the body, which is the visible house of life. Finally, we shall have
regard to the recuperative ministry of sleep, knowing that the waking life of

aspiration gives entrance to a higher sphere of activities in the repose of the outer man, knowing that there is a hygienic science of sleep as there is a hygiene for the waking world, and knowing that we have brushed but the fringe of such science. Our devices extend little further than the sanitation of an open window, or an elevated room. But there is an open window by which the soul goes forth, and leaves the physical vessel to the simplicity of a perfect rest. And the waking elevation of the interior man will conduct that travelling soul into things elevated of the unseen world. There is also the unattempted problem of environment in sleep; we must sanctify the hush of night; we must rectify the encompassing elements with sweet and invigorating aromas, and, once more, in all this ministry, as in other things great and small, the poets will be at hand to help us.

We are indicating in this section a work which has yet to be achieved, but the method of its fulfilment we by no means pretend to teach. In this single department of our subject there is matter in abundance for large volumes; at another time, and in another place, should our zeal be received by our brethren in the spirit which prompts it now, we may perhaps attempt something, and possibly others may appear who on these points will be better equipped for speaking.

CHAPTER THE FOURTH.

The Religion of Evolution.

I.

The True Religion of Humanity.

O F the starry promise of evolution we have written as best we may, and even as after a long ecstasy of imagination the poet returns cold, trembling, and unequipped to the actualities of that commonplace existence which he can transfigure for himself alone, and not always even for himself, so, and with such feelings, with the same consciousness of deficiency in power, we turn from our long vision, and looking upon the world about us, we endeavour to suggest to ourselves some further possible and reasonable course by which we can attempt to realize our grand dreaming. Organization for the ultimate accomplishment of an end which, however certain, is undeniably distant, must be ever difficult, and vulnerable to unfavourable criticism at almost every point. We have already laid down as a general rule of life that in all our dealings, whether with ourselves or with others, we must do all things in harmony with evolution; we must bring our consciousness, reason, will, and desire to act with and not against it. We must think and act and be in reference to the attainment of perfection in ourselves and in others, and of a perfection which does not refer exclusively to God and man's relation with Godhead, nor to the inter-relation of social humanity, nor to the excellence of the interior man, but to all three, and also to the development of perfection in the body of man. The practice of this perfection is essentially a religious practice, and we have already defined the necessity for a new religion of evolution—in other words, the religious idea must become identified with the law which accomplishes the construction of the race, which law, from the time that it is consecrated by the activities and aspirations of religion, will work with increased force. How best therefore to lay the groundwork of our design so that we can elaborate the principles of a universal religion, having a dual mission, the creation of an immediate correspondence between the individual and the universal soul, and such a modification and education of the exterior man, together with such a transfiguration of that man's environment, as will ultimately manifest in time and space the fulfilled design of Nature. Let us endeavour in all earnestness to grapple with this problem.

Let us consider, in the first place, that there is a royalty and priesthood to come, for the perfect man will be at once both king and priest—*secundum ordinem Melchisedech*. If we look into the far future of that millennial time from the standpoint of ecclesiastical polity, we shall find but two classes—that of the spiritual neophyte and that of the adept or the hierophant, which is simply the broad distinction between youth and maturity. The evolution of Aphrodite-Urania, or of Isis, the Mother of the Gods, and of Hermes-Apollo, will be accomplished in every grown man and woman, and will be in course of accomplishment in every maid and boy. If we seek here and now to inaugurate a universal religion of development for the speeding of the time of perfection, such a religion must consist:

(*a*) Of a practical doctrine, embodying the counsels of perfection in all departments of life, from the manner of the conception of the individual to the preparation for that change in the form of perception which we call death.

(*b*) Of an experimental method for putting those counsels in practice, and thus working for the attainment of the desired end.

(*c*) Of an external ministry consisting of ritual and liturgy, designed for the realization in a vivid manner of the grand hope which is before us, and calculated not only to keep it fresh in the minds of the members of that religion, but to stand as a public sign and witness of the quality of our profession.

But the great work of Human Reconstruction may be begun by any person vitally interested therein, even in his own house, and in his own family. It is indeed there that it should and must begin. The domestic hearth is the true Mystic Lodge of the New Life, and the Masonic and Rosicrucian analogies which abound therein may be elaborated with more profit than any vindication of Solomon's Temple spiritualized. There should we look to find the perfect Ashlar in the Master of the Household, and the great process of the hewing of the Rough Ashlar in the shaping of the Youth of the Household. There should the Spiritual Temple be created and visibly made manifest. There at each birth should Christ enter anew into the world. Each daily lustration should symbolize anew the one baptism of the Spirit, and each meal a sacrificial offering and a Eucharistic communion.

But if we would testify to the world at large concerning the grand religious and reconstructive work of development, and concerning the help which we can give therein, we must have a visible ministering body and a church of the New

Life. That must begin like the parabolic grain of mustard seed, set newly in the developing matrix of mother earth. It must be humble and small at first, and it must grow gradually, till, like the Apostolic Church of Christ, it takes possession of the king's palace and of the throne of the world. Like the upper room at Jerusalem must be the first synagogue of the true religion of Humanity, but the grand, universal, mystic Temple of the new mystic Jerusalem will stand after a few years as a sign unto the nations of the earth of the glory that in them is to be revealed, of the flower of human loveliness which is to unfold, of the day of dream and legend, of the day of prophecy and song, of the day of development and evolution, of the surpassing Day of Christ.

We are not prophesying or divining; we state a fact to come. There is only one doctrine in religion which can ultimately possess the world, and that is the doctrine of development. The law which has presided over the construction of the universal world can alone preside adequately over the construction of humanity to the end of eternal life.

II.

The Synthesis of Religious Belief.

There is perhaps nothing which modifies and transfigures humanity to the degree of the religions it professes. They shape man's destiny; they define his hopes; they control his nature; they influence, by modifying or exalting, his passions; they prompt his aspirations; they "assist at his birth and attend him in death." So it is needful before all things that we should possess an official religion which shall be consonant to man's development. Official religion is to be distinguished from fundamental religion. Fundamentally, there has never been but one religion in the world. There is and there can be only one way by which we can approach God, and that is by the way of the interior life. The reason is plain. God is the absolute reality, and there can be but one means of seeking Him, and that is through the reality which is in ourselves. So far as we can trace it, the interior life, and its revelations, have always been known in the world. "Everywhere it has been the same, and everywhere carefully concealed." It ruled everywhere; it was sublime everywhere; and everywhere it led mankind, or the *élite* of mankind which possessed it, into the eternal truth, into the divine light, into the perennial beatitude and joy. For him who possessed it the Mystics truly said:—*omnia unum sunt, et omnia ad unum trahit, et omnia in uno videt.* But the religious sentiment has clothed itself in a thousand forms—many barbarous, many grotesque, some grand and beautiful. There is a final transfiguration to come which will not pass away, because it will embrace all needs and all possibilities. It will be the most complete expression of the inner nature of religion.

When humanity has outgrown the shell of an official religion, as a shell it casts it behind. But religion does not die. To-day, when there is a general disintegration of all forms of speculative belief, the vital spirit of religion was perhaps never more abroad in the world, is more conscious than ever of itself; the secrets of spiritual truth were never sought more eagerly, and never did the positive reality which is behind all official religions seem more likely to become universally known, and accepted with zeal and enthusiasm. It is therefore a day of revelation, a day of many teachers, of intellectual going to and fro, and of continual interior ferment.

Now, the synthesis of religious belief must be the work of the twentieth century. It is not possible to intellectually assert any longer the positive and exclusive truth of any one form of exterior religion. It is certainly not possible for Mystics. We have discovered the actual substratum which is the heart of all religions. We are not only convinced with Max Müller that there is a religion behind all religions, but we also know what it is. We are in one sense convinced of the truth of all those that are worthy of the name which they bear. But we cannot mistake the veil for the reality, type for antitype, *signum* for *signatum*. And once we have come to recognize that the official religions are a veil of symbolism, a woof of parable, it is clear that without irreverence, and without sacrilege, we, at least, who know something of the thing signified, may consider after what manner the veil is woven, whether it requires re-adjustment and another fashion of emblazonment, or even whether it would be well to invest the realities of religion with a new veil of symbolism, of a lighter and finer texture. One thing is certain. If we would accomplish the evolution of humanity we must have a public sacrament, or outward sign of inward grace and beauty, an economy of the positive truth which shall be consonant with the law of progress—a religion of light and joy, a religion of peace and beatitude, a religion of mildness and beneficence, a religion of aspiration, of dream and poetry—of the aspiration which is the source of poetry, of the beauty which is its expression, of the inspiration which is its birthright, of high, supreme, emancipated imagining. We no longer believe in dragons, in winged serpents, and in the monsters of unnatural history; we do not attach actuality to nightmares, nor objective truth to the revolting horrors of *delirium tremens*. The *Inferno* of Dante is sublime, but our veil of symbolism, our tissue of parable, must be stripped of the mythology of perdition even in its most exalted aspect. The good, the beautiful, and the true—these are the ends of our aspiration, these the substance of our hopes. And our religion must be like unto these.

Its foundation should be also in the principle that man must inevitably work out his own salvation. Help he may have from beyond and outside himself, but the help from within is essential—it is the essence of conscious progress. It is not by the vicarious sacrifice of a Christ crucified on a Cross, but by the personal immolation of the lesser and meaner man, crucified on the altar of the heart, that the sins of the world will be washed out.

And now if we refrain from proposing a scheme of universal religion, it is not because we are deficient in clear conviction as to the lines which that scheme must follow, but we are conscious of deficiencies within, and however much we may be energized with mystic zeal, we would avoid, as becomes us, the errors of incompetent temerity. We look for a leader of men; awaiting his advent, help from all quarters should be welcome to all Mystics, and here a word may be added for thinkers of the agnostic standpoint.

It is the main thesis of our whole instruction that the processes of Mysticism are evolutionary processes, and that the doctrine of development is at the root of our practical wisdom. At the same time, there is a religious aspect of evolution which is separable from Mysticism, which could be followed to the world's profit were there no mystic science, and in this aspect it constitutes a kind of natural religion, which, addressing ourselves for the moment to the agnostic thinkers only, we would venture to recommend to their judgment as a possible field of activity. We assume that, when true to their name, they are the most negative and undogmatic of reasoners, that their judgment is suspended concerning the great issues of life, but that they are aware also of the incapacity of their principles to sustain the moral nature of humanity when it has cut itself adrift from the official mainstays of morality. Now, provisionally defining religious work as the construction of the race in the direction of its true end, we submit that a practical system for the creation of a correspondence with evolutionary law should not only enlist their sympathies, but should also command their co-operation. Mystics though we be, we should delight if agnostic philosophy developed an independent instrument for the creation of such a correspondence. However diverse the methods, we should be at work for the same end, and after the reason of the one law.

III.

An Order of the Spiritual Temple.

The attempt to initiate any new departure in the development of exoteric religion is inevitably attended with every species of difficulty. It has all the disadvantage which must attend a first experiment. It is almost impossible to distil the elixir of wisdom out of the raw matter of innumerable previous failures for the nourishment of the new-born child. The attempt also is peculiarly vulnerable to the easy charge of charlatanism at a period when no scheme, even the most altruistic, is absolved in general opinion from a concealed commercial motive. When it is possible to disarm this cruel, yet not always unwarranted, suspicion, the genius of criticism can fall back on the alternative charge of blind folly and enthusiasm. Even the sympathetic mind is alienated by the prospect of a new priestcraft, and the abuses of an irresponsible hierarchy. Above and over all there is the ominous precedent that the warrant of any such experiment is founded in the abortive nature of forerunning attempts. While, therefore, on the one hand, we do seriously and vividly realize the necessity of a religion of evolution which shall attempt to lead mankind along the path of reasonable development within and without, and shall make the cultus of the body a duty of the religious life as much as interior culture, the enunciation of a constructive scheme would be unwise in a work like the present, could we even assume our ability to initiate a felicitous proposal. The world has waited long for its deliverer, and it must wait, so far as we are concerned, a little longer yet for the manifestation of a true teacher. But we believe that he must surely come, and may even now be in the world, and we shall be more than repaid in our labour if this little book upon development shall in any sense speed his time, or in any way make straight his path. It is possible that a teaching society, composed of unanimous minds acquainted with the laws of life, might in the interval perform something, while we watch for the "heaven-sent moment," and for the "spark from heaven to fall." The inner, individual work can be performed without association, but its elementary sections may more easily and profitably be undertaken in a circle of like intention, and the principles developed in this book, concerning the progress towards perfection of the outward and inward man, have been to some extent, a subject of enquiry in a private circle which assembled periodically for harmonious intercourse within the bonds of common sympathy. The consideration of transcendental evolution in its religious aspect took shape ultimately in certain preliminary proposals, which we now offer for more general consideration, neither expressing our personal approval, nor in any sense advocating their adoption, but to indicate simply after what manner the New Light of Mysticism has been tentatively focussed already in a certain glass of mind. The purity of intention which prompted the proposals condoned the imperfections of immaturity and the haste of imprudent zeal for that circle in which they were originally planned. We select two sections from the written records of the debates, and we aspire in all earnestness for the more perfect pattern of a riper time.

The first section is concerned with *An Apology for Ritual.*

"You have been invited to this conference as something more than ordinary investigators of the mysteries of being, and as possessors of more than a fluctuating or passing interest in the principles and profundities of Mysticism. To you, therefore, who believe that advanced spiritual knowledge is the need of this advancing age, to you who, if a way may be opened, would do somewhat for the illumination of the world, we submit with some confidence the following proposition. That those persons who shall prove to be in agreement among us should meet regularly in private, and endeavour to establish a high quality of correspondence with the superior spheres, by accomplishing the spiritual exercises of devotional Mysticism with the subsequent object of putting Mystic Experiment in practice. We do not propose to you in the first instance an elaborate programme. Our design is to establish harmonious relations between ourselves, with a view to our spiritual self-culture in common, proceeding consistently throughout along the lines of the Mystics. We shall constitute ourselves into an informal transcendental society of unpretending seekers after the true light of Mysticism, of earnest and humble aspirants after the unseen grandeurs which have been revealed to the Mystics, worshipping the unmanifest God of the Sages after the most simple methods which have been presented by the Sages, invoking the superior hierarchies which mystic processes have unveiled in the past to the mighty men of soul, refining our interior natures, attempting our alchemical reconstruction, fostering our spiritual aspirations, and looking for that power which 'he shall receive,' say the Mystics, 'who from the clamorous tumults of this world ascends to the supernatural still voice, from this base earth and mud whereto his body is allied to the spiritual, invisible elements of his soul.'

"Such is, broadly, the proposition which we make to you, and if you are in agreement therewith we shall solicit your opinions in the second part of this conference on the best way of putting our design in practice, inviting your attention first of all to a matter of considerable importance which is closely bound up with our proposition.

"The exercises of devotional Mysticism which will be the object of our meetings will involve some revival of ancient Mystic Ritual, and we may say at once that this revival must be to some extent reconstructive in character. Mystic experiment and the exercises of Mystic devotion have been always connected with a certain ceremonial sequence, and they cannot be separated therefrom. It may be further stated that this ceremonial is wholly symbolical

in character. Now if there should be any difference of opinion at this conference, it is here that it will begin. There may be some among us who shrink
from the ceremonial element in the services of religion, who believe that the
worship of God should take place only in spirit and in truth, who would say in
particular that Mysticism is concerned only with the interior man, to whom
rites and forms are nothing. We have therefore to justify before you, in view
of this possible difference, the application of ritual and symbolism to matters of
religion; and, in the first place, we would draw your attention to something
which is taken rightly for granted in these objections. It is assumed that the
meetings which we propose to hold are primarily of the nature of religious
services. This is actually true. Now, what do we mean by religion, and, in
this connection, what also do we mean by service? Well, the word religion, as
you will know, is of Latin origin, and its philological significance is a close
consideration or pondering. It is, in fact, that thinking in the heart without
which the whole garden of humanity, the *hortus inclusus*, the Paradise of the
Soul, is desolate. But it has also a higher and more arcane significance, and in
this aspect religion is a readjustment or rebinding of man to that source from
which man originated. The word service as applied to religion means ministration to spiritual need. We have therefore the inward want and the outward
ministry; and religious service, being of necessity exterior, must take a shape
and form. The ordinary religious service is devised to minister to the ordinary
requirements of persons desiring to reflect religiously in themselves. But the
Mystic is conscious of higher spiritual necessities, and he must be served outwardly in another way. He is aware that there are resident within him faculties,
powers, possibilities of correspondence, which are commonly unknown, and that
the outward methods for their development must be more elaborate than would
be needed in the case of other men and women. This is a fact which has been
recognized through all the ages of Mysticism, and as a consequence the religious
ceremonial of Mysticism, practised in utter secrecy, has ever been more advanced,
more splendid, more suggestive, in a word, more developing, than that of any of
the great hierarchic creeds. The religion of the Mystics possesses then its
liturgies, its rituals, its vestments, and its official formulæ, which are all full of
meaning and beauty. They have a virtue in themselves because they stimulate
the mind of the beholder, and when you hear of the inherent virtues of mystical
forms, it is this quickening which is referred to, which gives new ideas to the
mind, awakens dormant faculties, and imparts strange, transitory powers. The
contemplation of the symbolism of Nature uplifts the mind of its student. The
symbolism of Nature transfigured by the alchemy of the poet, which is essentially symbolic, will elevate it still further. When the symbolism of Nature and

of poetry have both been modified by the action of Mystic instruments, a still higher grade of exaltation is reached—which is that of true illumination. To assist the induction of the prepared student into this condition is the object of Mystic ritual, because it is in this state alone that a correspondence can be established with superior things. We see therefore that a Mystic service—an outward ministry to the inward needs of a mind which has been modified by Mysticism—must be essentially symbolical; and we submit that in this matter of the methods it is our duty as disciples to follow the old masters. Nor is there need that we should do so as merely blind believers; we can justify the course that we shall pursue; we can discern the reasons which actuated them; we can see that they still hold good; and we can appeal to the universal precedent of all Mysticism, from the days of the Eleusinian Mysteries down to the latest development of mystic ceremony within the Church of Christ."

The apology for ritual was followed at a later debate by the outlines of *A Tentative Rite.*

"We have taken the opinion of this Conference on the question of establishing a series of permanent religious services of a devotional and mystical character, undertaken for our own self-instruction, and for our own spiritual culture. Substantially that opinion was unanimously in favour of the scheme. If there were any point of difference, it arose, as was expected, on the subject of the form of the Ministry, on the reconstruction of Mystic ritual. We then endeavoured to justify the application of external symbolism to the services of religion, defending the suggestion of ceremonial, and maintaining that the elevation of the senses by the appeals of an impressive ritual was natural, legitimate and useful. An objection—common enough—was put forward as to the invariable ultimate of elaborate religious ceremonial, namely, the aridity of formalism. But that is true only, or chiefly, when the form has survived the idea—when truth has departed from the sanctuary—when the interior and informing life has evaporated, and left only the outward image behind—when the inner meaning of the parable has been lost, and only the husk of its literal significance remains. It is clear, as we then affirmed, that the proposed service of devotional Mysticism must take an outward shape and form, and that this exterior form should correspond to the interior end; it should recall the objects of the ministry, and the defined ends of religion. If there be a veritable Science of the Mystics, the external operations with which it is connected cannot be vain and foolish. The outward senses are the ministers to the man within. If we attract, instruct, and elevate the one, we must assuredly influence the other. We have also to consider the importance of historic association. By adapting the symbolic ritual of the Mystics, we become associated with the Mystics. In

the words of Eliphas Levi, we enter that magnetic chain which began with
Enoch and Hermes, and will only finish with the world.

"But there are questions of more transcending importance than any that
are connected with association.   They are those of environment, conditions,
and harmony.   The importance of a favourable environment is sufficiently
exhibited in the natural order and in matters of daily life.   Within certain limits
we may control circumstances, but more largely still do circumstances control
us.   Within certain limits we may create our own environment, but in a greater
degree our environment makes us.   If we would encompass a certain end, our
circumstances must conduce to that end, and wherever necessary we must bend
them and modify them till we are surrounded with an environment which is
favourable to the fulfilment of our intention.   The present application of these
almost truistic remarks is too obvious to require enforcing.   If we would
accomplish the ends of the Mystics, we must surround ourselves with external
appointments which tolerably favour that end.   Interior recollection is impossible during the performance of a comedy; philosophical reflection would
be misplaced at a masque or a ball.   For the same reason we feel that a hall or
gymnasium are inappropriate to the exercises of religion; and, in like manner,
the bare walls of a Baptist chapel are a poor and ineffective impulse to the
poetic aspirations of an elevated and cultured devotion.   'The magnificence of
the cultus is the life of religion,' says an advanced French Mystic.   And why?
Because the religious sentiment, like all others, must find an outward expression, which will be grand in proportion to the sentiment.   It is the loftiest
buildings which cast the longest shadows.   In the presence of an association
of transcendentalists, it should scarcely be necessary to insist more strongly on
this point.   You, above all others, are aware of the importance of conditions.
The most experienced among you have affirmed that the conditions are everything.   Now, the adjustment of conditions and the refinement and elevation of
environment are the sole end of ritual in religion.   They are devised to adapt
the external surroundings to the inward intention, to elevate and refine the
external senses, so that no sensual grossness may interfere with the work within.
This last statement is simply equivalent to insisting on the importance of harmony.   To accomplish the religious, and especially the Mystic, work, there must
be a proper harmonious correspondence between the outward and the inward
man.   A ministration to the senses is therefore necessary—to effect a 'settling of
all things small and mean like a sediment.'   For this reason we use music in
the transcendental séance, we use music in the services of religion, and if it be
lawful and useful to make appeal to the ear, it is equally right and necessary to
call upon the other senses and endeavour to influence all in the direction of the

desired end. In their absence, no body of worshippers can accomplish more collectively than may be accomplished individually without any form of service.

"Assuming that you are for the most part in agreement with us on this point, we may proceed to describe shortly the nature of the service which should be established among us. It should be borne in mind that it is tentative in character, that its form is elementary only, that we hope, as opportunity arises, and as our field of possibility expands, to reconstruct the whole Mystic ritual and to establish a system of ministration which shall be adapted to the religious needs of the age, and shall be an adequate representative of the entire Mystic process.

"We are told by the Mystics that there is an exterior evolution on the physical plane, and an interior evolution on the psychic plane. There is a promise to the outward man and a promise to the inward man. They prophesy unto us of a glory to be revealed outwardly and of a glory to be realized within —of an exterior splendour and an interior light. This two-fold evolution will be represented in the ministry of devotional Mysticism by the liturgy and the ritual. The liturgy will be concerned with the inward man; in the symbolic ritual there will be a service of the outward senses, and as there is a solidarity between the two evolutions, so there should be a solidarity between the liturgy and the ritual. There are also four chief processes in Mysticism—Regeneration, Illumination, Dedication, and the Mystic Marriage, or communication with Deity. These will be represented in the four divisions of the service— Regeneration through Aspiration by an opening aspirational rite, Illumination by the instruction of lessons and discourses, Dedication by a sacrificial service, the Mystic Marriage by a Eucharistic rite. Three other ideas would also be involved by the Ministry of a Mystic service—a possibility of communication with the Divine, and the way and the means thereof, with the two who seek to communicate, namely, Pneuma and Psyche—the Spirit and the Bride. If we educe these processes and ideas into form on the exterior plane, we shall have definite points for our guidance:

"(a) The Temple into which all retire to establish correspondence with the Divine—and this is the Interior Sanctuary.

"(b) The visible body of the Church, corresponding to the physical body, and represented by the concourse of worshippers.

"(c) The Ritual of the Temple, which creates the conditions that are required in the exterior man.

"(d) The Soul and the Spirit which do reside in the interior man, and wherewith the outward man must be unified. These are represented within the interior sanctuary by the ministry of a man and a woman.

"(e) The Liturgy, or devotional service, by which it is sought to unite the three principles of man in a common aspiration and outreaching towards the Divine.

"(f) The high priest, also within the Sanctuary, who is the chief celebrant, the sign of the possibility which exists, the type of communication, the living symbol of the bridge between the seen and the unseen, the representative of God, the speaker who, symbolically, is commissioned from the other side of life.

"In the order of mystical ideas, the priest ministers to the Three Principles, but especially to the Spirit; the Spirit ministers to the Two inferior Principles, but especially to the Soul; the Soul ministers to the whole body. Our Mystic service will be shaped along these lines; they are not arbitrary; they are the order of spiritual procedure. The liturgic portion of the service will be compiled from the Mystics. It will be wholly aspirational and devotional, and will embody the aspirational Mysticism of the Old and New Testaments of all religion. There will be a hymnal portion, selected from the metrical literature of Mysticism. The instructional section will be derived mainly from the lives and teachings of the Mystics. We shall select from the concourse of the Sages fifty-two representative men, taken in historical order, beginning with Pythagoras and Plato. The lessons of each week will be taken from the works of one of these men, and the discourse will interpret his wisdom, or some important factor in mystical philosophy which may be said to take shape in him. During seven days he will rule our thoughts, and will be therefore the ascending star which will govern during that period in the spiritual sky. The lessons and discourses which constitute the second division of the service will be followed by a dedicatory rite, which will open with a choral hymn and a devout invocational litany. A solemn act of Dedication will then be made, and the seven-branched candlestick, which now overshadows you, will be lighted on the altar, representing the five senses, or faculties, and the two principles of the interior man, among other profound significances. The symbolic sacrifice of incense and perfume will be offered to the Divine Substance, representing the aspiration of the worshippers. Acts of Mystic Renunciation will then be made by all present, after which the priest, as the ambassador of the superior world, will proceed to the consecration of bread and wine, symbolical of the divine principles which constitute the food of the interior man. After the consecration, the priest will partake of the elements, and then all present, to signify the communication with Deity, which is the end of the Mystic process. The order of procedure will be as follows: The elements will be received by the deacon from the hands of the priest himself, for he stands as the Spirit in Man. The lady sub-deacon will receive them from the hands of the Pneuma, who is the proper mediator to the Soul, and she in turn will communicate them to the body of the worshippers, as she is the proper ministrant to the Body. After an interval of interior recollection, the service will conclude with an act of thanksgiving, a solemn charge, a benediction, and a final jubilatory hymn."

When prompted by genuine enthusiasm, propositions like these are pleasing, but of little practical value. The church of the future can become actual only by evolving, and the modes of its ministry must be left to evolve with it. The essential quality of life escapes in the ready-made ritual. We are not afraid of the development of another priestcraft, we believe in the magnificence of the exterior sign, and in the grandeur of outward worship; but, with full sympathy for the spirit which governs them, we must deprecate these designs, which have only the elements of failure. At the same time, it is pertinent to draw attention to their existence, for they are part of that spiritual ferment in which we all of us breathe and move.

PART II.
THE INWARD MAN.

THE INWARD MAN.

CHAPTER THE FIRST.

SOME AXIOMS OF TRANSCENDENTAL SCIENCE.

I.

IN the definitions of its most authoritative exponents, Mysticism is variously described as the traditional science of the sacred arcana of Nature which are derived from the Magi; and as the primeval religious, moral, and political doctrine of humanity. It has been connected with vulgar superstitions, but is itself neither superstitious nor vulgar. It is at once a science, an art, and a religion. "It unites in a single gnosis all that is most certain in philosophy and most infallible and eternal in faith." Its palmary province is to lead intellectual aspiration into the plane of absolute realization.

II.

Thus it can place the qualified neophyte in possession of a practical and even of a creative power; but this power in all its scope is available for the "flowers of intelligence alone."

III.

It can connect such intelligences with the operative energies of the universe, and thus enable them to perform within the domain of natural law that which is impossible to humanity at large, and is therefore called miraculous.

IV.

The Mystic can then control matter and adapt it thaumaturgically to his purpose because he works in accordance with the laws which govern it.

V.

These laws are not outside matter; they are merely the permanent mode of its manifestation.

VI.

But the search after arcane power is not the true end of transcendental science, and those who pursue it will miss the divine vocation and misinterpret the divine voice.

VII.

The true end of all Mysticism is union with God, which is accomplished in the knowledge of God, and is effected by the love of God. In comparison with this all other objects are vain and unprofitable.

VIII.

The knowledge of God is consequent upon a mode of the inward mind, and a mode of outward life.

IX.

The acquisition of the two modes which make for divine knowledge demands as a point of departure an exact philosophic theory, which is thus enunciated by the Mystics.

X.

The distinction between matter and spirit is not recognized by the true philosopher, who is aware that there is but one nature infinitely differentiated in the universe.

XI.

The present physical Cosmos represents simply a stage in the evolution of intelligence.

XII.

The law and order which exist in the Cosmos constitute the form of perception which alone is commonly possible to intelligence at its present stage of development.

XIII.

But the application of evolutionary law to the arcane potencies of the inward man will enable a prepared intelligence, by "rationally conditionating," to enter into a superior form of perception.

XIV.

The range, scope, and direction of intellectual vision determine the order in the manifestation of the one substance to the mind, which is a part of that substance.

XV.

The philosophy of intellectual vision is contained in the term direction; as the direction alters, so is the manifestation transfigured, and the exaltation of the one depends upon the elevation of the other.

XVI.

Birth is the entrance into our present form of perception after an infinite series of other and lower forms.

XVII.

Death is a natural transition giving entrance into another form of perception, the quality of which is regulated by the use or abuse of intelligence in an actual form.

XVIII.

The penalties of intellectual retrogression at the higher stages of evolution are heavy indeed. The abysmal lapse of Lucifer and the primeval fall of man were mythological realizations of this retrogression of the spiritual principle.

XIX.

It is possible for the Mystic to enter thaumaturgically into a higher form of perception. This fact is the Key of Celestial Magic.

XX.

It is also possible for the Mystic to enter barbarously, unnaturally, and suicidally into lower forms of perception, and this fact is the Key of Black Magic, and the terrors of the Sabbath.

XXI.

The spirits, or phantasmal duplications, of the so-called dead can occasionally be evoked by entering into another form of subsistence.

XXII.

Communication with extramundane intelligences not yet developed into the plane of humanity can be established by the Mystic, and a properly emancipated mind may exercise an absolute control over these rudimentary beings; but the communication is beset with perils.

XXIII.

The evocation of extramundane intelligences belonging to other hierarchies, and never to be humanly incarnate, is also possible. The lower orders of these beings are termed elementals, and here also the communication is perilous and sometimes full of terrors.

XXIV.

The two-fold peril of these communications constitutes the Magical Danger of the Depths.

XXV.

There are other extramundanes who have transcended the plane of incarnation without becoming incarnate, and these are members of the super-celestial hierarchies. They are grand, glorious, and beneficent; but the unworthy aspirant to participation in their condition of splendour may be overwhelmed by the majesty of their form of subsistence.

XXVI.

The peril of their evocation constitutes the Magical Danger of the Heights.

XXVII.

But these experiments are comparatively frivolous and foolish, and must be counted less than nothing when confronted with the grand possibility which is participation in the life of God.

XXVIII.

So ever have the higher Mystics abhorred thaumaturgic experiments and have regarded even celestial visions as an index of spiritual weakness.

XXIX.

Therefore is the mode of the intelligence to be shaped after its end in God, and the mode of the outward life is to be constrained towards the higher laws which fulfil the divine purpose.

XXX.

So shall we become true Mystics; we shall communicate with God in our spirits, and our spirits will communicate in God with all evolved intelligences, with the Paladins of achievement, the peers of eternity, the sacred and Holy Assemblies, with all that has been born in Him, without rites and without evocations, and without any danger of lapsing into vanity or littleness.

CHAPTER THE SECOND.

Grounds of the Spiritual Practice.

I.

THE psychological experiments of the nineteenth century have directed the attention of many earnest students to the Spiritual Mysteries of the past, and the present epoch of humanity may be deemed a ripe time for the general enunciation of certain philosophical convictions which have taken shape in the minds of a few earnest aspirants after the attainment of positive truth.

II.

It is believed that the lost keys of the ancient secret sciences may yet be recovered. Modern facts, regarded in the light of old theories, and old theories explained by modern facts, seem to have already brought a small number of unassisted seekers to the threshold of the Interior Wisdom.

III.

Certain circles of investigation, and certain unattached students working on individual lines, have set themselves to discover in the literature of Western Mysticism a solution of the great problems of existence.

IV.

Now, the religious aspirations of the age are distracted by the conflict of the sects, and those principles which are at the base of all religion must undoubtedly be sought as the source of illumination for the many minds which are weary of vain speculations and disputes that have no end:

V.

But while the existence of a Supreme Intelligence is being relegated to the rank of superstitions, that process is still in existence, and is once again being brought into prominence, by which the God-illuminated seers of old—Plato, Plotinus, Ammonius, Tauler, Vaughan, Theresa, Saint-Martin, and Jacob Böhme—accomplished an individual reversion to the fontal source of souls, and entered into an ecstatic communion with the universal consciousness.

VI.

In view of these facts, in view of the actual discoveries which have been made in the domain of psychology by various circles of investigation, in view of the needs of the age to which these discoveries can alone truly minister, we invite the attention of all persons who are convinced of the permanence, reality, and proximity of an unseen world, who believe in the possibility of communication therewith, who are enthusiasts for God and the soul, who know that the revelation of the indwelling Spirit and the overshadowing Deity can alone accomplish a conversion in the life of mankind—we invite their attention to the present philosophical attempt to establish the lines of correspondence between that world and the whole body of humanity.

VII.

To these it may be stated that a method of transcending the material world, and of entering into the realities which underlie sense-delusions, does not seem beyond the reach of the age. An acquaintance with this method will destroy the philosophy of the materialist; it will realize spiritual aspirations and the hopes of a larger life.

VIII.

To these also we would proclaim, on the faith of an unbroken historical testimony, and on the evidence of innumerable witnesses, that it is possible in this life, and in this body, to know God, and that the process is enshrined in the secret language of Alchemy, in the allegories of Transcendental Freemasonry, in the occult initiations of the Mysteries, and in the books of the Christian Mystics.

IX.

From the same circle of esoteric literature it is believed that there may be elaborated the true methods for

(*a*) The Interior Regeneration of Humanity.

(*b*) The Manifestation of the Soul in Man, or the Divine Virgin, and the Vision of the interior Diana.

(*c*) The Revelation of the Spirit in Man.

(*d*) The Manifestation of the Dual Flower, or the unification of the Soul and Spirit, which are *Pneuma* and *Psyche*.

(*e*) The Evolution of the Perfect Man.

(*f*) The Transfiguration of the Body of Man by the splendour of Spirit and Soul, or the physical glorification of Humanity.

(*g*) The Evolution of the Christ in Man.

(*h*) The Attainment of the Crown of Evolution in the Interior Translation and the Mystic Apocalypse.

X.

All aspirations of religion and all dreams of idealism admit of realization by the application of the arcane methods which were known to the Mystics.

CHAPTER THE THIRD.

The Holy Assembly.

I T is the universal testimony of all transcendentalists that their science has been ever in the world; this testimony has taken a concrete shape in the theological doctrine that the first man knew God, and that between God and His chosen people there has ever been an avenue of communication· Mysticism, therefore, comes before us as an inheritance from primeval times, a link of secret knowledge which connects with the unfallen state wherein all religions have believed, which is, in fact, the interior history of the soul's progress before it entered into its present form of perception. The perpetuation of the secret knowledge has been dimly limned in the patriarchal traditions of Genesis. Now, the transmission of knowledge in secret involves the idea of inheritors for that secret knowledge, and thus we are prepared for the further testimony which is catholic to all Mysticism and is concerned with a withdrawn brotherhood in whose hands this knowledge has remained, of which they have been living custodians, not mere tabernacles, for it has been increased in the ages, and one of the points of its progress has had the centuries of Christendom for a result. Our most direct knowledge of the science and its guardians is affirmed to be obtained by interpretation from the old canon of the Jews, the new canon of Christ, the great body of Kabbalistic tradition, and at a later period from the literature of alchemy. We ground these statements partly upon the consensus of mystical testimony, but also upon communicated knowledge from a source which we are not at liberty to identify. We do not here speak upon any authority of our own, while, at the same time, we would earnestly disclaim any desire to mystify. We aspire after *la couronne princière*, the Rose-Cross crown of the adept, not to be regarded as an arch-master in the mysteries of make-believe. We have no higher title than that of an informed student, who at the same time is sufficiently instructed in the unwritten code of mystic honour to be superior to the violation of a confidence, and not to make that confidence the excuse for a theatrical attitude. From our own standpoint, even the esoteric history of mystic docrine is of little moment—all literature, all authority, all history being swallowed up by the supreme importance of the personal experience. We ourselves must know these things; we must realize them in the life within; all things may help towards experience, but that is the grand end. The finger-post is not the path, nor is the way of knowledge to be confused with the science itself.[1]

And yet in the interests of that end, not only as regards the doctrine and the secret knowledge of the Mystics, but in its ultimate as regards all knowledge—all real knowledge—and more especially in the science of religion, it is our duty to affirm that "esoteric Christianity holds all"; but while this statement is final as regards the inclusive character of the Wisdom in Christ, it is not affirmed to the exclusion, in any degree or sense, of the Wisdom in Buddha. A crystal basin of pure and limpid water does not contain the less of heaven within its cool, translucent concave because it has a twin sister in its neighbourhood, which also mirrors and radiates. If the Stars and the Fairies have informed our heart with the fire and the life of song, we are not less or more a poet because there has been also until this last among us a perfect Christ of melody, whom we have laureated for his minstrelsy, who has carried unspotted for half a century the immortal bays of Wordsworth. Christianity, however, while it is not apart from Buddha—even as between two basins there may be a secret channel of communication—presents itself before us as the special revelation befitting Western minds, or, more accurately, as the appropriate Western presentation of the one universal revelation, which is that of the Divine in the universe to the Divine in man. It has, so to speak, come home to us, is among us, and appeals to us—even as the woman whom we love, though she would be beautiful in any garment, is more appropriately for us attired in the vesture of her native country than in the gold cloth of Florence, the drapery of Ypres, or the crapes and scarves of the Levant. It is in these that she has first received us; by these we have first become familiar with the suggestions and outlines of her spiritual beauty. Why should we desire to behold her in other garments? Let us rather look forward to the time when we shall see our Dian in glory. There is beauty in veil and vesture, but there is no coruscation of sheeny cincture to compare with the mystery of loveliness which cincture and veil conceal. The parable of the physical universe is full of divine beauty, but more fair is the Reality within. Allegories allure us, as with the glamour of a hypnotic disc; but the truth attracts us more, even as "the heart of the wooer is warm, but warmer the heart of the wooing." Bright is the virgin snow which gleams and glistens upon the gentle bosom of the hills, but when the snow melts and dissolves in running music into the light streams of the valley, it is brighter still to behold the sprouting of tender shoots among

[1] In the pages which immediately follow, the quoted passages are derived from the communication to which reference has been made above.

the grass, the first snowdrops of the season, and to feel the quicker pulsation of the blood of Spring. Let us expect, therefore, the day of the dissolution of veils, when we shall look into the eyes of Artemis.

Even as there is in Mercury all that is desired by the Wise, so in Christianity, when properly understood, there is all that is needed by the Elect; at the same time Buddhism and all revelations help, for collateral sequences of symbolism utter speech one to another, and allegory shows knowledge to allegory. All religions ultimate into the same primeval principles; one Spirit of Truth informs them all, of which they are all phases of partial manifestation, and modes of incomplete exhibition. It is the same in the sphere of religion as it is in the world of physical phenomena, where all that is about us, however much it may differ in depth and height, is the veil and the manifestation at once of one Reality, of one, undivided, undifferentiated, permanent, and absolute Noumen. " But while respecting all other societies, we shall do well if we are led by our Angel to remain in our own Christian Society," and enter into the Sanctuary of the Spirit through that door which is nearest to our hand, is likely to yield most easily to our touch, and to open at our knocking. It is necessary at the same time, and indeed before all things, that the Soul which desires to be illuminated should become—as in all other cases where there is a reality involved—acquainted with the interior side, in other words, with Mystic Christianity, and should enter into "a sympathetic union with the secret hope of the ages." Whosoever shall accomplish this "will perhaps learn something of the labours of the Initiates, and will obtain a glimpse of their knowledge concerning sub-natural and super-natural things." He will then be on the Royal Road, and if he can also show patience, in the Way of Attainment. He will, so to speak, "choose and find his God by a comprehension of spiritual life as it has become specialized in the West." Here it should be understood that there is no distinction in the quality of spiritual vitality. There is one life communicated by one spirit, but the degrees of receptivity are infinite. The East has chosen the special system of spiritual life which is called Buddha, and through that enters into illumination. But with us the same Spirit is of Christ, and though we may not gain less by going further, we shall do well to hold all things in one thing which spiritually contains all things, and is thus the one thing needful. So may we enter through Christ into the rest of Buddha, even as we trust that every earnest Buddhist will enter through the Wisdom of Gautama into the joy of Christ.

Now, seeing that there is an interior side of Christianity, it is evident that there are two aspects to what is called the Church of Christ. " The Church militant must *ex*ist if the Church spiritual *sub*sists." The spiritual Church is the intelligence which informs the Body; we can only make true contact with this intelligence by becoming regenerated or born again, which is to be informed with the life that governs, vivifies, and leads the Church. Thus, and not otherwise, can the Veil be lifted; thus only can we learn more, and especially "how much of exoteric Christianity is indeed true, but in a way so different to what its teachers think." The sole revelation which comes to us at present from within the Veil instructs us to regard the Esoteric Church in the light of "a Holy Assembly," or Inner Circle of Initiates of the First Order, who have subsisted from those primeval times the nature of which has been secretly and faintly shadowed forth in the pregnant allegory of the Edenic age. Whether the constituent intelligences of this Holy Assembly are in the body or out of the body we know not, God knoweth; but we may know, after a transcendental manner, how this sacred society has held on "hoping and working through the ages, helped by expectation and prophecy, fed by the occasional manifestation of a certain divine glory," elaborating in the withdrawn penetralia of the interior life those arcane potencies required for the manifestation of the Day of Christ.

The history of this great school of initiation is presented symbolically in the Old Testament, in which the exoteric narrative of the development of the Jewish people is made use of as a cloak or disguise for an inner and mystical record. The philosophical history of Greece makes evident, on the one hand, that the Eleusinian and other Mysteries were connected with this Holy Assembly, while, on the other hand, the records themselves make evident that there was a contact with the mystery of Egypt. At this point, if we are to deal ingenuously with our readers, it seems necessary to say that the historical evidence for these matters is not open to criticism, for the simple reason that there is properly speaking no historical evidence. There is no doubt that such testimony should be of the best and most indubitable character, considering the momentous issues that are involved, if an appeal is to be made to such witness. But it is not a matter of exoteric history at all, and the grounds on which we repose it are of another kind. That which is interior must be tested by that which is interior. That which is behind the Veil can but dimly be made evident or discerned from without; a hint here, an outline there, may give a vague apprehension of form and contour, but of essence or complexion nothing. Now, as things exterior are before all of the historical plane, so those which are interior are especially of the sphere of experience, and experiential also must be the kind of proof we seek. Those who earnestly desire to know (a) the Mystery of the Inner Circle, and (b) the interior evidence which it can present, may do so through "the mystic power of the Body and Blood." People take the Sacrament at times superstitiously, at others hypocritically, and at others flippantly, but it is a sacred act all the same, and "if taken as a neophyte, and in reverence to the Holy

Assembly, in memory of a great and glorious act which once took place within the earthly circle—a real event, long hoped for by the Initiates of the earliest ages—if taken in reverence for that, and in ' Remembrance of Me,' then one is admitted to the Adytum as a neophyte who in time may know all." We can make contact with the Celestial Inner Circle and its Lord when in a pure spirit we take the Lord's Supper at Church. The interior quickening, and, as it were, the electrical communion of saints which can and in some cases does follow the eucharistic rite will successively make clear to the communicant the points which we now proceed to enumerate.

(a) That in both the Old and New Testaments, every generic reference to the Jews—that is to say, as a chosen people set apart from the rest of the race— is to be understood as referring to the Initiates. The profane or outer world is, on the other hand, referred to under the term Gentiles—those who are not initiated into the Sacred Circle. Thus the so-called history of the Jews is not that of the exoteric ten tribes, but is to be regarded rather as the sacred books of a Mystic Society which is connected on the one side with Eleusinia and Egypt, and on the other with the Essenes and Gnostics.[1]

(b) That the Holy Assembly was illuminated in its labours by the occasional realization of the glory of the Shekinah, until at length, when the fulness of time had come, "and the Sun was in its right place in the equinox," the glory fell, and the Birth of Christ came to pass. " But we must think of all this as taking place within the precincts of the Temple, and as known only to the Initiates. It is a historical fact, but it belongs to the transcendental order of history. The hope of the ages was personified, and man saw God; the Mystery of the Inner Circle was completed."

(c) That the Hidden Life of the thirty years of Christ was passed within the sacred pale of the Holy Assembly, and was also known only to the Elect. "Complete on every plane, the Christ is finally manifested on the outer; but the outer only beholds, it cannot understand Him." The work of Regeneration is the work of this understanding; when it is accomplished, and the Christ is born into the Soul, then "the Collective Christ, born of the Collective Spirit of the Holy Assemblies for ages," is understood. "As yet we can only think of the individual Christ, not of the collective and universal." When we understand that and the Power and the Glory thereof, it will forbid the possibility of

[1] So far as the reader can be assisted by any literature towards an intellectual comprehension of these matters, he will perhaps be most assisted by the papers of Mr. Brodie-Innes on "The Esoteric Church," published in *Lucifer* from October, 1890, to April, 1891. There is also an interesting American work, called *Christ the Spirit*, which urges that "the Gospels were designed originally as an interpretation of the Hebrew Sacred Scriptures for the use and edification of a sacred Secret Society among the Jews"—that is, of a Society of Initiates of the First Order.

limiting the Christ only to the Individual Jesus, "though such an one was doubtless selected as convenient for recognition on the sense plane."

(*d*) That the Four Gospels were designed for the instruction of an Outer Circle, and as such have been transmitted to ourselves who are its descendants and heirs. Thus the Church has never been taken from the world. Its militant aspect—Catholic, Greek, and Anglican—with all its lamentable shortcomings, is the outer and visible sign of the inward and invisible Church. "The Inner Circle still lives; their Lord Christ still reigns over it, and works for His people." We, as the Outer Circle, at present know only the beginning of things; we see through a glass darkly; to learn more, we must lift the veil, and that is not done, as has been said, except through regeneration—that New Birth for which also the Alchemists worked. "Christ notwithstanding does not leave this Outer Circle comfortless." In due time, when people have learned more of these matters, "the Priests will arise who will be able to teach more, and in so doing there will take place that long desired and all needful cleansing of the Church, the true reform which destroys nothing that should remain. All now is outwardly veiled, all now is silent, and yet life exists. The door of the Sacred Assembly is not shut." At times the light breaks through, like rays from the uplifted host, streaming through incense clouds on the upturned, adoring face of the communicating acolyte. "If Christianity lay only in the historical Church, all would be dead."

Those who can accept this testimony concerning the transmission of mystic science, and concerning the locality of the centre of knowledge, will do well to attempt the experience of the Eucharist as a means of attainment. Undoubtedly, however, there are other ways that lead to the truth within, and it would be a poor indication of our spiritual and intellectual liberality if we neglected to recognize that Theosophy has offered us of late years another and distinct method. The means indeed are many, but the end is one, and hence the individual mind may not unreasonably be governed by its own particular bent.

CHAPTER THE FOURTH.

THE CATHOLIC DOCTRINE OF THEOSOPHY AND MYSTICISM.

I.

Higher Consciousness in the Absolute.

THERE is one fundamental point and principle of agreement between all religions and all the creeds which formulate them. They are unanimous in regarding man as having in some sense come forth out of God, and in like manner they all affirm that it is necessary for him to return into his source for the attainment of true perfection and beatitude. In like manner also, every religion is in substantial agreement with all others upon the nature of its claim, for they all indifferently profess to equip their believers with a perfect and true process for the attainment of the divine reunion. There is a multitude of claimants, but the claim is one, there is a multitude of processes, but again their end is one. Yet as they are seldom consistent with themselves, and never with one another, an increasing proportion of mankind has elected to come out of a "war and waste" of words, and to set aside both the claim and the claimants by rejecting the principle of agreement, and denying the end in view. Whether this is really a logical and reasonable position, whether it may not be an economy of trouble which in the end will prove improvident are questions which it is beyond our purpose to discuss. Concerning the divine origin of humanity, and concerning the ultimate nature of beatitude, we are acquainted with another quality of evidence than that which has been offered hitherto by any official religion. But amidst the conflict of rival orthodoxies, it may well be doubted whether there has been at any time a due justification of any individual claim. It is obvious, at least, that not one of them has been able to put their believers in possession, while in this life, of that hypostatic union with divinity which they profess to dispense in eternity. So far as individual persons have progressed in the path of that union, and have attained to any measure of that peace which passeth understanding, which some call the joy in Christ Jesus, and others call refuge in Buddha, while yet others do more variously denominate it, for the names are many, but the joy is one, and is indeed free consciousness in the Absolute of the noumenal world, so far as any have advanced herein, and have participated according to their measure in the Great Subject, it has been in virtue of a special faculty, only incidentally assisted by their special religious equipment. Of this faculty, from which infinite possibilities for its possessors may, in a sense, be said to depend, we must here speak under the name of INTROSPEC-TION. It is not adequate; it is like describing a house by its gate; but our language cannot supply us with a better, it is, moreover, familiar to us all, and up to a certain point all persons are acquainted with its meaning.

The faculty and its name alike are connected in a very close manner with the Mystics and their philosophy or science. This faculty is indeed the field of Mysticism. Thanks partly to the fashion of the moment, to which we have referred upon another occasion, but thanks, above all, to an existing sincerity of inquiry on the subject of transcendental truth, which was manifested in a variety of directions long before the fashion set in, it is now possible to speak with ease, that is, without much danger of being generally misunderstood, on the great object or end of Mysticism. Now, the fundamental principle and object of all true Mysticism is identical with that of religion in general. We affirm that the principle is the same, for the Mystics also regard man as having come forth out of God, and attest that it is necessary for him to return into his source for the attainment of true perfection and beatitude. We affirm also that the object is the same, for it is eminently the return into God that is desired and sought by the Mystic. We may, however, go further, and submit that the claim of Mysticism is at one with the claim of all religions—namely, that it is in possession of a perfect and true process for the attainment of divine reunion. Should any one be required to put a finger on the point where Mysticism becomes differentiated from exterior religion, it might be said that it is in possession not of an arbitrary body of dogma, handed down from antiquity, and to which we must subscribe if we would be saved, but of an actual and precise science of the methods and the means by which a man may work up towards divine union with a fair chance of attaining it in this life—at least in a certain mea-sure—and not having the reward of his labour put off till the harvest of eternity.

We see, therefore, that there is a central, or catholic, doctrine, or principle, which will be found to underlie all Mysticism, and that is man's divine origin and his divine destiny. If we may clothe it in more philosophical language, we would say that man's essential nature issued originally from the noumenal world, is now manifested in the phenomenal world, and, in order to achieve its destiny and attain its beatitude, must return, after a certain manner, into the noumenal world. In yet other words, the end of Mysticism is to attain higher consciousness in the Absolute, and this last expression brings us into contact with a subject which has recently enjoyed an extraordinary share of public attention and interest. We refer to Theosophy. One scarcely knows whether to speak of it as a science, a philosophy, or a form of religious faith. To some extent it partakes of the nature of all three, but at the present moment there is no call to enter upon an exact definition. We all know how Theosophy has been received by the world, and how an unexpected, and what might have seemed an incredible conversion, has brought the eyes of intellectual England into a focus upon it. Many of us will know also how it has been received by other Mystics—with suspicion on the one hand, and with open hostility on the other. Now, it is not in any sense necessary that one should hold a special brief for Theosophy in order that, as a mere question of truth and justice, we should desire this branch of Oriental Mysticism to be regarded, at least, from a proper standpoint.

Between all Mysticism—theosophical or otherwise—and Spiritualism, there is an essential and real difference, and, moreover, it is a difference which should be accentuated. Mysticism—and Theosophy, we take it, in common with other Mysticism, is an attempt to transcend the phenomenal world, the Aquastor of alchemical literature, which "stands for" something but is not the thing itself, and to enter into noumenal—into that world of abstract reality which is behind all forms and appearances. It seeks not to place its believers in communication with any species of spirits—whether those of the dead and disembodied, of elementals and elementaries, of planetary intelligences, or of any angels in the hierarchy. What it does desire to offer them is the attainment of higher consciousness in the Absolute. Spiritualism, on the other hand, is almost exclusively concerned with a special department of experience in the phenomenal world. True, it is that branch which has been called transcendental phenomena; true, in the matter of exterior, evidential value, it is very useful and important; it is improbable that any real Mystic would despise or depreciate the work that has been done in this direction, but all Mysticism is agreed that there is nothing in the phenomenal world—transcendental or normal—which can bring permanent peace or beatitude, that it is the source of delusion and not of truth, and that at no point of the external plane can we expect to impinge upon reality. Now, this is an essential difference, and it is in no spirit of hostility if we consider that it ought to be accentuated. But between Theosophists and other Mystics there is no such distinction. Both are agreed upon the variety of the phenomenal world; both are agreed that the noumenal is the only source of truth; both seek union with the Absolute; both believe this to be the end of our being; both hold that they are in possession of a path thereto. Would it not be well in this instance if we could efface or overlook accidental or minor differences? For our own part, we should choose, if it were permitted, to regard ourselves indifferently as Theosophist and as Mystic, because, like both, we are seeking higher consciousness in the Absolute by the one possible path, which is that of the Interior Life. And the categorical statement of this object, and of the way to this object, constitutes what we have ventured to term the Central, Catholic, or Universal Doctrine of Theosophy or Mysticism— that higher consciousness is attainable in the Absolute of Being, and that the way of its attainment is the Way of the Life Within.

II.

The Grand Hypostasis.

We have passed in preceding chapters through a splendid and prophetic vision. We have seen what is possible for the manifest and exterior man; we have defined to ourselves the nature of the visible glory and perfection which he can and may attain; we have shown how that attainment can be worked for; and we have put upon every Mystic, and upon all who accept our words, the divine and inexorable duty of shaping every action in consonance with the intent of evolution—of that grand law which is educing into actuality, ever more and more, the powers, capacities, and nature of the latent, or inner, man. But the outward man is the outline and the hint only of the man within; and we have continually acknowledged that the development of the one is in propor- tion to that of the other. The term development involves the idea of that which is behind, is latent, is hidden, being brought out into the foreground, into activity, into the sight of all. But behind all that is possible of exterior eduction, there is the withdrawn vastness and unmeasured profundity of the man within, which can never manifest on the exterior plane, which can never be covered by physical sight, nor be included in the embrace of the physical arms, nor approached by any instruments of external perception. This man is only to be known by the individual himself, and to him it can be known only through an extension of the field of consciousness, for consciousness, we agree with the German idealist Fichte, covers but a small portion of our inward nature.

Man is thus triune in another than the recognized manner. There is, firstly, the outward man, who is capable of a perfection, a beauty, a glory, a joy, and happiness of which at present we have scarcely dreamed. Then there is the interior man, whose mystery is illumined by the sun of consciousness, and whom only, as we have said, the man himself can know. There is, finally, an undiscovered field of being and subsistence not lighted by the radiance of con-sciousness, which does consequently lie outside all normal knowledge, but is still the true, ultimate, and absolute man—of which the conscious man is but a part and a fraction, even as the field of life incarnate which is covered by normal memory may be but a fraction and a part of our past — having an universal immensity, an abysmal deepness, a dizzy altitude, wherein lie the roots of all mysteries, and into which there is but one narrow path and one strait way of entrance, which is the act of Introspection. If we would know God, we must pass through this gate; if we would know ourselves, we must span the depth, the height, the distance of that withdrawn individuality, which at some point of its extension doth impinge upon Deity. Is it possible to undertake this grand, this sublime journey? The Mystics answer: Yes. Is it possible by undertaking it really to know ourselves? The Mystics answer: Yes. Is it not long, dangerous, and terrible? Well, perhaps in a certain sense, though not ever or in all senses, it may be all of these; but there is God the Absolute at the end of it. Is it lawful? The Mystics answer: Yes—because it has God for its impulse. Is it open to all? Yes, it is assuredly open to all, and yet there are few who are called to it. The faculty of introspection is a special gift, which is possessed and desired by few; and it requires special strength in all functions of the organic man. Mysticism, like alchemy, in the words of the purified "Lover of Philalethes" requires "the whole man," even as "when found it possesses him." The ill-balanced mind may be unseated by the prolonged experiment; the heart may wither in the isolation of a solitary life; aspiration, dizzy in the altitude, may collapse, and, returning with a great rush upon the physical, may become broken for further flight; transcendental desire frustrated may overflow upon the material, and may pursue satisfaction among the void and fatal pro-cesses of sin. It is for this reason that every saint has within him all those elements which go to constitute, under the influence of another force of attrac-tion, the worst forms of moral deflection: and it is also in this sense that some theologians have recognized in Baia and Pompeii more abstract possibility for holiness than in the little spheres of selfish comfort which circumscribe the possibilities and passions, the activities for good and evil, that make up the average man. It is a hollow commonplace to say that where there is no danger there is no glory, but while in peril itself there is nothing good or desirable, it is mere cowardice to shrink from it in the prosecution of a resplendent end. If it be ever so dangerous, that is no excuse for avoiding it. Why should we concede to the solicitations of our weaker part? Do not let us ask if it be dangerous; let us assure ourselves rather that the end is certain for those who survive the ordeal, for those who are faithful and true. As to this, our authority is the

Mystics, and they say that no such search, properly conceived and conducted, will ever fail. *Inquirentibus se remunerator sit.* Our authority, we repeat, is the Mystics; it is the Mysticism of all the ages, but it is especially Christian Mysticism, disencumbered, at the same time, from all dispensable specialities of dogma, and reduced to its true proportions by comparison with universal Mysticism, that we shall take as our guide now when we attempt to delineate in plain words what every man must do and experience in order to establish between himself and God a permanent and ineffable union, based upon a rational hypostatic theory, and thus enter in this life into the contemplation and possession of absolute truth and reality, so that he may no longer perforce content himself, as best he can, with the many methods of divination which prevail in the phenomenal world.

Strong minds have derided divination by stars and by teacups, by the tilts of magnetized tables and by parabolic indications in crystals. But when strong minds seek to find out God they also divine after their own manner. Thus, the strong minds of theology divine by the gift of faith, and they denounce those who prophesy by tongues. The philosopher divines by analogy, and he derides the simplicity of faith. The ontologist divines by design, and regards his conclusions, or "results," as equipped with an exclusive trade-mark of infallibility. But it is essentially all divination; and, for our own parts, with a mystical reverence, we venture to deride all, except the divination by poetry, which, best of all methods, interprets the grand parable of existence, though it is still a divinatory method, the cream and efflorescence of all—utilizing the prodigies of vision, extending the intuitions of faith, multiplying the analogies of philosophy, and perceiving purpose and intelligence everywhere. We venture, as we have said, to deride all, and we attach ourselves to those who know, seeking to learn in our turn, because at all risks, and at what price and peril soever, we must and will have God; for with the desire of the ages we desire the fulness of all beatitude, the sum of all pleasantness, the immersion within and without in delight and joy and love; and these only can be given us when we return to our first source, which contains the sum of all felicity, and in which we not only possess all things, but are joined to all things that can be lawfully permitted to our desire.

III.

The Consolation of Philosophy.

And now as to the end in view. We do not propose to make an absurd attempt to define the Absolute, being that ultimate which escapes definition, or to appraise the special quality of the rest of man in God. What we would wish to observe to our readers when they hear of the peace and joy in Christ Jesus, of the refuge in Buddha, of the beatific vision, of absorption, of Nirvana, of free perspicuity of thought in universal consciousness, and of a thousand and one other kindred terms—religious and philosophical, Eastern and Western—let them remember that the Catholic Mystic understands them to refer unto one state variously denominated, and it is that state which, for the moment, we have ourselves termed higher consciousness in the Absolute. For the rest, it will be well to bring home to us as briefly as possible one feature which must appear to be of special beauty and consolation, and is contained in that very conception of mystical philôsophy which, while it is the central, ultimate conception of the whole body of wisdom, is too often found to overwhelm a humble mind by the very terror of its splendour—from which the soul of the uninstructed disciple, not having as yet been taught to use its wings, scarcely as yet conscious that it possesses wings to use, does not infrequently shrink with a sense of the inadequacy of its nature, even as Elia the delightful, sitting and "drinking late" among his "bosom cronies," surrounded with "old familiar faces," shrank from the thought of another life, of a strange form of subsistence, and would gladly, were it possible, continue for ever in his old haunts, for ever wearing the same friendly garments of the flesh, a man with men around him, and saved from exaltation and grandeur among the pleasant littleness of the world we see.

It is in the theosophical or mystical doctrine of the Beatific Vision and absorption into Nirvana, that we must look for an adequate answer to a question which is ever recurring in all speculations on the eternal state, and on the quality of our participation therein. We refer to the touching and often melancholy problem of our possible reunion in the higher consciousness with those whom we have loved on earth. We have termed it a melancholy problem, because to most of us the hope of this reunion has always something of the character of a forlorn hope; the possibility is always presented to our minds as a matter which inevitably is somewhat remote and dim. The evidential gospel of Spiritualism has indeed come forward with its alleged tests of identity, and its hand-grasps from infinity, to tell us that the dead of earth are *there*, and that the other side of the world of life is truly the house of man. But it seems to promise us reunion with the departed at the expense of separation from God, because the other life of Spiritualism is simply a new form of environment, and as long as we are environed, and subsist in a separate identity, we are substantially apart from God. Now, the spirit hungers after God with an appetite which nothing can satisfy till it is united wholly and absolutely with the object of its desire; and it is only by a complete incorporation of the consciousness into universal consciousness, when God shall stand round His people as the hills stand round Jerusalem, that it can attain this union.

On the other hand, most presentations of the doctrine of Eternal Beatitude would seem almost implicitly to set aside the idea of a reunion in the midst of that Beatitude with those personalities which we have known, and loved, and been joined with, during our own personal period. If we take the Christian presentation, which received its fullest and most perfect development—and is in itself a most important and fascinating branch of transcendentalism—at the hands of the Latin theologians, we shall find that, almost by a common consent, the subject is dropped, for the Beatific Vision is so all-sufficient to the soul that enjoys it as to sweep away every faculty for any narrower form of happiness. We do not affirm that if we questioned St. Thomas on the communion of the saints and the angels, he would find no room for such intercourse in his system of divine bliss; and if our dead were redeemed, he might permit us, with all our beatitude, some pleasure in the knowledge that they shared our eternal reward; but in the elaboration of Nirvana in Christ, he has forgotten what has not seemed to him of moment, and the omission is, of course, characteristic of a celibate theosophy. Furthermore, the dogma of eternal perdition, which is in reserve for the majority of mankind, must inevitably take the heart out of any scheme of reunion, creating an eternal separation between the few handfuls of grapes which are left in the vineyard after a well-gleaned vintage, and the overflowing harvest which is swallowed up in the garners of perdition. On the other hand, if we turn to the Buddhist presentation of the doctrine, the weakness of human love is not likely to meet with overmuch sympathy from the ascetic spirit of the East. There may be communion between the saints who assemble in the heaven of Devachan previous to absorption, but those who are "reduced to impalpableness in the void of that which no longer is" can scarcely be expected to retain in their sublimated condition even the most ethereal affection for former partners in the grand jumble of material illusions.

It would seem, therefore, that those who are looking for absorption into God as the supreme end of being, as the only true rest, and the sole real bliss, must be content to lay aside with their mortality all the ties of earth, and to regard as bonds even the holiest affection which they have nourished for the humanity around them; while, on the contrary, if those ties be too strong, and if they be content to be bonded in the freedom wherewith love makes us free, and to be constrained by their human sympathies, they must, intellectually, be content also with the "spheres" of the Spiritualists, and with the pleasant and poetical puerilities of "Beyond the Gates."

And yet, dear friends, by the Light in the Beloved Eye, and by the Mystery which was revealed to St. John on the beloved breast of his Divine Master, it is not so—in all earnestness, there is another and a truer view, which, we think, needs only to be stated to ensure its universal acceptance among all thinking minds. There subsists, in fact, a complete harmony between both these desires of the spirit, for here, as in other matters, we most truly find that no pure aspiration of humanity is ever mocked. We undertake to show:

(*a*) That absorption into God is necessary to an effectual union with any being whom we may have loved on earth.

(*b*) That as long as we possess a separate identity and a distinct personality —as long as we are environed and separated—there can be no true union with any object.

Concerning the first proposition, we have only to bring home to ourselves the evident truth that we can lose nothing by possessing God, for in Him we must possess all things, since He is the sum of all. We are substantially, or, rather, supersubstantially, joined in God to everything which is good and holy, or is capable, under any circumstances, of becoming good and holy; and we possess it with a transcendental completeness, and a masterful grasp and hold upon its inner and real nature, which is not possible apart from God. To be absorbed into the Divine Nature is to be absorbed into the inmost and divine part of all natures which subsist in God. God forbid that we should be separated by God from any being which has a part or reflection of His own loveliness and beauty!

Concerning the second proposition, we need appeal only to those who have ever loved. They will understand us when we say that the most complete union of two intellectual natures, in the most perfect manner of love, is a poor, ineffective, and partial form of union, in which the essence of the idea escapes, just as the essence of truth is said to escape in the form of the logical syllogism. There is an inmost nature on each side which cannot be joined through the personality, which meets only as the lips of lovers with a sheet of glass between them. It is a transparent barrier and a thin barrier, but it must be broken before they can kiss truly. Cold and half-hearted are the unions of this earthly life; they are but the promise of a possible form of spiritual and interior union which can be achieved only in the noumenal world. It is in the region which overlies personality that we are truly united with those with whom we have here effected a phantasmal representation of union. Two beings can only be welded into one being, which is to say they can only be united, by a junction of the pneumatic roots of their natures—there is no union in the temporary interlacing of branches. But the basic juncture is in virtue of a common foundation, and that foundation is God.

Now, in view of this teaching, it is clear that the Spiritualistic conception of the life beyond is insufficient to the dual purpose of spiritual aspiration with which we are now dealing. He that would enter Godhead must be quit of his person, and he that would participate truly in the love of any other created being must also transcend his personality. But in the so-called spiritual spheres we are presented with a sublimed personality and a sublimed environment, and a promise of the eternal perpetuation of these barriers. We see, therefore, that in this matter of reunion—as in other problems—we get at an intelligible solution of a painful and perplexing enigma by recourse to mystic doctrine, which has been enlightened by the sweet reasonableness of a middle interpretation; and we must rise from its consideration much strengthened in our conviction that the Mystic is in possession of an instruction which alone is equal to all emergencies, and is intelligent and consoling in all.

And so even were it definitely true that while in this life the path of Absorption is a path of isolation and asceticism, we are not to condemn that life as cold, callous, and inhuman. Here only is another illustration of the old truth that we must lose our life if we would find it, and if we love it, we lose; we must bury love in order to find it in a true and higher form. If the Mystic separate himself from humanity, it is because he looks to return to it again, and to be united with it more efficiently and completely. The motto of the Mystic is the motto of the dying Monica—"Life in God, and union there!"

If the twin doctrine of Absorption and of the Loss of Personality seem to offer us all of God and all of humanity, while, at the same time, taking away from us nothing that we can have any desire to retain, do not let us be moved from its adoption by any plausible errors of criticism. Above all, let us be on our guard against the old specious objection that in Nirvana such individuality as may remain to us is at best only that of a beatified cipher in the enjoyment of a barren rest and a useless happiness. Many natures, conscious of an energy within them which has little scope for its possibilities in the achievements of time, forecast a period of higher activity in the world to come, and would regard themselves as debased by the prospect of the endless rest. But as there is one only Centre, so there is only one true activity of motion, and that is in the direction of the Centre; and to work rightly we must all work towards rest, and must then ultimately rest in the Centre, being identified with the Great Oversoul, whose force informs the universe. And, surely, in that last state, the Omega of our being, he is not useless who is henceforth part of the activity of God.

Nor can it be too seriously realized that the doctrine of the Divine Absorption is no more dependent on dogmatic Christianity than it is on Buddhism.

Those who accept it, and shape their life towards it as towards a goal and end of being, are no more constrained on that account to assimilate the whole corpus of the exoteric creed of Christendom than they are bound to accept literally the doctrine of the five Dhyani Buddhas. There is no doubt that the essence of the conception of Nirvana and that of the Christian Beatific Vision are one and the same; but it is an essence common to all true religion.

CHAPTER THE FIFTH.

THE FIVE ILLUMINATIONS OF IDEAL BEING.

THERE are five illuminations of ideal being which constitute the quintessential rapture of pure intelligence, the scale of ascension in the life of the world to come, and they also constitute five species of regeneration, five immersions in the deep waters of absolute beatitude, five openings of the interior nature, which are, in other words, the successive developments of new and sovereign senses, or faculties for the perception and portals for the influx of ineffable delight and joy. There is the illumination of Nature, which is, in its transcendental aspect, or its aspect of absolute transcendency, the revelation of the inner beauty of Earth and Heaven, and this is the soul's union with the essential Spirit of Nature, and its felicitous refreshment in the magisterial beauty, power, and dominion of all loveliness of the divine Egeria. This is the *Beata Pulchra* of Rosicrucian symbolism. As there is a higher aspect of humanity, which is the true humanity, so is there a higher aspect of Nature, which is veritable nature, the *Anima Mundi* of the Mystics, and it is of her in the first place we must seek enlightenment. Hers is the secret which we must learn before we can attain God, or the world to come, or the absolute of real being. By that blithe spirit we must be taught, as in a school of Natural Philosophy; we must be graduated in the scale of her mystery, and must submit ourselves in all humility to the enlarging ministry of her profound instruction. This is a spiritual direction which refreshes, invigorates, awakens, and enlarges being. We do not live truly until we have, *in statu pupillari*, matriculated in Nature and have studied her as she is, not by a scientific analysis but by a full heart of comprehension. There are many natural philosophers who know the courses of the stars, but nothing of the high altitudes which Egeria loves. They have spelled over the stratification of the rocks, and yet are they ignorant of Nature's depths. They have dredged the great seas, but they have never received the communication of the secret of old ocean. There are, in like manner, many botanists who are profound in the lore of plants, but yet are completely uninformed of the essential life of the living world around them. The love of Nature is communicated, but it cannot be taught. It is learned in pine forests at night, and on lone headlands looking out upon stormy waters, and on the pathless wastes of ocean, and under stars, and in moonlight, and wherever Nature is, as also in all aspects of Nature, it is thus communicated, when truly, and at any time, can the soul be enlightened by Nature. He that has had experience of this revelation has passed through the first Mystery of Godliness.

The second of the five Illuminations of Ideal Being is the Poetic Instruction, or the indoctrination of the Spirit of Poetry, which is impossible to him who has not first been disciplined by Nature. For out of the sympathetic knowledge of Nature is evolved the poetic rapture, and he only who is familiar with her parables can enter into the spirit which interprets her. That man who has qualified even as a neophyte in the school of initiation which is presided over by the Spirit of Poetry, as by a true and living preceptress, and has been edified even partially by her golden rule of interpretation, regards all things from her standpoint, sees all things in her light, acts only from her impulse, shapes himself and all his life in conformity with her law, and between the lines of all mysteries reads the music of her running commentaries.

Third among these Illuminations of Ideal Being is the Revelation of Universal Law, which is the great reconstruction of the human mode into its proper accordance with the divine mode. In all the manifested and visible life of earth there is but one section which is invested with the sublime and terrible power of departing from that which an enlightened poet and a profound seer has called the law of our being. To create or to destroy himself is possible to man alone, and the history of humanity is, in effect, the æonian chronicle of a grand aberration from the universal law. Those who would enter into true life must enter into the Reign of Law, and when a man has so ordered his life anew that it has become incorporated into the cosmic harmony, when his heart beats time to the heart-throbbing of the Great World, then does he accomplish in peace and joy the purpose of his being, then does he live with the world's life, progresses with the world's progress, and is lifted from the vortex of vicissitude by an equable and constant motion towards that in which there is no change or shadow of passing away. The indoctrination into Universal Law is not an easy achievement, but it is the gate and entrance of the inner life, and as such it has been written of in all ages of Christendom by the great doctors of contemplation. It is summarized in the word RESIGNATION, as the law of progress towards higher things is synthesized in the word DETACHMENT. Like all natural struggles, it is one in which the fittest alone survive. It consists in the sustained renunciation of all individual impulse to compete against the dominion of law. Unlike the Illumination of Nature, it is a hard and military schooling, for he who would learn of the Law must have overcome his lower self—that Nature which is to be left behind in evolution, that coarseness which is to be eliminated, that crookedness which is to be bent straight, that correspondence which is to be torn up. But when the strife has led on to victory, the recompense is a profound peace and a permanent ease of being, which is like the reduction of friction in machinery to a minimum point; and then the soul itself becomes an instrument of harmony, is at one with itself, is ordered lineally in all things without any deviation, and does always that which is right, because it is fixed in the way of rectitude. It proceeds therefore without jar, and without let or hindrance; it moves onward, as the law moves, to its own true and real end.

The fourth place among the Illuminations of Ideal Being is filled by the precious and angelic instruction of altruistic human love. This illumination stands fourth in the scale of progression, because he who attempts initiation into the mystery of this high and withdrawn spirit before he has been qualified by a due indoctrination derived from the Spirits of Nature, Poetry and Law, is beginning in the middle of his spiritual Euclid, and learns, as indeed he acts, too often not wisely for himself nor well for others. To this fundamental error of method may be traced the follies and failures of much that is called philanthropy. The ultimate tendency of all being is, however, so invariably towards rectitude that a man who has entered unprepared into the middle of our scholastic sequence may yet subsequently, if he so will it, complete the transcendental curriculum, only he then relearns, and after another manner, under a proper modifying control, what he has taught himself previously in vain. No humanity is complete, nor indeed human, unless it has been leavened by the altruistic spirit, which includes all that is best in loving kindness, and all that is tender in love. It is not necessary, nor indeed possible, that all Mystics should devote themselves without reserve to the service of man, but it is altogether necessary that they should be tinged and transmuted by a vital quality of real benevolence. Herein is the ratification of a contract which nothing can make null, which can be avoided by no true man, much less by the true Mystic. There are many modes of altruistic service, and those who acknowledge the enlightened rule of our philosophy very frequently experience an over-mastering attraction exclusively to what is called technically the service of God, but they can minister to man in God, and in some cases this may be the best and highest form of altruistic function. But ever should we remember, and vividly should we realize, that such pretended dedications as that of the desert anchorite to God alone, and the pruning of all tendrils of correspondence with humanity, so that the spiritual tree of life may grow up straight into heaven like the enchanted beanstalk, casting no cooling shadow, and offering no fruit to earth, is a divorce from the divine in humanity, and in

that respect makes us outlaws from the Kingdom of Christ. Now, the instruction of altruistic love is very certainly an advanced course of mystic training; to
the unskilled it is hard schooling in which they do little but mislearn, and their
record is one of barren energy and squandered zeal. But to the lettered scholar,
in other words to the initiate of the previous degrees, it is a profitable and delightful preception in which the infinite of our individual *ego* goes out to the infinite
of the *non-ego*, which passes mystically into an *alter-ego*, and is finally absorbed
into our higher self. When this absorption has been completed we become one
with all our instructors by a perfect assimilation of their instruction, and we are
made ready for the Grand Prelection.

When a man has accomplished in honour of mind and body the sublimity of
this instruction, he, having passed also through the previous degrees, is fitted
for the fifth and last illumination, which is the true Mystic Apocalypse, or the
Revelation of God to Man in a direct and immediate manner. Concerning the
possibility and the mode of this tutelage, beyond which, whether in time or in
eternity, whether in life or death, there is no other apprenticeship of spirit, but
only in life and death, an unending progression in the exercises of this wisdom,
we shall speak in another chapter. These then are the five Illuminations of
Ideal Being, successively delineated, of which the Crown is in the Mystic
Apocalypse, and of all it may be said that they are in truth but one course of
arcane academic evolution, which is that of the divine in man into the divine,
variously manifested, in the universe. Whosoever shall seek after these things
in the scholar's garment of transcendental aspiration shall be in nowise cast out,
so only that he is true to his aspiration, and permits that which can transfigure
the world without to also transmute the world within. So shall all things
beautiful on earth overwatch him in his learning, and do service on the day of
his Coronation.

We have said that the love of Nature is communicated, but that it cannot
be taught, and the five spiritual illuminations are essentially mysteries of spirit.
They are, nevertheless, open to all who can understand the operation of "the
passionate bright endeavour," wherein the toiler is transmuted, and by which
the higher man is awakened.

The awakening to the Love of Nature takes place under laws the operation of which are not to be traced by man. In no unprepared mind can such
awakening be achieved. There may have been a time in the springtide of
spirit when we bore the emblazonments of enthusiasm more royally on the
banner of boyhood—when no tasks were impossible, and no problems beyond
solution—in that time we may have conceived it possible to infect all hearts
with the love of Nature, all souls with the love of poetry, all minds with the

adoring love of light. But these dreams have passed away. We indeed may possess the spirit, but the great gift of the spirit cannot be imparted by its possessor. Could anyone awaken the heart to the love of Nature, he would have power over the withdrawn mystery of the biogenesis of soul. With some there is, consciously speaking, no defined awakening—only the gradual growth or unfoldment of a faculty possessed from the beginning. With others, there is a sudden quickening, an electric touch, and the man's soul has impinged upon the universal soul which informs the living world. "A flower, a leaf, the ocean"—anything, small or great—are sufficient to produce this shock, the life of the world without is changed into our life, and the man is reborn in Nature. In either case, he is possessed of that clear perception and of that vivid realization of Nature's ministry which distinguishes him by its presence from the common run of men who are not capable of perception into Nature, but through a coarse, untutored medium receive only a dim and vague impression.

No vivifying and informing love of Nature is separable from the poetic faculty, and according to the intensity of that love may be calculated the scope of the faculty in any given person. The awakening to the conscious love of poetry is usually consequent on that contact which we have already mentioned, in which the glory of the mystery of the universe is in part opened to the interior eye. But this second awakening, like the first, is essentially untraceable, and it is in this sense that the poet is born, not made, for in the matter of expression the poet is undoubtedly made by art. The "vision and the faculty" are gifts not to be bought or acquired; the "accomplishment of verse" *is* bought, and at the expense of no common labour.

There is a third awakening which may be said, in a manner, to complete the quickening of the intellectual man, and that is the awakening to the love of light. This is the first step towards transcendental development. When any man truly rises to the living cultus of the light, he transcends, by a willing act of conscious mind, the region of cloud and dimness. If he only be true to such awakening, the possibilities of all knowledge are in his hands.

CHAPTER THE SIXTH.

THE INTERIOR LIFE FROM THE STANDPOINT OF THE MYSTICS.

I.

The Life of Contemplation.

IF it were necessary to divide the science which is called mystical into two chief branches, it would be clear from what has preceded that we might speak of them as phenomenal and transcendental. This is not an actually accurate division, but it will serve a practical purpose by indicating a definite line of demarcation in a dual process. There is that which, under the term "Magic," comprises most branches of the occult or secret sciences, including the doctrines concerning the nature and power of angels, ghosts, and spirits; the methods of evoking and controlling the shades of the dead, elementary spirits, and demons; the composition of talismans; all forms of divination, including clairvoyance in the crystal, and all the mysterious calculations which make up Kabalistic science. Between the spiritual and psychological phenomena of our present epoch and these experiments of the past there is a strong basis of similarity, they are of the same value, and they serve a like purpose. To those who are in search of "a sign," they may be evidence of worlds transcending our normal senses, and they are valuable to that extent. But they are not true Mysticism, and those who pursue them are not real Mystics. With the entire world of phenomena, normal or abnormal, Mysticism has solely an incidental connection. The object of transcendental science is to get beyond the phenomenal world, to penetrate the veil of appearances, and, outside the spheres of illusion, to enter into the grand realities. It is to this second, more elevated, branch of what is so loosely termed transcendentalism that we desire alone to direct our attention. It must be admitted at the outset that it is not an easy subject, for it is concerned with the highest aspiration which it is possible for man to entertain, and the highest act which it is possible for man to achieve.

All transcendental philosophy recognizes and is based upon one great fact
—that the true light is to be sought within, and that the avenues of interior
contemplation—the withdrawn state, and the hidden life—are not only the way
to God, but that they are the way of the soul's peace. Now, it has been truly
affirmed by the Quietists, that "there is no real happiness save that which is
the result of a peaceful heart," so we see that the *Summum Bonum*, the supreme
and permanent felicity, of all human existence is also to be sought within.
Those who by the study of the soul have made themselves acquainted with the
highest mysteries of being, and, in a certain sense, have spoken to us as from
behind the veil, have denied truth and reality, as they have denied joy and
contentment, to the merely outward life. On their authority, therefore, we must
add to our previous affirmations that the true life, the life which is alone persistent amidst the everlasting flux of apparitions and evanishments, which is
alone real amidst the multitude of the things which seem, is also to be found
within. Men have sought it in the kingdoms of this world wherein God has
not anything, and have failed miserably in the quest. They have sought it
amid the splendours and beauties, the consolations and felicities, of exterior
Nature, but all her attractions and delights have been only the vesture and the
threshold of the "still rest and the unchanging simplicity" which are the
conditions of the grand reality.

What is there which can be offered to the mind of man that shall be of
higher value and of greater intellectual affluence than is offered us by the
interior life when it promises God and truth, light and the undivided permanence and beatitude of real being? It will be said that such amenities are
possible at most for only an infinitesimal proportion of our race, and in the
existing conditions of our environment that is unfortunately true; but the
value of the interior state is not to be estimated by the standard of social dis-
abilities. A thing is not less good, rather is it, in some respects, the more
desirable, because it is difficult of attainment, and can, therefore, be attained by
few. Let the quest be attempted by those whose surroundings make it possible,
and we may profit in a measure by their achievement if we cannot achieve
ourselves.

From a statement in an earlier chapter, it will already have been inferred
that the conditions of the life of contemplation are to be found in the word
"detachment." The Quietists speak of "detachment from the things of earth,
contempt of riches, and love of God"; and these terms of ascetic theology in
the West admit of being converted into the language of modern science, into
the terminology of that natural law which it has been attempted to follow
through a few of its ramifications in the spiritual world. The detachment in

question consists in cutting off correspondence with inferior things.   The isolation which follows is not to be confounded with that of the cynical philosopher who withdraws himself in disgust from a world whose beauty he is unable to discern, and with whose goodness he has ceased to be in affinity. The isolation of the interior life is devoid of pride and jealousy, it abstracts from the humanity around us nothing that can be given to humanity, and, like the lone inspiration of the Scald, its result in the ultimate to the world may prove better than a long cycle of familiar companionship in our ordinary daily life.   The suspension of correspondence with things exterior and phenomenal is the means to a higher operation, and that is the creation of correspondence with the absolute realities which transcend them.

According to Cornelius Agrippa, we must learn how to leave the "intellectual multitude" if we would come to the "superintellectual and essential unity," for that is "absolute from all multitude, and the very fountain of good and truth."   "We must ascend," he assures us, "to sciences in which although there be a various multitude, yet there is no contrariety, until at length we reach to that one inclusive science which supposes all below it, while there is nothing that can be supposed beyond it."   And above even this apex of attainment, and there only, he tells us, is the positive knowledge of a pure intellect.   Therefore—it is thus he ends—"let us attain to the first unity, from whom there is a union in all things, through that one which is as the flower of our essence; which then at length we attain to, when, avoiding all multitude, we do arise into our very unity, are made one and act uniformly."

Solitude is essential to such a work, and the eduction of the superior conditions is best effected among the primeval sublimities of Nature, in mountain fastnesses, in the divine desolation of the wilderness, or, as the Mystics themselves tell us, in the middle of the open sea.   For the majesties and splendours of the outside world are the threshold of the unknown grandeurs.   The gorgeous incandescence of the sunset is eloquent in Pentecostal tongues of revelation, but not to the exclusion of the all-permeating ministry of Night, which utters a *Fiat Lux* to the strong in soul.   *Dies diei eructat verbum, et nox nocti indicat scientiam.* "Day unto day uttereth speech, and night unto night showeth knowledge."   It is thus that we are advised by the voice of one of our illuminators, Thomas Vaughan—he that was the most translucid of all the English Mystics, he that was the brother of the Silurist poet, sweetest and most silver-tongued of all our devotional singers: "Translate thyself to the fields, where all things are green with the breath of God, and fresh with the powers of Heaven. . . . Sometimes thou mayst walk in groves, which, being full of majesty, will much advance the soul; and sometimes by clear, active rivers, for by such (say the mystic poets) did Apollo contemplate:

> All things which Phœbus in his musing spake,
> The bless'd Eurotas heard.

So also an advanced inspirational poet of our own spiritual era, Thomas Lake Harris, has revealed to us the spiritual ministry of Night, when thoughts more subtle touch

> The inner mind,
> And all the fettered inner wings unbind.
> When an infinite sight in the spirit is born,   .   .   .
> When we see, as the sun sees, creation below;
> And we thrill, as the earth thrills, with Heaven's warm glow;
> And we move, as the light moves, from world unto world;
> And we change, as the skies change, when morn is unfurl'd,
> And we breathe the sweet breath of the angels' delight,
> Till our hearts ope like roses in fragrance and light;
> Till within us, as round us, the Heavens are spread,
> And our thoughts to our loves, like twin angels, are wed.

It will be seen, therefore, that the first recompense of the interior life is the "seeing sense" of the poet, the possession of that strange instrument of interior alchemy, which dissolves the natural world, to discover in it a new and higher order.   A life led near to the heart of Nature can be sanctified by such a posses- sion.   There can be no doubt of the amenities of such an existence, for then the individual is in harmony with his surroundings, and this initial attainment will be possible to many who may be barred from the higher achievements.   On the other hand, the most perfect environment which can be offered by Nature to man is devoid of the softening, sublimating, and glorifying influences ascribed to it, when the heart and intelligence of the individual are without any instru- ment of correspondence with that environment.   No one was more intimately and passionately aware of the truth of this principle than Coleridge, and, indeed he has enunciated it in one of the most profound passages of spiritual insight which can be met with in the whole range of English poetry.   From Nature, he tells us, we can receive only that which we give:

> And in our life alone does Nature live.

Unless there be resident within us those undefinable qualities of appreciation, perception, and discernment which constitute the poetic temperament, there is no utterance from the heart of the external world to the heart of man, there is none of that electric and magnetic contact between the centre without and the centre within, and the local proximity is worthless.

The life of contemplation merely in the natural order brings, therefore, its own reward.

II.

Conventional Idealism.

It is eminently necessary to distinguish between true idealism and the conventional ideality which in all ages and nations has been proffered by pseudo-poetics as the true magic spectacles through which Nature and life must be viewed before the sensitive soul can experience any pleasure in the contemplation. It is possible even to misinterpret, and wrest to the destruction of poetry that truth concerning "the light which never was on land or sea," unto which we have so often had need to refer, that light which the mind of the observer must be able to diffuse over the universe before there can be obtained what is called its poetic perception. It is not the material projection of a phantasmal radiance for the creation of a curious illusion; it is the opening of an intellectual faculty which enables one to perceive what is, even as it really is; it does not read meanings into Nature, but it interprets her sure sense. It is not like the Veiled Son of the Starbeam, which, if you can once lay it loosely about the floor, will permeate space generally. It enables you indeed on the authority of George Macdonald, to "behold the same thing everywhere," but that is the one substance infinitely differentiated and permutating throughout the chromatic scale of creation. It is not a hypnotic process, and it is only in its false and distorting presentment that it is akin to the operations of certain Oriental fakirs, who concentrate their gaze on the umbilicum, and are rewarded sooner or later by the apparition of the uncreated light, after which they become God. It is not in reality requisite to surround oneself with a species of mesmeric atmosphere, and pass into a biologized condition, before we can discover any beauty in the phenomena that surround us. That is part of a gospel of hallucination and artificial glamour which most of all has contributed to make poetry "false in sentiment and fictitious in story." Ruskin was the first to expound to us the poetic fallacy which invests Nature with the biliousness of her observer, but that is not less a fallacy, nor less absurd in its confusion, which, on the one hand, invests creation with a fantastic and spurious colouring, and, on the other, ascribes to the crowd the faculties and feelings of a few exceptional natures.

If a person who is in possession of the mystical instrument of correspondence between God, man, and the universe which we term the poetic temperament—which may or may not be united to the gift of poetic expression—if such a person fare forth on some bridal morning of earth and sky, when the grass, let us say, is down over the wide meadows, and the haymakers are at work under a sun of June, what does he, unless indeed he is acquainted with the true use of his instrument? Most commonly, he stands at a poetic distance; the visible vibration of the hot, dry air is like a sudden manifestation of the "light" of Wordsworth; he is conscious that—

> To him the meanest flower which blows may give
> Thoughts that do often lie too deep for tears.

But he forgets that an opposite state has been described by the same seer, and that the peasants before him are essentially of that class to whom "a primrose on a river's brim" is simply "a yellow primrose." His poetic instrument is set to work on their picturesque figures; their life passes from that of the commonplace rustic into a superfine pastoral subsistence which is full of simple beatitude; the false process of artificial idealizing adapts, dissolves, and transfigures, and if all individual existence is not presently identified in a vague swoon of radiant impersonal being, the result is a Thomson's *Seasons* or a century of "rhymes and roundelays in praise of a country life."

One of the late Lord Lytton's minor tales of fantasy has a pretty conception in the matter of a magic mirror, which unveils to the beholder the scenes of his past life in a serene and pleasant atmosphere, with every particle of vexation and solicitude eliminated. To a certain extent this mirror is an allegory of memory, which exercises an intellectual selection in an unconscious manner, and present us chiefly with a survival of the fittest. It is for this reason that past times are so generally regarded as happy. It is a natural process, which softens the remembrance of sorrow, which mellows the joy that hath fled, which separates the tares from the wheat, casting one into the limbus of oblivion, and garnering the other into the storehouse of mind to provide food for the reflective part, and it is absolutely parallel, while from the standpoint of historic actuality, it is of the same value with the pseudo-poetic transfiguration which evaporates the commonplace of ordinary rustic life and provides the hollow mockeries of false poetry to invest it with the pleasures of an earthly paradise.

When the vindictive witch of Lord Lytton had empoisoned the magic mirror with her magnetic passes, the observer beheld his past no longer in its enchanted light; it was presented in actual facsimile, stripped of its ideal softness, every element of pain and care minutely reproduced upon the phantasmal picture. The transmutation effected by the hands of the fictitious enchantress is identical with that which would result from a few forward paces on the part of the poetic student in search of the picturesque, for the ideal beauty of the rustic's life, as we have seen in a previous chapter, is simply a matter of distance.   Standing far apart, giving free play to the fancy, such a poet observes nothing truly, though fancifully he may behold much.   Did he mingle with the rural group of haymakers, and become familiar with them, the spell would be quickly broken, and their life would be revealed to him as it is, with all its inevitable littleness, its narrowness, and its sordid prose. This is possibly the criticism of a Philistine, but it is sober truth, and in the recognition of this truth which is now taking place, we may look for a new and purer well-spring of English song, when bucolics and pastorals, whether passed under the seal of a great name like Virgil, or of a little name like James Thomson, will be relegated to the conventional paradise of the poetaster, and at least this form of false idealism will have disappeared.   Then we shall be contented, with Browning, to find in human nature, with all its unmeasured possibilities, unadorned by veneer or varnish, a "proper study" for the poet, and a sufficient source of encouragement and consolation.   One of the chief signs of this change is the revival of the romantic element which is now taking place in English versecraft.   Its great recommendation, indeed its essential character, is the rejection of artificial glamour, and recourse to the fountains of Celtic instead of classical inspiration.   The pioneers of this revival are not all in themselves great, but they represent a great movement, and they include some illustrious names.   At the same time, to look fairly on all sides of the prospect, it should be realized that if conventional idealism be passing, some of us are becoming more and more, in the matter of literary expression, mere slaves of form, and of form which has not even the slender merit of novelty, for it is borrowed in the main from French sources.   English minor poetry, under the influence of at least one prominent reputation, is devoting itself to the culture of such articles of literary *virtu* as those rondels and ballads, triolets and pantoufles, which are mere exercises of tiresome and worthless ingenuity, for which English is a language insufficiently elastic, while they are wholly inadequate to the depth and height and scope of true poetic feeling.   Even the formal anarchy of Walt Whitman is to be preferred before the inane formalism of these gimcrack poetics.   A great nature may find channels of expression in rhythmic prose, but in the petty gymnastics of French versecraft there is room only for an elegant littleness.

III.

The Castle of the Interior Man.

From the realms of the fantastic and fanciful, let us pass into the clear and lucid world of undefiled imagination; let us devote ourselves to the grandeurs of the mystic world; let us aspire towards the heights of the soul, towards a transfigured and glorious humanity, towards the ultimate end of evolution, the Sun which shines at night and the vision of immaculate Dian. Let these be our aim and our object; and then "the noble heart" shall find the Artemisian spring of "virtuous thought" pouring forth in the spiritual order, the living waters of a "glorious, great intent."

In the supernatural order, as it is understood by the orthodox religions, there is an immense literature concerned with the cultivation of the interior condition, and with the spiritual advantages which may be reaped from it. In the supernatural order, as we have seen, the end is God—that, at least, is the supreme, ultimate, and perfect end; and with the Quietists the life of contemplation consists wholly in the soul's surrender without reserve to God, that it may be filled with His own peace. We are told that this state stills all passions, restrains the imagination, steadies the mind, and controls all wavering; it endures alike in the "time of tribulation and the time of wealth," in temptation and in trial, as when the world shines brightly on us. Martyrs, confessors, and saints have tasted this rest, and have "counted themselves happy in that they endured." A countless host of God's faithful servants have drunk deeply of it amid the daily burden of a weary life—dull, commonplace, painful, or desolate—and to each one of their disciples the Quietists promise that all which God has been to the most exalted in the hierarchy of the saints, He is ready to be unto them, if only they will seek no rest save in Him. But the Hidden Life of most Christian theology is after all but the threshold of the true interior existence which is the subject of Mysticism. The devotional literature to which we have hitherto referred, can at most promise to man that joy and peace in well-being which is the consequence of harmonious correspondence with a certain supernatural standard, which is called the will of God. But these are the elements of the experience, and it is to the Mystics that we must look for more. They are in possession of a science which claims to comprehend the Divine Essence or ultimate reality of all things, and to impart, while even in this life and in this body, the blessedness of an immediate communion with the Highest—"free perspicuity of thought in universal consciousness"—an ecstatic immersion of the spiritual substance of man in the pure substance of Deity—all peace, all truth, all light, being seen, and known, and enjoyed to an infinite degree by virtue of a community of pneumatic sensations established with an infinite form of subsistence.

The secret processes which constitute the science of the Mystics accomplish the development of the interior life through a series of successive stages, from the New Birth or Regeneration to the manifestation of the Divine Psyche, the alchemical "vision of Diana," the interior translation, which is the Soul's flight towards God, and, lastly, the transcendental union which is known as the Beatific Vision, and is equivalent to Nirvana in Christ. Concerning these steps, and concerning this ecstatic state of final being, which is the crown of the whole process, we must speak in detail later on, but at this point it will be well to give a short synopsis of the whole consecution, as regards scope and development, founded on materials which are derived from the Mystic literature of the West.

The union of God with the Soul is the principle of all mystic life. But this union, the fulness and final consummation of which cannot be absolutely experienced till the ordeal of physical death has been withstood, and till eternity has been achieved, can be accomplished even upon earth in a more or less perfect manner, and the literature of entire transcendentalism has no other end than to unveil to us, by a full and profound analysis of the different stages of evolution in the spirit of man, the diverse successive degrees of this divine development. Seven distinct stages of the Soul's ascent towards God have been recognized by Mystics, and they constitute what has been emblematically called the Castle of the Interior Man. They represent the seven positive processes of psychic transfiguration. The first link in this arcane sequence is called the state of aspiration, which, from the pneumatic standpoint, is the concentration of the physical energies upon God as the object of thought; this state commonly derives some assistance from the ceremonial appeal made by religion to the senses. It has, however, a higher aspect, comprised in the second evolutionary process, which is called the condition of Mental Aspiration. As the first is the exaltation of the senses, so is this of the intellectual part. Here, also, the illusory phenomena of the visible world are regarded as informed with an inner pneumatic significance, to divine which is an important end of Mysticism. In order to make progress therein, and so attain the third stage, it is necessary that the aspirant, shaping all practical life in conformity with this theory, should perform no outward act except with a view to its inward meaning, all things which are of time and earth and man being simply figures and symbols of Eternity and Heaven and God. The postulant, as he advances, will perceive that the inmost thoughts of his own conscious being are only a limited and individual speculation of the speech or Word of God, concealed even in its apparent revelation, itself a Veil of the Divine truth, and something which must be removed, or effaced, for the contemplation of the truth absolute which is behind it. When he has reached this point the Mystic will have entered on the third stage of his illumination. This is the most difficult of all. It is termed by the Mystics the Obscure Night, and here it is necessary that the aspirant should become void in the interior man, should empty himself completely, should defraud himself of all his normal faculties, renouncing his own predilections, his own thoughts, his own will—in a word, his whole self must be made void. Aridity, weariness, temptation, desolation, and darkness are characteristic of this epoch, and they have been experienced by all who have ever made any progress in the mysteries of mystical life. The fourth condition is denominated the Absorption of Quietism. Complete immolation of self and unreserved surrender into the hands of God have repose as their first result. Such Quietism, however, is not to be confounded with insensibility, for it leads to the sole real activity, to that which has God for its impulse. The fifth degree in the successive spiritualization of the Soul is called the state of Union, in which the will of man and the will of God become substantially identified, and the individual, as a consequence, is energized by the first influx of the Divine intelligence which elaborates the eternal purpose. This is the mystical irrigation which fertilizes the Garden of the Soul. During this portion of his development, the now regenerated being, imbued with a sovereign disdain for all things visible, as well as for himself, accomplishes in peace, serenity, and joy of spirit the will of God, as it is made known to him by the Word of God supernaturally speaking within him. On the extreme further limit of this condition, the Mystic enters the sixth state, which is that of Ecstatic Absorption, or the Soul's transport above and outside itself. It constitutes a more perfect union with Divinity by the law of positive love. It is a state of sanctification, beatitude, and ineffable torrents of delight flowing over the whole being. It is beyond description, it transcends illustration, and its felicity is not to be conceived. Love, which is a potency of the Soul, or of that *Anima* which vivifies our bodies, has passed into the Spirit of the Soul, into its superior, divine, and universal form, and this process, when completed, comprises the seventh and final stage of pneumatic development, which is that of Entrancement. Renouncing all that is corporeal about it, the Soul becomes a pure spirit, capable of being enlightened in a wholly celestial manner by the Uncreated Spirit, whom it beholds, loves, serves, and adores above and beyond all created forms. And this is the end of Mysticism, the perfect union, the entrance of God and heaven into the interior man.

There is evidence to show that this process has been accomplished in all ages and among all nations. With it the Egyptian hierophants would seem to have been acquainted in that "early dawn and dusk of time" which preceded the first epoch of the Mosaic dispensation. This also was the end of the Mysteries in their primeval and undefiled condition. And when, scaling the "mountains of our ignorance," we look forth upon the immeasurable antiquity of far Oriental countries, upon India, China, and Japan, there also was the positive philosophy pursued with the same objects, and by rigorously parallel processes. In the beginning of Christianity, it was known to the Gnostic ascetics and to that wonderful circle of withdrawn *illuminati* and grand masters in transcendentalism who comprised the theurgic school of Alexandria. The writings of Hermes Trismegistus are the disguised history of the evolution of the human Soul, and the doctrine of reconstruction is developed in the Old and New Testaments. From adepts of Egyptian wisdom and from Jewish keepers of the secret keys of knowledge, from Greek initiates, from Platonic successors, and from the first hierophants of esoteric Christianity, the absolute tradition, with all its processes and all its mysteries, passed on to the mediæval alchemists, to those *bizarre* writers and profound thinkers who have succeeded in persuading centuries that they were in search simply of the transmutation of metals, when under the cover of physical experiments they wrote also of the Soul's transmutation, and rectified the secret *Sol* and the true *Luna* with the energies of Deific elements.

It is unnecessary, however, to have recourse to the remote Oriental world for instruction upon the highest mysteries of arcane science. There is a fund of wisdom, a fund of light, and a great body of positive and practical doctrine in the Western Mystics, who devoted their retired lives to the attainment of Nirvana in Christ, and even in the order of phenomenal achievement they did not fall behind the East. The history of Christian supernaturalism informs us that in the seven stages of transcendental absorption the body of the Mystic was seen to rise from the ground and to poise itself mysteriously in space. Possessed by interior visions, he became insensible to all that was passing around him, and, at the same time, his physical senses, which had suspended correspondence for the moment with normal exterior environment, were ministered to in a manner which we should term magical; he saw, heard, felt, tasted, but on another plane of being, and occasionally his indescribable ecstasy was manifested in the apparition of lights and halos about him, and in the diffusion of an unearthly fragrance. Thus was the Mystic of Majorca transfigured, so to speak, on Mount Randa, and attained through the sublimation of the senses to the possession of the Universal Science.*

* See Appendix IV.

CHAPTER THE SEVENTH.

THE NEW BIRTH, OR THE GRAND PALINGENESIS.

CONCERNING that star of our life, which is the ungenerated soul of man, it has been said that it has elsewhere had its setting, and that it "cometh from afar":

> Long, long since, undower'd yet, our spirit
> Roam'd, ere birth, the treasuries of God,

whence our actual physical birth is nothing but "a sleep and a forgetting." That may well be a truth of the eternal heaven, which in the ode of a master of melody seems to reflect something of heaven's highest music. Ever has this Light from the East, which, with something of a Promethean aspect, was brought to us long ago by good old Joseph Glanvill, appeared to the philosophic mind as an enlightenment upon the mystery of our origin, and as scarcely less than he claimed for it, "a key to the grand mysteries of sin and misery." Has it not come unto us all, perchance under "a moon of flowers," or, it may be,

> In a wan autumn night of falling stars,

and we have realized not only that

> Strong is the soul, and wise, and beautiful,

but that there is nothing more ancient than ourselves among all the galaxies of heaven? Then does the keen and crisp light of those untold and innumerable luminaries speak unto the light which is within us as sister may speak unto sister, with a familiar confidence, which assumes a common knowledge, concerning the things that have been, and that past which is not of mortality. Blessed be the starry radiance, blessed be its silver speech, and blessed be the unknown capacity of the responding soul, because the soul does indeed answer; the Star of ou interior Mercury is sublimed towards the stars of the zenith, and there follows, in the language of the alchemists, "a supercelestial conjunction and union between the astra of the firmament and the astra of inferior things"! This conjunction is termed the *Ilech supranaturale*, or "primal Ilech of the stars." The dateless origin of our interior being, the divinity of our extraction, the eternal pedigree of the Spirit, seem part of those lessons from Nature which she imparts to those who have created a scheme of correspondence with her own interior mystery. The communication is full of import, and it is among the precious title-deeds of our inheritance.

But, spiritually, it is of the highest importance that we should distinguish between the mystical doctrine of regeneration and the fascinating legends which are concerned with the soul's travellings, and the metamorphoses of Pneuma and Psyche, after much the same manner that it is necessary also to distinguish between the subjective rest in God, and that great body of traditional history and glamorous revelation which is concerned with the Land of Souls.* The New Birth has no traceable relation either to the age or youth of the spirit. Until we have fathomed the mysteries of being, and have attained in God to an all-embracing knowledge of ourselves, it would be unbecoming in those who, before all things, are governed by divine reason, to say that there is no such connection. There is a harmony and an inter-relation between all things that belong to the spirit; as in objective life there are no isolated facts, so in interior subsistence there can be no unrelated truths. But that man must be born again in the deep sense of Christ and the Mystics does not mean that he must be reincarnated, whether on earth or in another planet, even if reincarnation be otherwise an indispensable part of the eternal plan; but that upon this earth and in this planet, he must become a new creature. If we accept this statement as containing the keynote, and embracing the actuality of this fundamental process of Mysticism, what are we precisely to understand by becoming a new creature? How shall it be possible for us to unmake or remake ourselves? After what law or principle shall we cease to be that which we have been and attain to be that which we are not? Do the terms of the statement represent a process which is at all possible to man? Perhaps the true answer to these questions will be best reached by a reference to the operation of the New Birth. There is a large body of literature which contains the experiences of the life within, and it is written by those who, happily for themselves and for the world, have passed through the process of regeneration as through the white waters of baptism; and that literature is substantially unanimous as to the mode and manifestation of these experiences. Not only by the terms that are employed but by the descriptions so far as they have been interpreted, we conclude that the New Birth, like that of the physical man, though the fermentation and gestation thereof may extend over many days, is accomplished with a certain suddenness. Even as in alchemy the operation of the fire and furnace proceeds during the mystical space of what is called the philosophical year, whereas the

* See Appendix V.

transmutation of the elements is accomplished by the change of an instant, as it were in the twinkling of an eye, following at once on the projection of the powder or stone, so is this pneumatic transmutation accomplished without let or hindrance, and the man is made anew. There are two words which are especially applied by the Mystics to this process, and both are in direct relation to the suddenness of its nature. It is known as an interior illustration; it is likened unto the opening of an eye, from which there pours forth the loving radiance of a divine spirit, and it falls upon the face of the seer. It is even as a lantern lifted suddenly in a dark place. It is the manifestation of the moon's wonder upon the turbid blackness of troubled waters. It is the sudden flash which followed the *Fiat Lux*, when the bosom of primeval chaos was ripped by the vivid apparition of the creative beam. If we seek in modern science for a comparison with this illustration, the phenomena of electrical energy will be found ready to our hand.

The process comes also before us under the old word CONVERSION. It is the common and conventional name; it has become almost intellectually unclean under the manipulation of many hands, and almost out of all application has it been distorted by those who have misused it. It is with many, and in many cases, a practical synonym for cant in sentiment and vulgarity in religion, for the outward chalk and the inward refuse of the proverbial whited sepulchre. And yet, after all, the name is not only good and true, accurate and philosophical, but it is in many ways the best and the happiest which could be offered for this application. It has in some respects a wider scope than is possessed by the term Regeneration, for it might be taken to include that deep mystery of growth in godliness which must follow upon the New Birth, even as growth follows upon birth into physical being. The word Regeneration, however, is more vividly explanatory in its character, for a second birth presupposes a second conception. Now, there is only one thing which is conceived, and that is life. Thus the New Birth is, in the first place the infusion, and, in the second, the bringing forth of a new life. Consequent upon this statement there is one manifest conclusion. All life is unattainable and communicated, and even as in the physical order it is impossible that we should beget ourselves, so in the harmony of the spirit there is no spontaneous generation. An older science than biology has enunciated this truth after the *bizarre* fashion of its Veiled Masters. To make gold, say the alchemists, we must first have gold, and they who spoke after this manner were instructed in the deep things of life and of the spirit. Behind their metallic mask there is the face of Psyche and the uplifted intelligence of Pneuma; at the back of their laboratories there is a door giving entrance to the fane of God; and the flame of their physical furnace is a metaphor for the chemistry of Christ. To obtain the philosophical gold which is not the gold metallic, but a living substance—an *aurum vivum*—we must possess that gold which they have sought for vainly who have fossed in any mines, for it is like unto a certain kingdom which our king hath foreshown to us—it is not of this world; it is of the order of the celestial quintessence. The life of the spirit is communicated from the spirit of life, and even as no person by taking thought can add a cubit to his stature, so is it impossible by any taking thought of our own to generate the Bios of the Beyond.

But it is not to be supposed that the communication of life is arbitrary. The wind indeed bloweth where it listeth, but the guarantee of its freedom is in the certainty of its operative law. So also is it with the birth of the spirit; it is performed in virtue of a supreme and abiding principle. There is no room for the repulsive suspicion of an indiscriminate distribution. There is no one passed over and there is none left out. To some it cometh in the spring of being; to others in the fall of the leaf, and in the day of the garner; and when it manifestly comes not at all, there may be many lives which make up our endless life. If it be not to-day, it will be to-morrow, or in the century and the age to come. Communication is easy: creation hard and long. We are not then ill dealt with in that we can never be the authors of our life after either order of being. We are not the victims of a divine caprice, but our development in this, as in all things, is governed by a law that never errs, respecting no persons.

At this point we may affirm our central and fundamental principle—*the communication of spiritual life which is signified by the New Birth is a question of conditions.* In the physical order, the primordial germ of life was manifested upon this planet at a certain favourable moment. There is no science of biology which can tell us how that germ was generated, but at the right time it appeared, and it was fostered by the ministry of conditions. Hence all animated Nature began, and continues by the willingness and the coöperation of environment. So is it also in the life of the soul, and the preparation of the New Birth lies irredeemably in our own hands. In this respect, every man and every woman is the tiller of the secret garden of their interior being. From the four quarters of heaven, on the wings of the four winds, the seed is borne, though we know not when nor how, and if the soil be ready the germ will sprout. It is the same in the spiritual mystery of life and birth and growth. There is a soil of the supernatural vitality; there is a fructifying sun of love; there is a ministry of spiritual watering, by which the increase is given.

Notwithstanding, therefore, that the creation of any life is beyond the potentiality of our nature, we can all attain, as we are all indeed elected, to the

New Birth. And although the quality of any life is a mystery, there is no mystery in the mode of this achievement. Three chief points may be interpreted concerning the process from among the enumerations of mystical writers. There is the Science of Attitude, the Science of Activity, and the Science of Fertility.

Concerning the science of attitude, it is needful that we should dispose the materials of our being in such a manner as will favour the manifestation of a fresh nature, and make them, in the first place, a fitting receptacle for the germ of a new life; and, in the second place, an adaptable substance on which that life can work. Now, it is clear that the New Life is identical with life in God—that is, in which the consciousness is united with God—and the old life is that which we have all of us led, which some of us may be still leading, apart from divine consciousness. It is not necessarily an evil life; there are no penalties that are indispensably attached to it; it is often very generous, very beautiful, and very free; many sweet and fragrant flowers of humanity are continually produced under its influence; at times it may well be a life of

Summer Isles of Eden lying in dark purple spheres of sea.

We must absolutely detach from our minds the old dark doctrines of the utter reprobation of the natural; no doubt in the harvest of God there will be some use found for the flowers of the field as well as for the corn in harvest, and the blessed gospel of beauty will save and redeem much which might be rejected by the narrow gospel of utility. But we must recognize that there is a distinction between the life of Nature and the life of grace, and it covers the field of comparison which was instituted of old between natural and supernatural being. That comparison is derided at the present day by persons who regard themselves as progressed; especially among the uninstructed class of modern spiritualists, we find the denial of the supernatural world figuring among the current cant of their shallow philosophy, and the sentiment is not infrequently echoed by some who should be better acquainted with the proper meaning of language. The attitude of mind which is necessary to the New Birth is then that which has God for its motive, divine union for its object, higher life for its interest, and the deep things of the spirit for the ambition of its purpose. The desire for the knowledge of God must precede divine union, and it is eminently one which may be nourished by all persons, and in every department of life. It corresponds in the main to what the Mystics have termed *purity of intention*. In the BOOK OF KNOWLEDGE AND OF THE SOUL, this interior attitude is represented as holding a rank so elevated, and a height so excellent, that alone it gives value and preciousness to all our actions. "Like unto a spiritual alchemy, it doth convert all it touches into gold, diamonds, and rubies." But this purity of intention is not possible in any positive and vital sense when apart from the divine intention. In its emotional aspect, it most definitely takes shape before the mind as the hunger and thirst after righteousness. Philosophically considered, it may be identified with the love of truth and devotion to truth. In this sense, however, we must understand the entire and undivided devotion of the whole being, for "as it is impossible," says the writer of *Man the Spirit*, "whatsoever be the extent of thy possessions outside of thy God, that ever thou shouldst be contented until thou dost possess Him, so, after a certain manner, thy God cannot be satisfied with thee, whatsoever thou shalt give Him, until thou hast devoted thyself."

Thus, the first method in the adaptation of our interior substance towards the New Birth consists in the creation of an attitude of correspondence with God.

The science of activity is an extension of the science of attitude. It is motive taking shape in practice, and in this department of mystical wisdom the course is so plain that it will admit of statement within the compass of a very few words. One purpose only must possess and animate our actions; whatsoever be the diversity of their character, both in and by them all we must approach to the divine union. *Omnia et in omnibus Christus*, says a terse mystic aphorism, and when we understand rightly what Christ is, it holds the sum of the practice of all perfection. Commonly speaking, there is little doubt that the path of this maxim is a path of tears and thorns, because it must be traversed prior to our entrance into the Promised Land of the New Life. Negatively taken, it simply means that in all things we must "cease to do evil," and positively that we must "learn to do good." There can be no qualification or compromise; there can be no distinction between grave and venial trespass. We must absolutely touch nothing, think nothing, do nothing, which does not make for God, and this certainly is a task so hard that there is nothing in the Herculean labours to compare with it. It will, in many cases, mean the uprooting of the associations of a life and of the tendencies inherited from generations. There is, however, no possible escape, and we must cast round us as best we can for sources of encouragement and consolation. Let us, therefore, remember that the way of the Mystic is ultimately of roses and lilies.

Let us concentrate our attention upon the splendour of emancipated mind, and realize that we are operating on our own natures for the utter annihilation of all darkness, superstition, and ignorance—that our own manumission will help towards the world's liberation, and towards the day of Christ, when all dogmas and creeds shall be destroyed, when Christ shall purge His Church, and there shall be henceforth no exoteric Christianity. Let us think of the amber-tinted and aureoline atmosphere of that supreme Hour of Romance in which Christ shall come, and there shall be given a happy ending to all stories, when God shall wipe away the tears from the eyes of Judas, when Barabbas shall be compensated for his environment, when the lost thief shall be dowered with incorruptible treasures, and the Destroyer shall be a Prince of Peace. Let us think also that in the mystic universe we possess a divine licence of unfettered thought, and do enter into the one Catholic hierarchy which forbids hell to the believer, the Eucharist of the flesh, the imputation of righteousness, the resurrection of the body, and virgin birth. Then, lastly, yet most of all, let us derive inspiration from poetry, knowing that also has its day to come, when "the chimes of the lyrical summer" shall "dissolve on the lips of the sea," when all the lighter parts of life shall trip to ballad music, while out of the heart of the world shall "the deep things of being, beyond hearing and seeing," be poured through the flood-gates of the soul to the measure of a mighty melody, and out of the infinite distance, down paths by the planets impearled, shall the song-embassies of inspired messengers interpret to us the harmonies of the spheres.

So shall we pass fortified through the science of activity to that of fruit, when bitterness shall have passed from the struggle. It is then that the sudden illustration will appear, and we shall be conscious of an interior quickening. For attitude and act become fertile after one manner; the confirmation of motive is in the affirmation of doing; that which is performed at first hardly we at length with ease accomplish; when all difficulty is removed there is a joy in the achievement, and when that joy is once experienced it may be said that the cities of the nations fall, all barriers are effaced; we emerge from the forest darkness and the undergrowth of the tenebrous way, the "splendour falls" upon the wide meadows in front of us, the "cataract leaps in glory," and lo!

> The long light shakes
> Across the lakes,

and broods upon the "castled walls" of the Promised Land! We have passed through the Mystery of Regeneration; we have become a new creature!

CHAPTER THE EIGHTH.

The First Sublimation, and the Spiritual Elevation of Sense.

THE process of Regeneration, as it has been delivered in the preceding chapter, is a kind of *Minutum Mundum* of the whole mystical achievement. It is also an economy or parable of the higher sequence of experience. It contains all the potencies and all the elements—no foreign substance has to be introduced subsequently. It is now in all simplicity a question of the development of the germ, and, that accomplished, the splendid flower of the light and joy of the wise will put forth its seven blossoms by the gift of the grace within, and will bear its twelve fruits full of divine sustenance. In defining the special nature of the mystical developments which are consequent upon the New Birth, we shall then be merely extending our researches into the elements and potencies with which we have dealt already, for it is the same spirit and the same quality of life which work and unfold through all.

Now, the states of the stone in alchemy, when interpreted on the superior plane, may be broadly accepted as exhibiting the external manifestation of conditions which are achieved in the interior man. As a fact, they are absolutely analogical to the inward phases of evolution. It follows, therefore, that a proper use of the analogical method will unfold to us the entire elaboration of the man within, through the instrumentality of Hermetic or alchemical literature alone. Hence also it would be quite easy, as it would further be quite legitimate, with due respect to the memory of the illustrious Francis Bacon, who has ridiculed the presentation of the truths of one science in the terminology of another, to elaborate interior progress in the exact words of alchemy, and along the exact lines of development affirmed in the operations of the stone. Regarded from this standpoint, the first process of mystic transmutation, or the achievement of spiritual chemistry, is the PURGATION of the interior being, which is the cleansing of the desires of the heart. There is the state of DISSO-LUTION, in which the soul dies to itself and to the exterior world, that it may live in a transcendental union with the Grand Totality. There is the SEPARATION of the subtle and the gross, which is performed, as the alchemists tell us, by

means of heat, or, in other words, the desire of God. There is the CONJUNC-
TION, which is the gathering of the interior forces, and their concentration
towards the one end, which is attained partially in the spiritual CONGELATION, or
unification of potencies. This is the White Stone of the alchemical allegories.
During this period the spiritual work has proceeded in the interior man, without
any assistance that he has been conscious of receiving from the superior world.
In the next state, however, that of CIBATION, the soul is fed from above, and
by that spiritual sustenance the whole being is sublimated, and it shines, say
the Mystics, with a glittering whiteness. The two final processes are called
FERMENTATION and EXALTATION. In the first, the spiritual subject, having
melted like wax under the divine influence, is augmented with the spirit of life.
The second is a rectification of elements, and it is followed by the MYSTIC
UNION, which is the conjunction of God and the Soul, the immersion of human
in divine consciousness, giving "free perspicuity of thought" in the universal
being, which constitutes the bliss of Nirvana, the beatific vision, and the perfect
rest in God.

But perhaps it is better, on the whole, to retain the distinctive terminology
of Western Mysticism, although at the head of this chapter we have set, out of
veneration for the Masters of Azoth, and as a link which will connect us with
them, and with the radiance and the mystery of their great work, a suggestive
reference to the experiment of their FIRST SUBLIMATION. There is a general
sense in which all the mystical conditions of the interior man may be regarded
as varied phases of ever sublimed being, but that with which we are now
dealing is the sublimation of the senses, the first state of aspiration, which,
philosophically speaking, is subsequent to the vitalizing process of the New
Birth. Here it is necessary to indicate that priority in the order of thought is
not invariably connected with priority in the order of time. The aspiration or
sublimation of the senses may begin either before or after the actual attainment
of regeneration, and it is frequently partially accomplished in many persons
who never receive the gift of the New Birth, and never make any progress in
mystical knowledge.

In considering the first state of mystical aspiration, we must have recourse
once again to the importance of the physical man, and with that we must
compare also the importance of conditions. That is a false and artificial
Mysticism which despises the body of man, which seems to exist chiefly for
the purpose of making man hateful in his own sight. There are exercises of
devotion which seek, with singular aberration, to magnify the Creator through
an illiberal and grovelling vilification of the work of His hands. It is regarded
as a reasonable act to invoke the Lord of the universe after the fashion of the

following terms: I am a miserable worm in Thy sight, O God—foul, filthy, and full of all uncleanness; I am not worthy to approach Thee; there is nothing whole in me; I am all sin and disease. It is only Thine infinite power which can redeem me from my sordid state! But is it necessary to grovel in a condition of moral leprosy before we can come to God? No; rather is it part of that philosophy of make-believe and that science of false attitude which are hateful in the sight of the Divine. Let us have recourse, on the contrary, to the grandeurs of mystical theology. Let us remember how Saint Chrysostom describes the subject Man in terms which we have already quoted—the most resplendent and glorious image, and the most exquisite portal and epitome of the unseen world. Illuminated Plato defines him to be the horizon of the universe—that is, the vessel of the Hermetists, the thing containing and the thing contained. Saint Ambrose is lost in the contemplation of the magnificent work of humanity, the one subject beyond which we need suppose nothing for itself supposes all—the divine image, the celestial substantiality, the divine Virgin, the eternal Christ, and the life of the world to come.

> I sent my Soul through the Invisible,
> Some letter of the after-life to spell,
> And by and by my Soul return'd to me,
> And answered, "I myself am Heaven and Hell."

The poetry of the naturalistic school may not have struck the true key. It is impossible, indeed, that the essence of verity should be contained in any school—much less in a college of interpretation which has uniformly mistaken *signum* for *signatum;* but it has approximated more closely to the eternal realitiesof God than have others of the didactic discipline when it has affirmed that there is nothing common or unclean, notwithstanding that in another sense there is a mystery of uncleanness even as there is a Mystery of God.

In an attempt to elaborate the possibilities which reside in the outward man, there is perhaps little in the resources of language that has been left unapplied to enforce our conviction as to the importance of physical humanity. We are Mystics of the Christian illumination, but we absolutely require to be set apart from the errors and the insanities of that blind asceticism which has perverted the science of self-denial and misread the mystery of mortification; which has despised the body, and by the excesses of a mistaken discipline has provoked the flesh to rebellion, instead of bringing it under the subjection of law. ·For the grand purposes, the high and luminous achievements of the mystic wisdom, the man needs all his powers, all his faculties, all his avenues of perception, all his physical and intellectual instruments of communication. And he needs them, moreover, refined, tempered, elaborated—in a word, cultured to the

highest pitch of excellence and the last degree of perfection. For this reason
it is well that allegorical Masonry has indispensably required of its brethren
that they should be whole men. If, therefore, in one sense it be true that all
Mysticism demands that we should deny the senses, it is still more true, and
true after a higher order, that those which are the outward ministers of the
mind and man within should be ever subject to the transfigurating ministry of
the whole mind and the whole man. The first state of Mystical Aspiration
issues therefore from the culture of sense. The first state of Mystical Sublimation is the transfiguring and subliming of sense. The culture of the physical
senses is a needful, an indispensable, preliminary of interior culture. It is, in
particular, necessary for the outward manifestation of the inward light. How
shall it be possible through a coarse, troubled, and gloomy medium that there
should be any adequate penetration of any secret glory enclosed by that
medium? By the culture of the exterior man, and by the refinement of sense
and its perceptions, is man the outward educated towards the appreciation of
higher things. It is, of course, of a preparatory nature. When culture stops
short at the senses it transfigures nothing but sensuality, and then we have the
subtle mysteries of what may be termed transcendental vice, and the educated
iniquity of Greece and Rome.

The essence of the sublimation of the senses is in their elevation into the
region of religion, and it is our immovable philosophical conviction that one of
the most important aids towards this species of elevation is to be found in
religious ritual. It is efficacious where others fail; it is possible where others
are difficult; it is direct where others are involved by the intellectual mysteries
of indirection; it is approximate where others are remote; it supplies an official
instrument available to all when other instrument are almost impossible to
attain. But there are many methods and there are many instruments. There
is a law and there is a mode of sublimation for each of the five senses, and one
also for that which, in a sense, is the development and extension of all—we refer
to the pure heart of altruistic love. The law of sensuous sublimation, in its
broad and general aspect, is based on the receptive nature of the five senses and
the active quality which characterizes these affectional instruments; and it constitutes, thus regarded, a species of practical education towards the best quality
of giving and receiving.

The sublimation of the receptive sense of sight is founded on the intellectual and mystical principle that the eye is not satisfied with seeing, because
there is nothing in the manifest universe, appealing through the faculty of
vision to the interior man, which can permanently fill the soul. We must
approach the interior realization of the divine beauty which abides in the

noumenal world through an imperative aspiration towards the ideal perfection which is shown forth to us in form and colour. The eye must work upon the manifested beauty of the world and man the mystic work of the transfiguration by interior light. We must aspire, in the first place, with an intense and reasoned longing towards all that is beautiful about us, understanding that the highest expression of phenomenal loveliness contains the most natural analogy, and the closest external approximation to the beauty of noumenal being. We must, in the next place, conform our life and mind absolutely, and in all things, to this highest standard of actual beauty which has been permeated and transfigured by the tinging potency of the ideal. Above all actual beauty, there is the archetypal perfection which we conceive but cannot see, and above that archetypal conception there is the reality of which it is the reflex. We must, finally, become convinced, and this in a vital manner, that in the perfection of such a conformity, and so alone, we shall approach the withdrawn loveliness of the noumenal order.

When we have thus accomplished the mystical consecration of the eye and the regeneration of the faculty of sight, we may proceed to the sublimation of the receptive sense of hearing, and to the culture of that faculty by the divine mystery of sound. This sublimation is based on the principle that the ear is not filled with hearing, for above all possible achievements of poetry and music there is the transcending ideal of melody and of the grand intellectual harmonies which on earth are never heard. Within "the silent, doorless, lonely entrance-gates of melody," there abides, however, a capacity of sense sublimation which is unknown to the other perceptive faculties, and thus it is that sense which of all our physical avenues does most minister to the ideality of mind, is most removed from the phenomenal, and is therefore most in touch with the ultimate of the things which are. Now, there are two orders of melody—that which is the result of harmonious vibrations impressed upon the universal instrument of the material atmosphere, and conveyed by that instrument to the wonderful medium of the physical ear, and there is the silent music of verse, which is independent of physical vibration, which appeals to the interior ear, and vibrates in the atmosphere of the soul. Of these orders the higher is that of poetry, for it is most in touch with the inner world, and speaks most from the heart of things. In the order of external melody, there is the Voice of Nature, the Voice of Humanity, and the Voice of Art, and the second is the greatest of these, for the word of man is the image and reflection of the eternal Logos, and it is also that which is most in touch with poetry, though all are correlated; for poetry is another aspect and another presentation of the word of man. To accomplish the sublimation of the faculty of hearing, we must understand the mystery of melody; we must aspire towards the ideal of the dual music, the harmony of thought and sound. We must above all things love poetry and music, and enter into the interior understanding of their most perfect modes, knowing that in their highest manifestation they most nearly approach, and most adequately reflect, the harmonial law of the universe, and that unutterable music which is the mode of true being.

These are the two palmary divisions in the sublimation of sense, but all our senses help us towards the comprehension of existence, and so the first state of Mystical Aspiration requires the transfiguration of all, the culture of all, the higher ministry of all. The faculties of taste and of smell are more seemingly, though not perhaps more intimately connected with the general sense of feeling than are those of ear and eye. They are both capable of a singular refinement, and he would be a poor idealist who should regard either as an inefficient aid towards the perfect life. Physically speaking, there is no doubt, and indeed it is generally admitted, that the keenness of the olfactory instrument is a test of the general delicacy of the other organs of perception, and an educated palate is not altogether wrongly regarded as an index of general culture. The ministry of fragrance is a very beautiful, very subtle, and permeating form of sense-ministration. It has a mystical action on memory which at present is an unexplored region of psychological experiment; its chief utility is in its action as a refining agent over the whole nature, and in some of its phases, as, for example in the salt fragrance of the glorious sea, the whole mind is informed and enlarged with the freshness of the primeval world. Benediction and salutation for ever unto the waste grandeur of the mighty waters!

> Aye, salutation to the open Sea!—
> The mist-clad Moon is motionless and mild,
> But thou beneath art urgent, restless, wild;
> Her dim light silently descends on thee.
>
> Thou art instinct with vibrant melody,
> Which oft by ministry of song beguiled
> And charmed my spirit as an awe-struck child,
> And that deep music still seems dread to me.
>
> It opens up immeasurable heights,
> Unsounded depths, and distance unexplored,
> Wherein the seeing faculty of thought
> Beholds the birth of spiritual lights;
> Till, all her lost capacities restored,
> By Nature's own great Soul my soul is taught.

And the benediction of the poet be upon thee, if this set not forth thy worth!

O manifold in aspect and in voice,
Spread wide thy space, increase thy nature's depth,
And thy white-crested surges seen afar
Bleach in the balmy wind and multiply
In thy divine, immeasurable wrath,
And in thy might, for ever!   When the clouds
Disperse above thee in the central watch
Of the dread night's deep noon, a thousand stars
Diffuse awhile tranquillity and light
On thy deep-breathing breast, and joy be thine—
Joy in the revolution of the sky,
In thy returning moon, auroral light,
Sun's splendour, pageantry of evening red;
And God through all in majesty and might
Informing thee!

Unerring then is that instinct which surrounds our home with flowers, and short in intellectual eyesight is the prejudice which banishes them from our bedrooms.   Possibly, of all ministrations to external sense, that of fragrance is the most purely ideal, for the mind is not capable of conceiving a higher quality of perfumes beyond those of which it has experienced the riches.

As there is a rapture of roses, so also there is a sublimation of savour, and if we would transfigure the sense of taste, and aspire by this avenue of perception towards the relish of the life to come, we must avoid all gross food and all unnatural diets.   We must minister to the culture of the palate by the denial of the desire after flesh, which in its own order does analogically the same violence to the absolute standard of idealism that is accomplished in the intellectual order by the violation of the standard of truth.   If we would accomplish the First Sublimation, we must refrain from the pots of Egypt and the abominations of Babylon.   We must minister to the needs of the body by the refined delicacies of delicious fruit and the delight of good wine, by which the mind is matured and enriched.

When we have thus accomplished the transfiguration of the four senses by the aspiration to the beautiful and the good, we shall find that the fifth faculty of feeling is already modified towards perfection, and we shall be possessed of that refinement of sensation which is the highest point of culture, whereby we at once enter into the ideal world, for in its superior aspect it includes that gentleness of dealing, that poetry of social ministration, which constitutes good will towards men, and the permeating influence of universal charity.   We shall then have accomplished the First Sublimation, and there will follow the at-one-ment of the senses which is their separation from inferior desire, and their immersion in that spiritual enchantment which may be called the divine *envautement*.   In this state we shall have no further need of ritual to assist us in the work of religion, for all life and all Nature, separated from the mean and the commonplace, will become for us a religious ritual perpetually in celebration about us, and we shall see, hear, smell, taste, and feel after the sublime manner of the life to come. The First Sublimation is the accomplishment of the divine in sense. We shall have collected and unified all the romance of sensation into one flower of feeling which will spring upward, full of fragrance, and woven of many spells, into the superior world. May the energy of Azoth make actual in those who read, and as much in us who write, the splendid possibilities and promises of the First Sublimation !

CHAPTER THE NINTH.

THE INTERIOR SUBLIMATION, OR THE ASCENT OF THE MIND.

THE aspiration of sense, when apart from the elevation of mind, is, we have seen, only sensuality in an exalted form, but the operation of the law is the guarantee and the protection of the law, and the perfection of the First Sublimation is impossible apart from the second, wherein it is completed and intensified. Thus, the two processes are not separable in the order of time, though they are successive in the order of thought. The basis of the Interior Sublimation is in a spiritual theory of life, and its intellectual correlations and consequences have all mentality for their horizon. Now, the spiritual theory of life has an intimate connection with that mystery of universal symbolism which is the special patrimony of Christian Mysticism and alchemy, and with that doctrine of the illusion of matter which is generally regarded as the keynote of Oriental Mysticism. The experience of the Second Sublimation offers, therefore, a harmonic adjustment between the two chief branches of transcendental philosophy.

We have passed in the aspiration of the senses through a pleasant region, full of light and depth and richness, tinged with the rose red and royal violet of exterior beauty. We have indicated after what manner the path of the life within is a way of joy and flowers. Now, the work of the Second Sublimation is performed amidst a blaze of splendour, wherein joy is caught up to the mountain heights of ecstasy. But it is the experience of a keen, cool, and crystalline pleasure; we pass from the close magnolian hush and laden fragrance of a floral valley to the uplifted freshness of an airy pinnacle which has all earth beneath it and only blue heaven above. The state of mental aspiration is the first evolution of the interior light, and the first introduction into the unspanned universe of the interior man. Far is the voyage and high the venture; those seas are "sailed with God"; it is the apex height, the concentrated essence, and the sum of all quests, it is the romance of all travelling, the poetry of all exploration. There are no mysteries in Udolpho to compare with the wonders and mysteries in the Castle of the Interior Man, its forests perilous eclipse the

Romance of the Forest; it is the land of all legend, the home of all imagination, the rolls of elfin emperors are stored therein, and there also are all the archives of wonderland.

As the First Sublimation, in a sense, includes the second, so does the second contain and suppose the whole process, for as the first was a work of refinement and purgation, of the separation of the gross from the subtle, so is the second one of enlightenment and of clarifying. Once more, as the First Sublimation was concerned with the transfiguration of sense, so is this with the mind's transfiguring. In another aspect it is the emancipation of mind from sense, not by the annihilation of sense but rather by a redemption of the body which takes place in the first process. In itself it eminently constitutes a redemption of the whole mind, for it is an interpretation of the universe which gives the true key to the significance of the message of the material senses, and enables us to distinguish the seemingness from the actuality of things. It destroys the letter, sets free the spirit, and saves true life from the deadly operation of misread materiality. It is therefore the emancipation of mind from the bondage of Egyptian darkness, that is to say, from the shadow of the veil of Isis and the darkness of the hieroglyph. This is therefore the domain of initiation. It is also the domain of activity from the standpoint of pure intelligence, and it involves both a theory and a practice. The theory is that fundamental doctrine of mentality that the truth is to be sought within, and that without is the world of illusion, not indeed of the illusion of imposture or planned deception, but the instructing illusion of parable and the illuminating deceit of symbol; for these things are light and teaching when their quality has been ascertained, while at the same time they do daily through long lives deceive and almost undo the overwhelming majority of mankind. The practice is the outcome of one central, perfect, and indeflectible resolution, the ability to make and abide by which may be regarded as an adequate test of Regeneration. It is the resolution to act intelligently or understandingly in all things, with due regard even at the time of its conception to the momentous consequences that are involved in every activity. For any man who is only and absolutely governed by a clear intelligence, in the world of action equally with the world of thought, is of the quality of saints and adepts, and is constructing his nature towards the powers and prerogatives of the world angelical. He is without either fear or weakness; he is directed by an instrument of judgment, a criterion of conduct, and a standard of motive which are poised lineally with the making of all order. Once more, in all action and in every thought, he is permanently united through intention to the supreme mind and the eternal will. Thus, the essence of the Second Sublimation is contained in the word Conformity, and in its highest developments there is the consciousness already of that contact between the individual and the Universal Mind which is a foretaste of mystical union. Now, the man who acts intelligently does no wrong on the exterior plane, nor in the interior does he conceive amiss; and we would accentuate this point to make plain that the Interior Sublimation is no light achievement, for it is the conquest of sovereign reason. At the same time, we regard it exclusively as a work of delight and joy, however difficult may be the practice of conscience, for it is the putting off of darkness from the inner man. It does not consist in the construction of any recondite or arbitrary theory, but in the active acquisition of light, in the passive receptivity for light, and in the correspondence with light, of which the balance and the accord are the perfection of interior attitude.

It is neither possible nor needful to lay down a rule of outward life in the order of the Second Sublimation. We have only to remember that the mind must rule in all, and that in all things we must be modified by the sweetness and the reasonableness, as in all things we must be led by the rectitude of pure intelligence. This is a counsel of perfection, without which there is no progress in the achievement of the Mystic. The first rule of the inward life in the order of Mental Aspiration is full of grace and gentleness, and it brings its own reward. It is the elimination of preconceptions and prejudice; it is the gift of a free mind, which recognizes, on the one hand, the unevolved possibilities that reside in pure intelligence, and, on the other, the limitations of reason. If once over the wide waters of the world of mind there pass the flash of intuition, which is the radiance of the clouded moon of soul, it is within our ability to realize the significance of that light, and we shall never more be the bondmen of mere reason, but shall ascend into the royalty of thought. Unilluminated by this loftier light, reason is gross, groping, slow, and laborious; it is the sphere of hereditary prejudice, of sordid motive, of selfish prudence, and the perverted zeal of bigotry; it is the region of secondary causes, of obscured insight, and of the fear of the unknown. But intuition is swift, keen, clear, uninvolved, penetrating, without fear, positive, and apart from all error. Reason feels, intuition sees; reason is halting, uncertain, suspensive, ever ready to deflect into the side issues, but intuition is lineal in all things and never misses its mark. At the same time, it is not the abrogation of reason that we must seek, but the elevation and ascent of the mind. We have not to oppose reason, but to supplement its activity. It is the vessel of a higher faculty, and the shrine of a concealed god. If we break the pitcher the wine is spilt, if the shrine be laid waste the presence departs therefrom; therefore, reason must be transfigured and glorified, and the way of its glorification is the way of the illuminative life, full of moderation, suavity, and, mystically, as a perfumed garden of great and good intention. Now, the chief field for the elimination of prejudice is that of religious **belief, and we** must seek therefore emancipation from the bondage of creed **and dogma.** This involves a recognition of the first principles which govern **the search** after truth. Its axioms are of a commonplace character—that is **to say,** they are of the quality which everyone acknowledges and few act on **consistently,** because few realize them—as, for example, a thing is not true because **it has been** taught us; and, again, we should reject what is unworthy in religious **doctrine** without regard to consequences. Now, the special quality of mind **which is** must adapted for fertilization by the desire of the higher life is **precisely that** which is most likely to be hindered by the apprehension of unknown **possibilities** in the unseen order, so that, on the one hand, we must be prepared **to regard** the emancipation with which we are dealing as by no means so easy **as will** appear to the "advanced thinker," who takes credit that "he believes **in nothing,"** unless it be "the pagan origin of Christianity"; and, on the **other, we** must realize that even the reasonable rejection of points in religious **doctrine is no** evidence of itself that the mind is experiencing the Second **Sublimation.** There are many broad thinkers who are exceedingly shallow, just **as there** are many narrow currents which penetrate to a great depth.

The second rule of the inward life in the order of this process **is emanci-** pation from the bondage of sense, and it has already been set down **after what** manner we are to interpret this counsel conformably with the solemn impor- tance of the physical man. When the First Sublimation has purged **us** *from* the grossness of desire, the interior comes forward to deliver us from **the** delu- sion of our sensuous part. But it is a discriminating deliverance which **deprives** us of nothing that is precious, for it is essential that it should liberate **only** and not defraud. We touch here upon ground that has been practically **travelled** already, for it is part of the philosophical theory of life that is at the base *of* the First Sublimation, and it is the key of our entire work. But it takes a practical shape in the recognition of the symbolical ministry of the phenomen*al* universe, and in the realization that our inmost mind is an economy or type of the universal ruling Mind. God is verified herein as the true beginning and end of all intelligence, and union with Him is the condition of our perfec- tion and beatitude. Here an essential part of the process will be the putting to heart of the eternal doctrine of vanity. Vain in themselves are every type and figure; vain are all phenomena; vain are all earthly beauty and all earthly joy apart from the divine. We must empty them of their supposititious reality and the fraudulent element of their satisfaction, and when we have filled them with sovereign reason and infused them with true life, we can reasonably find joy in them, a living ministry, and an abiding source of rest.

When by the consistent application of these two rules we shall have become elevated and imbued with the generosity and nobility, become liberated in the grand manumission, and enlightened by the illumination of a clear, disabused, and undeluded mind, we shall enter into the fruition of five refined qualities of consolation—(a) The intellectual message of Nature, which is truly Protean in that it can be adapted to interpretation after a thousand manners, and therefore does more than preach sermons since indeed it imparts revelations, with commentaries of infinite suggestions.   (b) The intellectual message of romance, for the transfiguration of mind is the evaporation of the commonplace. (c) The intellectual message of poetry, which is the romance of aspiration, desire, motive, and activity at the elevation of white heat.   (d) The intellectual message of philosophy, which will no longer be dead but living, no longer arid but fruitful, and the consolation of this message will be deeper than was dreamed by Boetius, for we shall possess the key which will open all its treasures, and the instrument which will separate the living gold of all systems, so that we can be garnished and enriched by them all.   (e) The intellectual message of parable and allegory will finally constitute the whole universe as a wise instruction towards the creation of the interior kingdom of light.   Like a five-fold fountain of living water, these consolations will continually refresh our minds; by them shall we also be illuminated as with the radiation of a burning pentagram.   So shall we desire more and more the quickening of intelligence; so shall we be prepared by receptivity towards higher truth ; so will our intellectual forces in all things make for God; so shall we hunger after the supernatural, thirst for the world beyond, die unto outward things, that again, after another manner, they may be renewed alive in us; so will all the forces of our nature, as of all Nature, propel us towards the life within, and we shall enter into that which is beyond contemplation, beyond trance, and the love and life of God shall encompass us, loving and living, when we dare the withdrawn mystery.

CHAPTER THE TENTH.

THE OBSCURE NIGHT.

N OW, the two sublimations, when regarded in their narrower sense, have a merely preparatory aspect; they are not the interior life, but the process which makes for it. They are the quickening of transcendental activity, not its gratification. Between that quickening and this gratification there is a period of darkness, which, under one or other form of presentation, is found in all schools of initiation, and in all records of transcendental experience. It is called by the Christian Mystics the Obscure Night. It is the mystical Mystery of Aridity which so frequently figures in the spiritual treatises of Latin theology. It is the Black State of the Matter of the Alchemists. It is the portentous darkness of initiation, the passage of the Soul through Hades, the Kingdom of Pluto, and the mystical death of Tartarus, which precedes the evolution of the inner light and the eduction of the withdrawn glory. Its Masonic symbol is the hoodwink of the candidate. It has been described as the "discovery of a fearful mystery," as "dark, delusive, and dangerous," but at the same time it comprises a salutary and indispensable experience, even as it was required of the epopt that he should pass through the power of Pluto before he could be suffered to participate in the Elysian light. It is true in transcendental development as it is true in song, that,

> Each Orpheus must to the depth descend,
> For only thus the poet can be wise,

and there also is the entrance into wisdom for the Mystic. It is, briefly, that state in which the eye of mind has turned inward upon itself before it has received the illustration of the light within. It is the first attempt at the exploration of an unknown world, where all, truly and needfully for the moment, is doubt, darkness, danger, vague vastness, and unintelligible reverberation. "Therein," say the alchemists, "are heard the noise and voice of many strange and devouring creatures, some of which are escaped with difficulty, and almost each has a different sound." Doubtless there were many among the old pursuers of the Mystic Quest, who, like the "lover of Philalethes," were acquainted with the method and the way, but were deficient in the fortitude required for the initial experience, and chose rather, with that inquirer, to remain in the "alchemical garden" of the transcendentalized senses without proceeding further. For it is in this initial experiment that half of the labour is comprised, and success herein almost ensures the battle. It is the final mortification and fermentation of the old nature, out of the corruption whereof the new nature is in course of generation. It is that arcane putrefaction of which the alchemists appear to distinguish several species; it is that one in particular which they term the dry and philosophical putrefaction, which is also a sublima-tion of elements. It takes place in the dry water of the Philosophers, or very sharp vinegar—having that quality therefore which is ascribed to death itself, namely bitterness, and possessing an affinity in typology to that other symbolical vinegar which was offered to the Supreme Master in the supreme crisis of His dereliction. It belongs only, we are told, to the Sun and Moon—that is to say, it deals with the superior principles of Pneuma and Psyche. There is a close connection between the philosophical process which bears this name and our mystery of the New Birth, for the property of alchemical putrefaction is to destroy the old, original nature of a thing, after which ensues the introduction of a new nature, and occasionally it is stated in the words of the Adepts them-selves, that the process has the same result as a second generation.

Once more then, it is evident that the Obscure Night is successive to the two Sublimations and to the New Birth in the order of thought, but not in the order of time. As interpreted by Christian theosophy, it is that state in which the soul has become disgusted with the vanities of this world, but has not yet found peace in God. In the language of our positive philosophy we should say that the phenomenal has ceased to satisfy, but the noumenal has not been attained. The soul has not yet been enlightened by that divine light wherein it beholds the King of glory; it is aware intellectually of the excellence and the merit of spiritual things; but as yet it has neither tasted nor seen after what perfection of indescribable mode the Lord is sweet. The savour of earth has evaporated, the joy of earth has become flat and insipid, but it has not discovered that Great Compensation which puts meaning anew into truth and fresh possi-bilities into the fountains of natural joy. It is the state of voidness and emptiness which must be experienced by every neophyte in the science of trans-cendental life. Thence shall we pass to the refreshment of that heavenly dew —*ros philosophorum* and *ros rosarum*—which "conquers dryness," say the alchemists, "by the aid of an earnest heat."

It is eminently a period of trial and of temptation, where the soul passes through the bitterness of Calvary, and the Christ within seems forsaken by the

Father. It is also a period of contradiction and of that special quality of con-flict which comes of the Spirit of Perversity; for in spite of the disillusion which belongs to it and the pessimistic realization of vanity, both mind and sense are strongly drawn back towards the old form of subsistence. It is Israel in the desert yearning for the flesh-pots of Egypt and loathing the lighter food of the spiritual manna, which has not yet worked in the interior man the whole pro-cess of leavening, and of modification. It is the turning-point of spiritual illumination, which is part of the hypostatic union between the heart of man and the heart of God, and many spiritual natures have never passed beyond it. It is that state which never was transcended by Cornelius Agrippa—who died in the toils—but was passed by William Postel, and was escaped with an arrow's swiftness by the ecstatic intelligence of Thomas Vaughan. Even as the Catholic is instructed that he should desire the healing agony of the purga-torial fire, and "without a sob or a resistance" should contemplate his passage through the purging lake, so should we long for our own entrance into this mystical state, for it affords an indispensable experience. Now, the two Sub-limations are the gates and ways thereof. Those who, like the children of Israel, remain wandering in the desert of the Obscure Night, and enter not into the Promised Land are consumed all their lives in a bitter struggle with the enemy, and they never truly partake of the permanent peace of God. Yet God has not left them or forsaken them, and they die towards Jerusalem, nor do we know in all mystical history of a single instance in which one of these brave combatants has been permanently overwhelmed in the struggle.

The entrance into this state follows naturally on the completion of the two Sublimations, and is occasionally begun in the midst of them.

There is no need to seek it, and it would be equally unwise and impossible to attempt its creation within us. Like all spiritual conditions, it will, at the proper time find out its proper subject. It is the inevitable outcome of a certain mode of acting and being. It is the first consequence of the soul's self-surrender into the hands of God, and of the direction of the current of our being towards the mysteries of the life within. During that period of bereavement which con-stitutes the essence of the experience, the greatest help will be derived from the application of intellectual principles to the concepts of religion, and of their elevation to our personal profit. It is *par excellence* the period of what is termed the religious consolation, and it is also the day of invocation. In this connection it will be useful to regard the act of prayer under three chief aspects. There is the act of aspiration, under which presentment the two Sublimations are both a form of prayer; there is the act of supplication, which may be truly regarded as a tender ministry to the weakness of our nature; and there is the act of invocation, wherein the soul, collecting all her forces, summons to her assistance all intelligent and loving energies in the universe.

The Obscure Night is also the stage of transcendental experiment, because, as we have seen, it is a stage of uncertainty and doubt, wherein the fallen angel of the lesser or material man afflicts the emancipating intelligence with the scourge of mystical unbelief, tempting us to deny our inheritance and to forfeit our starry crown. Prudent transcendental experiment at this point will at times fortify the mind, for it is well that we should realize albeit in the phenomenal order how we are surrounded with Principalities and Powers, encompassed by strong hosts and by mighty angels, even as we shall afterwards realize within, that we are encompassed and surrounded by God. It is indeed the only stage when the communion of the spiritual circle can be participated in with any real profit. Verily, it is a consolation, and one which enters wholly into the order of religion, to know that the dead live. And yet we must ever remember that the possibilities of these experiments are the possibilities of that threshold which is full of strange dwellers, and our precautions can be never too great; nor can that intercourse be too rigorously guarded. We do not recommend these instruments; we shall do well to dispense with such aids, for death is the secret of God, and it is high service for ourselves and for others to conceal the King's secret. Let us rather aspire to that higher communion which is established with the Holy Assembly in the rite of the spiritual Eucharist. To make contact with that plane is to enter into the divine energy which evolves the Day of Christ, and in ourselves it will speed the royal time which the sacred college of magian inheritance is speeding in the whole world. And so, well and swiftly, in harmony with all law, and in correspondence with the true order, shall we find within us the Obscure Night passing with serenity and sweetness into the Morning of the Soul.

CHAPTER THE ELEVENTH.

The Evolution of the Interior Life.

I.

The Absorption of Quietism.

THROUGH the darkness of the Obscure Night—faint and slow, then permeating and suffusing, then overwhelming, absorbing, rapid, bright, glittering—there comes the gleam of a rising radiance—the Eos of Light, the Celestial Convolvulus, the Morning Glory comes:

> And radiant on the hills the Morning stands,
> Her saffron hair back blown from rosy bands,
> And light and joy and fragrance in her hands.

This is the Soul's awakening. Now the Soul awakens after the manner that the sun rises, for in herself she never sleeps. It is the mind which becomes illuminated by her knowledge, and we are lifted into a higher sphere of consciousness. This is the first state of transcendental knowledge, and the first experience in the positive unification of potencies. It is called the Absorption of Quietism; but what are we to understand by this *bizarre* term, which seems in a vague and half-realized fashion to open the gulf beneath our feet and to expose the height above our head, till we pause dizzy, possessed once again by the fear of the unknown, facing once more the portents of mystery, and stung by the electric shock of the "awe which freezes words"? Well, we can express it by an equivalent phrase which will restore light and serenity, assuring us that there is truly balm in Gilead, despite the raven's watchword and the pessimism of the questing mind. It is in all simplicity the possession of the Soul in peace. Here is a gracious and gentle message which will dissipate every disquietude and inform all doubt. It is not the peace which passeth understanding; that is the inheritance and the recompense of a later stage in the divine experience. It is the ethical and philosophical peace which is the consolation resulting from philosophy and the reward of correspondence with law. In one of its aspects it may be defined as the first repose of attainment. Contemplated from the theological standpoint, it is the higher life which is generated out of the immolation of the meaner self. Symbolically speaking, it is the interior manifestation of the Divine Virgin; it is the extension of the field of consciousness into the region of the soul. It is that state in which the man may, in another form of parabolical language, be said to meet with his eternal complement, and it is therefore the acquisition of the science of the Soul. It is the union of intuition and reason. Of this union, as of the conditions that follow it, there are several degrees and phases, for it can, in the first place, be intellectually realized by many persons whose life is incompatible, through the barriers of environment, with the full possession of the Soul. And it can, in the second place, be experienced in that condition of the life of contemplation which is best expressed by the transcendental term Absorption, whereby the reason is taken up into the higher faculty, and we see with the Soul's eye—not that intuition is the single quality of the Soul, or that it can be said to be described therein, for the Soul has indeed many qualities, and the psychic state has many modes and privileges, but this is the key of all, as it is also the poetic mystery of transfigurement. This condition of the interior life is not one that is to be induced automatically, and for this reason hypnotic experiments are dangerous and fatiguing, though undoubtedly it is possible by hypnotism to enter partially at least into the state, and mesmerism, here as elsewhere, may be made a "steppingstone" to occult knowledge. It is a stage in interior evolution which comes to the prepared subject, and therein is accomplished in all fulness, and in all completion, the civilization, refinement, and exaltation of the rational mind. It is the first entrance into the participation of the divine nature. It is a return into the subjective condition; but it must not be supposed that it is ever permanent in this life. It is an occasional, with most a rare, felicity, and it can even be sometimes enjoyed by those who attain it amidst the activities of physical life.

In this union of mind and Soul we have the first key to the transfiguration of the body of man; for the operation of the Soul, as we have affirmed already, is necessary to such an illustration. Those who have achieved this happy state are withdrawn into the mystery of all poetry. They are filled with gentleness and benediction; they enjoy a calm rapture; they abide ever amidst the delicate spiritual colourings and the magnetic atmosphere of a continual moonlight which enchants all. They divine their origin, and they know their end; the other world has passed into them; they are at once chastened, subdued, informed, elevated; theirs is the poetry of sentiment and the thought deep as the sea; through their eyes, as through a glass of mystery, one may look into the

land of souls, to see Jesus and Mary, the far-away softness and melancholy tender-
ness of Buddha as of a pearl-grey sky in the evening. The refined beauty of a
transfigured desire is upon their faces, till we look almost for the sudden out-
burst of the Artemisian crescent over their brows, or a chaplet of flowers of
light. Theirs is supernatural vision, theirs the lone region of prophecy, theirs
intuition, theirs insight, theirs the gift of interpretation, and the Soul on the
plane of the timeless communicates with her sisters in the timeless; the royalty
of reason receives its crown in insight, the exiled King ascends his throne once
more, and re-enters into his inheritance. And the light radiates, the light grows,
the light increases, the absorption deepens like a dream, the dream heightens
into vision, the vision becomes full and unclouded; it includes the past and it
comprehends the future, till we know that there is neither past nor future, that
which is before becomes as that which is behind. The true, ideal, inviolable
Virgin is revealed in us, she has descended towards us, or we have risen to her,
she is identified with us, she dwells with us, and out from the illumination of
her glory, and down from the transcension of her height, there comes the
desired illumination, with the glory of dream and legend. It permeates, it
illustrates, it informs, it possesses all our being. It has "slept in death through
the wintry hours" and the long night of matter, but it "breaks forth in glory":
we may crown ourselves with roses and lilies from the Paradise of the life to
come; for the life is no longer to come; we have achieved in beauty and we shall
reign in joy. We have achieved the divine unreason of the impossible in
matter. Look on us, for the Eos is within us! Look round us, for what is
"the starry shemaia of Chaldæan lore" in comparison with this new heaven and
this new earth, which we have created out of the environment of the green
world without us!

Now may we proceed, in the law of eternal reason, to the instruction of the
New Humanity, the fruit of the Soul's delight. Glory be to God in the highest,
and on earth peace unto every Soul! Salutation from the Centre of Peace,
health from the source of healing, strength from the tower of fortitude, fragrance
from the mystical Rose, beauty from the *Turris Eburnea!* And, O thou God of
splendour, the end is still remote, for there is a quickening of light in the Soul,
and even as the prophetic stir of life, which in the deep mazes of a forest be-
tokens the coming of the morning, in a mystery of spiritual twilight, and in the
holy hush of love, she whispers the crowning secret of a light that is still to come.
Bend o'er us in the benediction of thy dews, while old trees in the living stillness of a summer evening breathe and move around us, bless and bend down,
O opal sky! Descend, thou dewy stillness, burst forth, O radiant music of
mellow-throated merles in the dim, empurpled mysteries of impenetrable

thickets! That which is above shall become as that which is below, the divine shall incline to earth, the mind shall be exalted into divinity, the Virgin shall rejoice of the Spirit, the Son of God shall be manifest, and the eternal Pneuma shall manifest in the divine vehicle—the *antimonium spirituale et essentiale* of the sublime alchemist Basil in the midst of the *Currus Triumphalis*. Prophesy unto us, O immortal Soul, prophesy, immaculate Psyche! Beyond the ecstasy of thy absorption there is the absorption of another ecstasy. Thou hast awakened in us, and in thee there is another awakening. What moons shall pass? Lo, in the spiritual heaven the young moon of promise is uplifted like a bended bow! Long may it wax and wane, so thou abide with us; our eyes are all on thee. Till the fulness of that second advent ever shall the rapture of thy presence increase in us! Yea, even until the day dawn and the day star arise from on high, till the Orient *ab excelsis* visit us!

II.

The Psychal Union.

So enters the illuminated mind into the second psychal state, which is the further revelation of the Soul in the mystery of arcane science, wherein that unspotted sibyl reveals ever and continually to the mind, by the gift of her pure intuition, the withdrawn purpose of the eternal will of God. Therefore do we adore thee, O Psyche, with all the litanies of our mystic rite; we worship thee with body and with mind—plumed angel of interior lucidity, light of joy and sanctity, bird of the wilderness of God, in the desert of mortal life ever abide with us!

Now, the secret of comprehension in the Soul is that also of a common comprehension in the psychic potencies of the unseen. It is the entrance into the spiritual body which is the Church of Christ. It is the guarantee of communication with the Sacred and Holy Assembly. It is not a communication of persons, but an interior union, and its fruition is the Spirit of Christ, which is absorbed in us. This is the celestial and Iris-light of supreme promise to those that can evolve spiritually. But after what manner can the Spirit of Christ be said to have birth in us? We have spoken of a quickening in the Soul, as of a new and higher light, but we know that the Spirit is eternal, monadic, not separable. Therefore the quickening in question is of the consciousness only, which rises into knowledge of the overshadowing Pneuma. The Spirit does not really descend into us, but we are elevated into the Spirit. If we inquire after what manner, we can obtain some light from the analogical processes of alchemy. There is a progressive unfoldment from the white to the red state of the Philosophical Stone. The white state is spiritually interpreted as that of Soul-consciousness, and we have expended our reasonable enthusiasm on the joy of this condition. The Stone, however, is Man, in this connection, and the Stone at the red is Man conscious in the Spirit. The evolution from the white to the red is performed alchemically by the elevation of fire, and the quickening of the consciousness into the divine knowledge of the Pneuma is performed by the exaltation of that interior heat of which we everywhere read in the Mystics. It is the eternal fire and energy, of which the material energy and fire are the exterior translation and the representative type. It is that love of God which is not only the instrument of communication, but the thing communicating and the thing communicated—that love which is the centre and the source of souls, the font of spirits, the universal and infinite principle of all interior life. So has the fountain of all mystic achievement been defined by the great transcendentalists to be simply the force of love elevated to a divine degree and endowed with an infinite power.

The revelation of the Spirit is like a dawn breaking in the sky. Hast thou seen it breaking slowly over wide marshes, or a waste and shoreless sea? There is an illuminated patience exacted of the lone wanderer who is waiting for the "heaven-sent moment," and for "the spark from heaven," who is waiting for the day's brightness and the joy that cometh in the morning:

> See the earliest Rose of Morning
> Fills the eternal East with light!

It is indeed the Rose of Hermes, the Mercurius, the Messenger; it is indeed the "Holy Rose," the "awful Rose of Dawn," which kindles and is unfolded of God, as it were, out of the very soul of heaven, even as in the limpid depths of the heaven in the soul of man; yet seems it not unto those who, like the blue mountains, "watch and wait alway," to be almost a thousand years since the light began to break? Coldly on the grey waters, faint on the far away mists of the ever withdrawn horizon, pale and dainty coral on the low, still clouds, it comes, it is here—a universal flash simultaneously diffused and all-possessing; we have entered suddenly into glory. There is a blaze of beauty, and the blue above is reflected in blue beneath. Thanks be to God—Light-Bearer, Light-Bringer, Prometheus! We may spread our sails in the morning; the darkness is over and done; the splendid space of the spell-weaving moonlight is also swallowed up in glory. We are conscious no longer in the Soul, for Psyche has become conscious in Pneuma.

But before we speak of this truly divine condition, this pearl and hyaline of the mind, this grand illumination beyond which, when all its possibilities have been explored, there is no possible illumination through the limitations of mortal life, let us abide a little longer in the lower rapture of the State of· Union. It is then that condition in which we know God intuitively through the moonlight medium of our Soul. There are degrees and gradations therein; the faculty itself is the birthright of many persons who never extend its field, who never test its powers; it is especially the gift of that softer phase of our humanity, which, in itself, embraces both phases; it is *par excellence* the faculty of the woman. Beyond the sphere of its beatitude few Christian transcendental-ists have ever passed, and it is for this reason that Mysticism in the West seems to be the feminine side of theology. It is rich in loving sentiment and enshrined monumentally in the imperishable beauty of its luminous literature. For all spiritual Mystics who have risen towards God in Christendom, and have left us any records of their experience in the poetic romance of Christ, have spoken at length of this period. They tell us that the end for which God has created man is that he may become glorified in Him and by Him, and that by the appli-cation of a divine energy, He, even in this life as truly as in the other, doth overflow the Soul with happiness by a psychal comprehension in Himself. He has placed no limit to the capacity of our nature for happiness, and He ministers infinitely to our faculty, which is the only adequate ministry, for it alone quenches all thirst, satisfies all hunger, and extinguishes all desire in fruition, or renews it eternally, in satisfaction. Here in this life we are told that it is performed by grace, there the operation is in glory; here it is a work of infusion, or of such an activity in this our environed mode which takes an aspect of infusion as its result, there it is a work of immersion. And the reason is in this, that here we can escape, if we will, into the refuge of matter and the senses; there, to our joy or our sorrow, we cannot escape our God. There is an infinite possibility of sorrow possessed by the Soul of man, for we see that from the standpoint of the Mystics it has an infinite capacity for joy. But it is the sorrow of the Morning Star, of lapsed, but light-bearing Lucifer; it is not the black and barren sorrow in the perdition of orthodox theology, and amid the pangs of material fire invented by an implacable asceticism. In the depths of that sorrow are the cooling waters of the well of God's mercy. Perish Christianity itself before we believe in hell! Perish the hope of the Mystics! Frustrate be the desire of the saints! We shall find disillusion in the midst of the joy in God ere hope shall end for the sinner. In the wisdom of the tran-scendental, calmly and assured do we rest that God has never made a heart ache except with love for Himself.

Now, there is only one bond of our union with God, and that is in His love and His service. The divine and secret master of the Soul, who is the sphere of the Soul's intuition, instructs us in the mysteries of His **magnificence**, mercy and bounty, and when we have arrived, says the *illuminé*, **Louis de Blois**, at this exalted state of union, the Soul perceives itself to be **enlightened by the** rays of eternal truth—in other words, it has entered into the first **consciousness** of the Absolute. It perceives truth through its own medium—a **little while**, a little further, a step higher in the grand ascent, and we may **perceive after** another manner, and this will be that higher consciousness of the **Absolute, of** which we have already spoken by the magnanimous privilege of God ; **wherein** the seeing eye of the spirit is gifted with direct vision, and the mind **becomes a** pure instrument of positive knowledge. But even in this lower state **the Mystics** tell us that faith enters into perfect certitude, hope into the altitude of **its energy,** love into a living ardour. Herein is the hypostatic union of the Soul **with God,** and the peace of the mind, the peace of the heart, with the peace of **chastened** will, are among the qualities of such a condition. In this is our **sanctification,** in this our salvation, in this the source of all our coming glory, as of **the whole** scale of our beatitude. It is the first revelation of the hidden life, **and** it *is* within the reach of any one who learns to do all things well. But **to reach** it there is the absolute necessity that we must never sin, and must act in **all things** under the law of beauty. In this gentle sphere of hallowed and **hallowing** illusion where God in His love has environed us, the most appropriate **type** and symbol of this State of Union is a loving and recollected **participation,** performed reasonably, in the Eucharistic rite.

III.

The Ecstatic Absorption.

And so the mind enters through its joy in Soul, and the Soul enters through the love of God, into the life of the Spirit. It is again like a New Birth, or, in another aspect, it is like a descent of Pentecost, but in reality it is a purely evolutionary process. It is the extension of the field of experience, which is equivalent to an extension of the consciousness, for the Soul takes in life as it takes in knowledge, and it lives in proportion as it learns. This fact is the key of all mystic processes, and it is, in particular, the way of entrance into that state which the transcendental philosophy has termed the Ecstatic Absorption, wherein the interior man becomes acquainted with his highest principles. In this he is more and not less man; he has acquired the true humanity and enters upon the maturity of his nature. False is that view of life which connects our human subsistence inseparably with foibles and follies, and imagines that man of necessity is founded in weakness. The elevation of the mind is the conquest of our true and ultimate domain, wherein we possess ourselves in all things and enjoy all things in ourselves by the virtue of an intimate participation in the universal.

What we have affirmed in the order of experience will suggest the conclusion that after all transcendental experiments, and despite the many subtleties of certain mystic tabulations, we have no ground in the certitude of real knowledge to regard the interior man as otherwise than one and indivisible, and current classifications of his component principles as other than definitions of successive steps in the development of his interior experiences. This opinion is in harmony with the consensus of theological thought in the West, and should not be regarded as unconsonant with the statement of esoteric experience, which we have been elaborating up to this point. It is not to be hastily set aside, for in view of one maxim of Mysticism which we have already quoted, it is stamped with "the seal of Nature and of art"—in other words, it has the presumption of simplicity in its favour. On the other hand, there are several philosophical schools which are of high importance in our science, and that do regard the separate classification of the spiritual principles in question as representing a distinction of qualities. Herein much depends on the point of view of the observer, and it is at least certain that they are separable in the distinction of spheres of experience. When a certain mode of life, either here or hereafter, has closed for all practical purposes, not indeed the avenues of attainment, but all moral likelihood that those avenues will be made use of, then the Pneuma may be said to have departed and there is a shrinkage of consciousness as the sphere of experience contracts. Yet the man may be regarded as one. The problem in practice does not seem of matter or moment, and the disciples of the Christian tradition concerning the monadic nature need not regard themselves as divided either in fundamental doctrine or in positive knowledge from the Oriental initiates who differentiate the sevenfold man. We are not expounders of the divisional insanity which counsels us to agree in differing, but we earnestly labour and desire that the several colleges of mystic thought, which we do embrace and love alike, should ever bear in mind that they are inseparably united by the aspiration after absolute science, and that no variation in details, nor any dissimilarity in methods, can possibly divide them in truth. As regards the debated point on which we have touched for a moment, if, on the one hand, the monadic view seems to leave open to the most retrograde intelligence the dim and remote possibility of again rising, and therefore is sealed with God's charity as well as with the simplicity of God, yet, upon the other, the extension of the field of consciousness into the world of the

Spirit presents itself before us with such an influx of miraculous individuality that the experience partakes somewhat of the communication between separate identities; and as in the consciousness of Soul we appeared to become united with a new nature of ineffable feminine loveliness, so in the consciousness of Spirit do we seem to have effected a union with a mighty and masterful being. which has, as it were, a male aspect. It is the period when that which is without becomes as that which is within, when, in the words of the alchemists, the body becomes spiritualized and the spirit is made corporeal. There is an absolute unification of all potencies, and according to a traditional saying of the Divine Master, it is during this period that the kingdom of Heaven is realized —that kingdom which is not of this world, but is established within us when the Son of Man cometh.

In the mystical ladder of ascension, on the stairs of the House of Life, this state is tabulated as that inner ecstasy whereby the mind is not only illuminated with a perfect knowledge of the will of God, but by the fortitude to perform it. It is the transport of the Soul, and it is known both to Mystics and alchemists under a special conventional name. It is the GRAND ILIASTER—"The passage of the mind or soul into the other world, as took place with Enoch, Elias, and others." The science of God's will and of the union of our own with God is the withdrawn mystery of this beatitude. Here it is necessary to distinguish between the imperfect theological sense in which the old religions have understood this will of God and the higher sense in which we as Mystics make use of it. With us it represents conformity to a supreme and eternal principle, not to the absolute mastery of an irresponsible mind. While we are anthropomorphic in so far as we believe in the Fatherhood of God, and sensualists in so far as we believe that in union with God there is attained a very rapture which we must express in the language of the senses for sheer want of any better vehicle of communication; we do not identify our doctrine with that of a personal Deity, which simply means that our conceptions have become emancipated from the limitations of a narrow theology. We hold that the efficient cause of the differentiations in the one substance which are presented to us as matter and mind is something transcending either and infinitely greater than both. Mind is the highest principle with which we are acquainted in the sentient universe, and we express the transcension of our conception concerning the noumenal oneness according to the highest possibility of our language, but without being deceived by our language. So also with regard to the will of the Noumen. Of that eternal, omnipotent, and omnipresent energy our finite will is the type and the image; but here the type is transcended by the antitype in a manner which escapes our definition, and when we speak of the will of God it is in the terms of a symbolism, with due regard to an enduring and necessary disparity. No doubt in the fulness of supreme intuition, in the union of the Mystic Wisdom, the mind will attain a higher knowledge upon the effulgent problems of the ultimate form of subsistence, but it will not be expressible knowledge on account of the limitations of language. How shall we hope to give a voice unto the things which are in the words of the shows which seem, whatever grace and beauty abide in the pageant and spectacle, whatever possibilities reside in the silver-tongued speech of humanity!

In the state of Ecstatic Absorption, man, united to his Spirit, obtains divine knowledge immediately, no longer through the medium of his Soul, and still less through the ordinary faculty of reason, with its imperfect companion light of conscience. He rises into the region of the true and eternal conscience, which is the identity of the idea with truth. He is in possession of an instrument of knowledge which transcends the intuition of the psychic part, because thereby he not only perceives truth, but the principle of all verity. Intuition is a perceptive faculty, but in the Spirit there is a positive science. The condition itself is denominated the ecstasy of absorption, for, with one exception, it is the highest conceivable mode of delight, it possesses the whole man and takes him up utterly into itself. It is also the highest form of that illuminated love of truth, which is a necessary part of the knowledge of truth. These things are counted among the Secrets of the King, and we have already said that they exceed illustration. Those who under the happy auspices of a truly spiritual magnetism, projected by a master of the heights, have felt their whole nature unbind slowly and dissolve in a sea of holiness, have experienced, before dissolving into that transcendental sensibility which is dead to outward things, the elementary felicities of the Ecstatic Absorption. The subjects of a Gregory or a Dupotet have occasionally passed away in bliss 'into the magnetic sleep. What must be that to the infusion of will-power on the part of a Saint Francis or a priest of Ars? But he that is absorbed by the Spirit may be said to be entranced by Christ. Herein is the true healing; the man is made one with himself in a celestial harmony. He is above all the order of the Magi; he has become a true Mystic.

IV.

Entrancement.

The last mystery of love and wisdom is the entrancement of the interior man. It is the second stage of the Grand Iliaster, the flight of Elias, the passage of Enoch. It is that in which man, unified **with his Spirit**, is unite' in the Spirit with God. For how many persons in any **generation**, or in an age, the attainment of this union is possible during life **on earth**, God alone knoweth. In its completeness it is possible to none, for, **in that sense**, it is an eternal reward; but a high degree of the experience is **attainable in** all probability by a far larger proportion of minds than even **many advanced** Mystics would appear to have supposed. We must also remember, **and herein is a** chief counsel of consolation, that in the merely intellectual real**ization of the** Seven States there is a great joy and also a great enlightenment. **There is no** person in the universal world to whom this slight share in mystic **processes can** be really forbidden by his environment. The most hard-driven **being can** progress by this shorter way, and the aspirational passage of the mind **for the space** of one hour daily through the states of the mystical Stone will fer**tilize all life**, and both within and outwardly will beautify the whole nature. It **is in** this sense that we must interpret the exhortations of the Mystics concer**ning what** they have termed the Practice of Peace, and the devotional exercises com**prised in it**. "As the peace of the interior and the repose of the mind with**drawn into** the hidden world of contemplation, constitute the best disposition and **the state** that is most desirable for the high ascension of the Soul into the blessed **heaven** of perfection, we must daily and frequently make a particular exercise **therein**; that we may establish ourselves more and more in a solid and in**violable** tranquillity." In this way we can also attain to what the old Christian **Mystics have** termed the Seven Gifts of the Spirit, and the Twelve Fruits of the **Most Holy** Counsel. This Shorter Way is after all the best, and it is perhaps **the indis**pensable, preparation for the Long Journey. It prepares the way of **the Lord** and makes straight His paths. We commend then this exercise of devotion to all who aspire towards perfection, and we can promise them in its practice a precious and unmistakable reward. For many it will come in the mode **of** that "sudden illustration," which is the form of the new conception, and then all the universe of Spirit is laid open ; our salvation will be truly in our h**ands**, and it will be difficult to miss beatitude. If the practice be accompanied by a fortitude of endeavour towards the construction of individual life in the direction of evolution, the operation can scarcely stop short at the enlightenment of the rational faculty, and as we believe that all heaven and all earth conspire with the man who would enter into perfect harmonial correspondence with natural law, failure may almost be expunged from our language, and we may look for a great ascension.

Now, as the Psychal Union was the immediate communion of Mind with Soul, and as the Ecstatic Absorption was the union of Spirit with Mind, so is the State of Entrancement the participation of the individual Pneuma in the Divine Spirit, and unto this have the Mystics applied another name, which is that of the Mystic Oneness, to indicate the substantial, the spiritually atomic, the ineffable union which it is possible for us to contract with the Grand Mystery of the *Fons Deitatis*. We have briefly affirmed the mode which belongs to this finality of transcendental evolution. It is the crown of life, the consummation and conclusion of all things in the microcosmic order; it is the day of interior rest, the entrance of the Spirit into the compensation of its true home; it is the millennium of our being. Hereunto we are all called, and in a sense we are all chosen, and yet as we have inferred already there are few persons in any generation who may be said to achieve this end. The literature of Christian Mysticism has many references to the state of Unified Spirituality, but we are inclined to the conclusion that at least in some cases the Psychal Union was confused with the Divine State. No doubt the interior life of the Mystic is impossible to the majority of mankind, because there is no question that its other than intellectual realization requires special exterior conditions. It does not demand wealth, nor, on the other hand, does it expect of us what, at this day of complexity, would be the pleasing aberration of selling all we have and giving it to the poor, who would misuse it, that we might follow on the imperative summons of the Christ abiding within us. It needs rather the "elegant sufficiency" of Thomson and the "rural quiet" of the *Seasons*. Having regard to the peculiar nature of the processes, we would affirm, without prejudice, that, given the required faculties, a man may best enter into the penetralia of the life within if he be possessed of a small portion, the modest competence of, let us say, two hundred pounds a year, of a wife who is also gifted and will develop along with him, finally, of an embowered house where the gradient of a green lawn goes down under the shadows of beech and willow to the banks of a quiet stream. We know of no better environment than this for those who would achieve eternity by the withdrawn way of the Quietists. The palace is impossible, the city is difficult, wealth reduces the avenues of development to the space of a needle's eye, the desert is a barren hardship, the monastic life too often the deliverance of the mind into the bondage of dogma. But we have indicated that manner of existence wherein is the felicity of true ease, giving scope for a higher labour, and the amenity of reasoned content, wherein transcendental aspiration may obtain wings to fly. Thus environed by simplicity, a man may put in practice the doctrines of interior perfection, and at the same time may educate his children under the enlightened law of evolution for the adornment of the age to come. For, regarded from the highest standpoint, there is no virtue in a celibate vocation, however solemnly it may be consecrated by the rites of a mistaken religion. Let us rather create in our own homes the portal of the Holy Assembly and the synagogue of the new temple. Between this work in transcendental education and our own interior progress, there need, however, be neither clash nor rivalry. That progress is not of a day or of a year, but of all life; and the higher stages are not unsuited to the mellow period of maturity. Energy is stultified in operations of haste and violence; so should we be governed in all things by an enlightened moderation and a grand patience. Crowns are often won by waiting which are sometimes denied to work; but at once to work and wait is a great secret of progress. Hence we counsel all persons who would follow the interior life along the lines that we have indicated to set themselves firstly, in all earnestness, to such a conquest of environment as will place them in tranquil possession of that modest mean of life whose panegyric we have recently pronounced. If they die in the midst of the attempt, they will die in the peace of Israel, and in the grace of the Holy Assembly. But they will probably live to achieve it; commonly the Mystic is not denied his ends, and no one desires earnestly to look upon the face of the Father without, at least, being permitted to lay hold of the hem of His garment. When we are thus rationally insphered, we can proceed to the larger work, but so regulating action that in its first stages we may bring up children to eternity in the light of those doctrines which will ultimately possess the world. For the Mystic it is eminently possible to make the best of both worlds, and indeed it is part of his vocation. When he has fulfilled his duty without, he may seek his reward within; meanwhile, in his illuminated homestead he will be creating a centre of applied law which will hasten the day of perfection, the day of the great general election, when the universal franchise of enlightened humanity will return an informed parliament to accomplish the federation of the world, and a wise ministry to rule under the law of Christ.

At this point then we close our delineation of the interior way. We have spoken with a certain measure of accuracy concerning the earlier stages, and of the higher transcension so far as our development will permit. Whatever the deficiencies of our labour, we claim, at least, that we have been controlled by the love of the light. Those who in this age have beheld Diana, who "possess the gift of God in secret," may possibly be constrained by our labour to uplift a purer light and a less erring "Guide of the Perplexed."

CHAPTER THE TWELFTH.

CONCLUSION.

OUR intellectual exploration into the summerland of transcendental philosophy is now ended. We have found that the law of evolution sets outwardly towards beauty as it does inwardly towards truth. We have shewn forth the nature of our coming physical perfection; it is summed in the word Transfigurement. We have also delineated those interior processes which make for the light within; they are summed in the term Illumination. And this illumination and that transfigurement constitute our New Light of Mysticism, our Star in the East, rising over the wide world of the life to come, our Star of Development and of AZOTH. We hold that our instruction is full of pleasantness and beauty because it compels no one except in the law of love, which operates in altruistic joy. It is tender to all weakness, it is alive to all arguments of disparity, it does not engage the frail disciple under the terrors of a penalty to the whole sum of perfection. It appreciates not only every stage in the progress but every step in the direction; it has, therefore, all reasonable sweetness, as it has all mystic reason. We have striven to purge these pages from the "vanity of dogmatizing"; we have countenanced no superstition, we have condoned no prejudice. We are grounded in devotion to the light, we aspire unceasingly after divine tolerance, the unbiassed mind of Christ, the generosity of Buddha, the free openness, and that sanctified indifference in doctrine which we regard as a test of illumination and in itself illuminant. We are assured in our hearts that, though many martyrs have been glorified in dying for their creeds, there is no creed worth dying for, and this conviction doth itself prepare us for the certitude of real knowledge. So have we eschewed in this treatise many fascinating theorems.

It will be seen that in developing the doctrine of the interior life in the second division of this book, we have only elaborated its theory in connection with experience. As far as practicable, we have excluded all reference to matters and possibilities, which, however interesting in themselves, lie less or more outside the direct domain of transcendental sensation. One among these, and in some respects the most important of all, from the importance that has recently been attached to it, is that of Reincarnation. It is outside our duty to pronounce on what is outside our subject, and yet it seems well that this book, which includes our highest dreams and our purest hopes, should not go forth without some allusion to an opinion which enters into the philosophic creed of so many persons who command our intellectual respect, while they possess our mystic love. Unto all such we would, therefore, say that the limits of our own philosophic faith are not defined by the limits which we have prescribed to our treatise. Yet is there nothing in its pages which opposes the sublime teachings of the ancient Pythagorean wisdom. Indeed the experiences of the interior life through all its stages, as they are sublimed successively towards Godhead, do in some respects present themselves to the mind with a more winning reasonableness as so many triumphant recoveries of anterior memory, of the consciousness of submerged pre-natal states, leading upward to the last and the highest, which also is first of all—the remembrance of our primeval and eternal being in the pure font of Deity. No doubt the experiences of the interior life impinge upon many lives and absorb many spiritual histories. Mad were the physical theory which would assign a date in time to the elements which form our body, and the Spirit, which is not of time, we may well believe to have been before the world was with God. The affinity which the Soul feels for Christ, our brother, has deep down in its nature the fibres of congenital union; and we doubt not—how should we doubt it when *Nihil Obstat?*—there is neither let in reason nor hindrance in experience, that the First Communion of the Soul was never made on earth. And we look for another Eucharist, of which we shall partake perfectly in the joy of the timeless. That which came forth out of God has been more than joined in God: the few who accomplish on earth that state of Mystic Oneness, whereof we write and dream, do celebrate a silver wedding, and there is a golden wedding to follow.

With the potencies of the invisible world and of the interior humanity at our command we need not despair, if only our policy be as profound as our ambition is high, of being one day masters of the world. But this can be only accomplished by the complete purgation of our motives, by the elimination of all that is mean and unworthy from our arcane science, by the definite abandonment of tawdry and pompous speculation, by weeding our garden of gold, frankincense, and myrrh, from the tares of inane assumption, and by identifying our whole nature with the ultimate end of evolution, which is the PERFECT MAN. Those who have attained to conviction on these subjects should do their best to disseminate their knowledge by every prudent means, so that literature and social life, and the high places of religion and of culture, may be permeated and saturated with ideas involved in the new mystical system. For if it be true at all, it is of that which we call God, it is a ray from the source of truth; and we are not perishable dust, we are not mere protoplasm, we are not for ever circumscribed by the narrow circle of simple faith, we are the heirs of the great everlasting; we can know as well as believe, there is no room for the atheist, there is no room for the gospel of matter; the illimitable possibilities of eternity open about, beyond, above us, the universe is not greater than our life is long; the infinite path of progress, the Holy Mountain, the City and Land of God, are within the horizon of possibility, and the vital realization of these facts, with all that they involve, is the NEW BIRTH.

Addressing ourselves, therefore, to the earnest students of esoteric science, to the seekers after light and the Gnosis, to those who would achieve and reign from the highest pinnacle of spiritual perfection, if there be anywhere a path thereto—to those who are hungering and thirsting after an absolute conviction concerning the deep things of the unseen world, but are in want of a warrant for their faith, we reverently commend the revived light of Mysticism. We support no arbitrary theories; we plead for no special views; we have no opinion to offer on the hypothesis of the Astral Light, nor on the *modus operandi* of visions and evocations; we neither reject nor countenance existing explanatory systems; we have no definition to submit concerning the limits of magical possibility, nor do we assume to know why magic is possible at all. We are concerned with a single fact—that mystic science is the sole system of thought or experiment which has ever pretended to direct mankind to the demonstration of the soul, and therefore for the soul-seeker it is the only and the one system which has any claim on consideration. If we are genuine seekers for the soul, then, in God's name, let us try Mysticism. But let us divest our minds from puerilities, imbecilities, and horrors, which have been too often associated falsely with that divine name—not denying the association, because it has existed, not explaining it away, but setting it absolutely apart. Difficulties concerning it may be settled when we have dealt with the grand, the supreme question: Can esoteric science, at its best and highest, actually provide us with the definition we require? Once more, let us try and see, for herein is our only hope.

The new Mysticism is in need not of believers, not of theorists, but of patient and well-equipped experimentalists, willing to test all methods, that they may acquire knowledge in a substantially unexplored field of experience. It is not in want of dabblers, of persons who can plash a little in the shallows of palmistry, who can perform small feats in thought-reading, who can divine dimly in coffee cups, who because they are addicted to the trivialities which fringe the borders of mysticism, and to some mild elementary experiments, believe themselves interested in occultism. The sanctuary of esoteric science is closed to the frivolous, not by an arbitrary decree, but by the law of their own nature.

Perfect counsel of supreme Buddha, assist us towards the grand end! All ye Teachers and Masters—all ye leaders in divinity—all ye sons and daughters of illumination—abide with us! Fast no longer falls the eventide, but the joy cometh of the morning—abide and help! Energize our hearts, inform our minds, actualize our grand imaginings! City of intelligence, city of love, be thou builded within us! Temple of humanity, shrine of the life beyond, therein we erect thee now! We salute thee with a final pageant of poesy. May the Benediction of Light be upon us, and may all who beautify these pages with the radiance of intelligent eyes be illuminated with a Royal Diadem!

L'ENVOI.

One moment, Brethren, and our task is ended!
Whatever here may meet deserving blame,
Whate'er is worthless, as our own we claim,
That so the Mystic's lore may be defended;
But whatsoe'er to noble thoughts and splendid
Achievement prompts you doth the Seer disclaim,
That mystic praise may fill the trump of fame,
And that new life with glory be attended,
Which in this book begins. It seeks to be
A living influence in the hearts of all—
Oh, from yourselves it seeks to set you free,
And unto native heights your souls recall,
Whence come fresh breezes from the Eternal Sea
To strengthen against future lapse and fall!

APPENDICES.

APPENDICES.

THE special quality of mystery which agnosticism has restored to the mind is to be valued only as an introduction to the mystery of the Mystics, that is, in so far as there is an avenue to its solution. There is ultimately no romance in a labyrinth if we are deprived of the thread of Ariadne. Mere physical science, in so far as it has introduced us to new fields of speculation, has not provided fresh pastures for the imagination, which is a creative and illuminative faculty, but a new exercise for our ignorance in the regions of unfulfilled possibility. We submit that there is no true fairyland of knowledge apart from the knowledge of the transcendental. In the past there was a wide area of spurious wonderland founded on the mystery of darkness. Science, in a measure, has exploded it, and in turn has created another realm of darkness, in which there is another wonderland which we regard as equally spurious, for the true fairyland is located not in darkness nor ignorance, but in the mystical mystery of light. In some of the supplements which follow we shall have occasion to illustrate the mode in which certain historical places are invested with romance and with meaning by the action of this light, and in the present note on the connection between imagination and science we may appropriately explain our standpoint by a geographical reference.

Now, whether or not it be true that in much knowledge, as in overmuch washing—we appeal to all artists in alchemy—there is that peculiar quality which was characterized as vanity by the wisest of men, it is undoubtedly true that modern geographical knowledge, and modern geographical methods, have well nigh eliminated all old elements of romance in travelling. For example, the division of France into innumerable petty departments is one of those devices of practical utility which have evaporated every particle of poetic flavour that once attached to such historic and high-sounding names as Provençe and Languedoc. So much for the classifying labels of politicians and map-makers. In this respect possibly few countries have suffered more severely than has England. Where, we may ask, is "the island valley of Avillion"? Where is the Forest Perilous of Arthur? Where are those dim, remote, and illimitable worlds of ghost-haunted marshes once situated in the Wild West of Britain, and wherein was the mist-encompassed castle of invincible Palmerin? They have been improved out of existence by the prosaic quest of the Ordnance Survey. There has been no chivalry in Europe since Don Quixote, and the valour of La Mancha was a comedy because it came after the Renaissance. It is impossible nowadays to fare forth in search of adventures, because every road is a beaten track, while every duck-pond and every dunghill are faithfully indicated in the pocket county-map. Little of the true spirit of an old traveller can inspire the breast of a modern railway passenger, who starts from Land's End to John o' Groats with a fair chance of reaching his bourne in safety, and fortifies himself in case of accidents with a *Tit-Bits* policy of assurance. Every element of uncertainty has been minimized to the last extent; every fraction of topographical ignorance can be reduced to a point without parts or magnitude, thanks to Murray's guide-books, and as, in this connection, some quality of ignorance is essential to the faculty of wonder, and as the romantic, thus falsely understood, is inseparable from the fabulous, it is exact to say that where there is much knowledge geographically there is little of this species of romance.

Now, it is this species which modern science, including geography, has annihilated, but at the same time it has afforded to those who delight in it a really substantial compensation, a comfortable competence for the fancy in some-what remoter realms, to say nothing of the infinite convenience to man the physical, an amenity of modern knowledge which must be rated at a high figure in the most parsimonious computation. It has revealed to us the indestructible energies and the cosmic forces, the law of continuity and the unknowable, at all of which it requests us to bow down and adore, and we adore and bow down accordingly, investing them with much the same misty magnificence which was once attached to the Castle of Tintagel, and the scenes of the Welsh Mabino-gion. It has instructed us also in the gospel according to words, and in a choice assortment of colossal myths and overwhelming marvels. We can "put a girdle round the globe" in something under sixty days, and imaginary travels like those of good old John Mandeville, Knight, are consequently out of the question; but we have our revenge in the star-depths. It is still open to us to populate the spaces of the air with the creations of the nebular hypothesis, and what with refractions and aberrations imagination will never want her kaleido-scope. When we have exhausted these worlds we can still imagine new, and if we invoke the assistance of the theory of natural selection, we can produce more marvels of natural magic than were ever encompassed by Apollonius, Paracelsus, or Eliphas Levi. Indeed, science, with its substitutes, as an aid to imagination and her counterfeits, might be the subject of a philosophical treatise.

If we are dissatisfied with resources like these, we can acquire, without much stress or hardship, the freedom of wider fields. Overlapping all regions, permeating everywhere, and ever anxious to be all things to all men, there are the length and height and depth, the complexities and magnitudes, of the immeasurable world of humbug, which in the days of Arthur and Perceforest, of dragons and hippogriffs, of enchanted castles and knightly romance, were really an unexplored region. It is the true land of Proteus, the modern Fairydom, full of transformation and illusion, of accommodation and suppleness, and always open to the exploiting mind. Before its board of directors the Round Table recedes into a barbarous obscurity, its paladins of finance eclipse the peers of Charlemagne, its enterprises breathe a hardier spirit of adventure than any chivalrous quests of old, and the Land's End of that country few persons are likely to reach in safety. Thus, the ministry of the modern world to the make-believe section of romance and to the faculty of fanciful pretence is so peculiarly abundant that their disciples can afford to dispense with the old delusions, may condone the offences of topography, and, despite its commonplace, may continue in their railway journeys the inexpensive precaution of the newspaper policy of assurance.

For ourselves we prefer the pure romance of Mysticism to any possible extensions of physical science into romance. But if it were possible for us to regard the transcendental as also a delusion, it appears to us that in the matter of imagination it belongs to the superlative order. At least there are splendid possibilities for fancy in the night side of Nature, in the doctrines of ghosts and goblins, in apparitions of the living, in thought-transference, in multiplex personality, and the philosophy of psychical research. Surely much profit in the fantastic order must follow on adopting the immaterial philosophy, and regarding that momentous hypothesis, the infinitely divisible atom, as a fiction of the dialectical schools! Surely in the teachings of theosophy and the Mystics there are sovereign consolations for imagination even apart from sober reason. Are we mathematically inclined? Then is there space of four dimensions, wherein it is an ordinary occupation to square the circle, to tie knots in an endless cord, to calculate our own logarithms, and to pass matter through matter at will. But if, on the other hand, we are evolutionists at large, we may contemplate with profound satisfaction the "passage of the life wave from planet to planet," the mysteries of pneumatic development, the spiral ascent of reincarnation, and the evolutionary achievements of a "fifth-rounder." We may acquire (in imagination) the "interior breathing," and renew youth and its delusions together; or, if we are bent upon a larger exploit, we need only fix our eyes on the lotus and repeat those mystic words, *Om Mani Padmi Houm*, till "the dewdrop slips into the shining sea," and then we shall have entered Nirvana, that washless ocean of romantic vacuity, in which even a perfervid imagination can wish for nothing. Yes, even caricatured by the terminology of the chimerical—yes, even under the guise of a delusion—we should still choose Mysticism!

APPENDIX II.

THE SECRET OF FREEMASONRY.

THOMAS DE QUINCEY, the immortal consumer of a daily dose of 60,000 drops of laudanum, was a man of many words, and of these some were sufficiently bitter and satirical. Writing on the subject of secret societies, he once said that Freemasonry was the great imposture of the modern world, even as the Eleusinian Mysteries were the great fraud of antiquity. It must be admitted that in the course of its existence the Masonic Brotherhood has numbered in its ranks some exceedingly strange personalities. The transcendental trickeries of Cassanova, St. Germain, and Cagliostro must rank among the most entertaining scandals of history; but the rogueries which are grafted for a time upon great institutions are not to be identified with essential elements which go down into the heart of institutions, and are part of their bone and flesh. It would be preposterous to suppose that a passing shaft of De Quincey has clung like a stigma to Masonry in the popular mind, but it is certain that those persons of average intelligence and education who are not attracted by its mystery are still frequently repelled by the conceptions it presents to them. A vast institution which includes upwards of ten thousand lodges in all parts of the world, and considerably over one million members, which in the mere matter of paid-up capital must be enormously rich, and of almost incalculable resources in the collective wealth of the Brothers—where is the limit of its possibilities? Each of these lodges is a storehouse of extraordinary symbols which cannot be generally interpreted—what do they mean? Every one of these million initiates is bound by solemn vows to an inviolable secresy—what do such pledges conceal? Is it some colossal conspiracy which has been elaborating for centuries, and possibly is now ripe for universal revolution? Alternately favoured and proscribed in most countries where it has openly and conspicuously flourished, long persecuted and still consistently denounced by the Church of Rome, accredited more or less definitely with most of the social cataclysms which have convulsed Europe, identified in methods and ends with the dark policies of plotting Illuminés and Carbonari; though in

England it may be a benefit society, abroad it is a political league, and where
the surface is all mystery and secresy there must be some volcanic danger in
the depths. So reasons the ignorant and nervous mind. There is a literature
of the subject which exhibits it in another light; but it is practically unknown
to the vulgar, who at most are acquainted with the bogus revelations of Carlile
and a few kindred retailers of "the secret out."

There are just three elements in the mystery of Freemasonry which deserve
to be briefly appraised. In the first place, the brotherhood has existed for an
indeterminate number of years, of which the first unit is occasionally denominated the night of time, and it is unequipped with any adequate materials for
its own history. Apart from the fabulous extravagances of romantic theorists,
it has no notion of the date, place, or circumstances of its origin, and it is
wholly improbable that the researches of the most painstaking antiquaries
would succeed in disentombing its past. This element of mystery may, therefore, be accepted as of an essential and unavoidable kind. Its natural consequence has been the gradual growth of a second species of mystery in the fables
which have been devised by imaginative persons, who have produced many
marvellous histories designed for the enhancement of its dignity. Their name
is legion; a moderate computation at least would fix them as numerically
equal to the "Arabian Nights' Entertainments," and their collection, would
any one undertake it, might be worthy of Scheherazade herself; it is all
glamour and enchantment, and as each is exclusive of the other, as they
begin with Adam in Paradise and end with the alchemist Ashmole, there
is an enormous variety of legend and a very satisfactory chaos. But as we
have ceased to write folios on the Druids, and on the origin of Stonehenge
and Carnac, as the archæology of to-day is content to confess itself ignorant
about many matters which gave monuments of erudition to our ancestors, what
is fabulous in the history of Masonry may also become a thing of the past;
the adept may be content to be ignorant of what he cannot possibly know, so
that this element in Masonic mystery is not of an essential kind. There is,
finally, the secret of Masonry. There is that profound and abysmal mystery
which the rope and plummet of the vulgar have never sounded, though it is
more than broadly whispered that all initiates who have bottomed it have discovered themselves *in vacuo bombinans*, like the famous chimera of the school-
men. In spite of Carlile and Johnson, in spite of occasional revelations of
expelled and seceded associates, the secret of Masonry would appear to be still
undivulged. Now, in an association which has existed in the open light of
history for at least two hundred years, which, moreover, is credibly averred to be
as ancient as old night, which numbers, as we have seen, ten thousand lodges

and a million members, and has occasionally initiated that sex which is the chartered libertine of the great world of gossip—in such an association, it is plain, from the nature of humanity, that there is no secret. Had there been such a treasure in such a storehouse of mystery, it would inevitably have been spoliated long ago, oaths and adjurations notwithstanding. As it is, the vacuous nature of the great arcanum of allegorical architecture is its permanent protection. Curiosity has attracted thousands to the ranks of the brotherhood, and they have returned to inform us that there is no cause for mystery, that there is nothing to tell, and of course they have never been believed.

There was possibly a time in the past, between the epochs of chaos and Solomon, between Solomon and Eleusis, or between Eleusis and the " Artist Elias," when Masonry may have had a secret. The doctrine of analogy—in other words, the principle that there is no smoke without fire—would lead us to conclude so much ; but it has melted, like its early Grand Masters, into "the infinite azure of the past." The prophet has, in fact, departed, and has left nothing but his footprints to be cherished by his less favoured successors. The secret of Freemasonry is therefore a mystification rather than a mystery, but it is an inheritance from the past; it is not a conscious imposture; it has been hallowed by the curiosity of the centuries; it answers well as a *modus operandi*, and may therefore pass unchallenged in an age which has elaborated the gospel of utilitarian philosophy.

The society, however, has an object, though its secresy be its sole secret, and the universal diffusion of such a brotherhood is in itself a substantial indication that this object is catholic or universal in character. The dutiful children of the Latin Church are taught to believe that it is atheism in religion and anarchy in law ; there are others who affirm that it is the transmutation of base metals into gold, and that it is only the wealth of the society which pre-vents this object being practically prosecuted by its members. Many erudite persons, on the other hand, are assured that the sole purpose of the entire order, whether here or at Pampelavuso, is to execute a tardy vengeance on pope and king for the butchery of Jacques de Molay, the Grand Master of the Templars. It is equally certain in the opinion of yet another section that the restoration of the Stuart dynasty is the sole end of the Royal Art. All of these theories have been proved times out of number to the satisfaction of those who hold them. Yet the world has been preserved from universal cataclysms, few persons as yet manufacture gold; the dust of five centuries has collected above the ashes of the Templars; and the House of Hanover remains unmenaced by the mythic dynasty of Bavaria. The truth is that, as usual, popular opinion and romantic theory have mistaken the transitory purposes of individual Masons for the grand ends of the united brotherhood.   Some Continental lodges have undoubtedly meddled with politics, and hatched plots in the penetralia of their temples under the mask of the square and compass.   The grand luminaries of the Reign of Terror were most, if not all, of them Masons, and the Grand Orient of France in the days of Maximilian Robespierre seethed in a sea of blood which was of a redder dye than her allegorical Rose of Morning.   But this was an incidental aberration at a period of fever heat.   So also in the middle of the eighteenth century that form of the golden passion which was known to our ancestors under the name of the Philosopher's Stone, took possession of the strongholds of the fraternity, and Masonry, both in France and in Germany, was practically divided between those who were in search of alchemical secrets, and that extraordinary crowd of Mystics who were followers of Weishaupt, Martinez Pasquales, and the more celebrated initiate Saint Martin.

The true object of the Masonic fraternity differs from the aims which have been ascribed to it precisely in that way wherein a universal institution would be expected to differ from a fanatical craze.   In its vulgar aspect, its purpose is benevolence and providence; in its esoteric significance, it is an attempt to achieve the moral regeneration of the human race; by the construction of a pure, unsectarian system of simple morality, to create the perfect man.   It is therefore at one with the intention of evolution, and at one with the end of Mysticism.   Whether it has consistently pursued this sublime end, whether, as a body, its members have conformed their daily lives to this ambition, is another question.   It is sufficient for our purpose to indicate the true aim of the fraternity, which, even at a period of generous indifference like the present, has continued to be misjudged.

APPENDIX III.

THE ROSICRUCIANS OF NUREMBERG.

THAT the body of the Mystic can be modified by alchemy is affirmed by Roger Bacon, or the treatise which has been commonly attributed to him, but even an elementary acquaintance with Mysticism and its history will modify the mind of the student, and will invest its localities and landmarks with the iridic atmosphere of glamour and enchantment. So also the traveller who is illuminated by any quality of mystic knowledge will ever find therein a certain transfiguring instrument which will illustrate his wanderings. For most historic places are connected with Mysticism, and all such have in this sense their secret history, sources of suggestion and poetry which are free to the chosen few. For this reason it may be truly affirmed that the most romantic associations which are connected with the great cities of the past do not invariably stand out foremost among historical landmarks, and this is certainly the case with that pre-eminently grand old town which is said to be for Bavarian Franconia what Munich is for Bavaria proper—the metropolis of its district. In an age when the sense of the picturesque was rudimentary among the races of the West, a respectable gentleman of the eighteenth century, who commemorated his perambulation of Germany in a goodly volume which found favour with Pinkerton, has recorded the fact that Nuremberg was an ugly town, which daily diminished in population. To us of the nineteenth century this same element of the picturesque has become almost a ponderable agent in that exceedingly composite atmosphere through which modern culture views the world around it, and new and old impressions of that city which was one of the keys of mediæval Europe are naturally in curious contrast. The opinion of M. Reisbach, who was gathered to the dust of the Fatherland in 1786, may therefore be compared with the poet of a recent day, who gathered the "nobility of labour" and the "pedigree of toil" out of every crevice in the pavement of that "quaint old town of toil and traffic," which was equally famous for its contributions to the world's universal exhibition both of arts and crafts.

> In the valley of the Pegnitz, where across broad meadow lands,
> Rise the blue Franconian mountains, Nuremberg the ancient stands.

So sings Longfellow, who, perhaps, of all English-speaking poets, was most permeated by the spiritual influence of Germany. For him, at least, the pebble-paved streets, the innumerable rambling mansions, rich in grotesque sculptures, in splendid oriels, and in broad, hammered-iron balustrades, the steep, slanting roofs, glowing with red tiles, the dormers, the gables, the door-posts, have established Nuremberg among the foremost, if not as the first, of all European cities in the ideal catalogue of the traveller in search of the picturesque. It is visited accordingly; comparatively, it is well known, and its history may be found in the guide-books. It is a town of art and song, for it is the birthplace of Albrecht Dürer, who has been called the "Evangelist of Art," and it was equally the birthplace of one, at least, of the Corporation of Meister-singers, the gentle cobbler-poet, Hans Sachs, who, work as he might at his last, was yet able to bequeath to posterity some thirty-four folio volumes of inimitable verse and prose. It is the birthplace of Adam Krafft and of Peter Vischer, whose sculptures still glorify the Gothic church of St. Laurenz. In a certain sense it is, therefore, *par excellence*, one of the centres and fountain-heads of mediæval Christian culture. But in the history of the commercial progress of Europe it also figures pre-eminently. There was a time, it has been said, when its power and glory were felt through every clime. This was in the fourteenth and fifteenth centuries, when its prosperity was at its apex. The industrial and scientific life of the country was concentrated within those old walls which environ it to this day, though the fosses are now luxuriant gardens, the embrasures are filled with lilacs, and the crumbling stones are colonized by bright-coloured climbing plants. "Greatest and most wealthy of all the free Imperial cities, the residence of emperors, the seat of diets, the focus of the trade of Europe, the most important manufacturing town in Germany, the home of German freedom, and of almost innumerable inventions," such was Nuremberg in its prime, and so much the guide-books will tell us of it. Nor will the intelligent traveller be at a loss to understand how and why it degenerated during the seventeenth century into that condition of ultra-legitimate dulness which, according to Shelley, is the presiding genius of a nameless place that, in other respects, is "a city much like London." He need only consult his Murray or his Badæker to learn that it was the discovery of the passage to India round the Cape of Good Hope which helped towards the decay of Nuremberg by deflecting the commerce of the East away from Central Europe. When the lonely reign of the Spirit of the Cape was violated by Vasco de Gama, "on seas which mortals ne'er till then beheld," the knell of Franconian commercial prosperity was practically sounded, and from the world's workshop it became the world's toyshop, as it remains unto this day, for it is the headquarters of the

German toy-manufactures. The ruin which originated with the adventurous hero of the *Lusiad* was completed by the Thirty Years' War, and thenceforth Nuremberg was, and is, the shadow of its former self, a city of memories. Therein "all that appertains to the present century is suddenly shut out from the senses." Under the shadow of its old castle, and by its dreamy river-side, one is overwhelmed by the presence of the past. But for a full appreciation of the place and its associations, it is necessary, as already hinted, to go beyond the guide-books, and to discover that Nuremberg was the seat of one of the most extraordinary secret associations which are known in all history.

That "open secret" of Masonry, with which our previous Appendix was concerned, transmitted from the architectural guilds of early Europe, and recruited from all quarters of the globe of mystery, is a child's device in comparison with the arch-secret of Franconia, which consecrated Nuremberg for ever as the Eleusinia of Germany, for it was there, in the first blush of the seventeenth century, were to be found the earliest traces of what is *facile princeps* in all the wonder-world—the Rosicrucian Mystery. Even were it true that nowadays nobody seriously believes in magic, that nobody vexes the planets with astrological calculations for the discovery of the future in portents, that nobody struggles to transmute lead into gold, that Cardinal Richelieu was the last person who attempted to renew his youth, that all these and kindred respectable superstitions of antiquity have been engulfed in that light of the world which is called physical science, and are essentially things of the past—even then they are part and parcel of the great empire of curiosity, which a French writer has paradoxically defined to be the one permanent realm in a world of everlasting mutation, and they cannot at this day be mentioned without awaking a weird and fearsome interest. Introduce the adept of the Rose-Cross among the group of historical figures which are present to the mind's eye in the tortuous streets of Nuremberg, and straightway the whole crowd disappears, he only is the concentrated centre of attraction. Nobody, of course, believes in him; visions of Cassanova, Cagliostro, and the long sequence of "illuminated" rogues and charlatans are called up by his presence, but, impostor or what not, he is a grand mystery, a historic riddle, and what is the bent and somewhat rotund figure of the poor cobbler-poet, staggering under the weight of his folios—what is he beside him? What, even, is the grave and almost stately carriage of Albrecht Dürer, what are the Twelve Wise Masters, compared with him? The Man in the Iron Mask is not more impervious to scrutiny than he who is enveloped in the folds of that violet mantle which is embroidered with the singular and inexplicable red cross. Tyrannous and irresponsible, the old magistrates of Franconia are said to have been like the old doges of Venice, and the statement is suggestive; but even Marino Faliero, in his city of lagoons and barges, is dwarfed by the side of the inexplicable Christian Rosencrantz, and it is distinctly good food for the imagination of the mystical dweller in Nuremberg to know that, from whatever dictionary of phrase and fable the Rosicrucians may have derived their name, they once had a "local habitation" in that city of departed greatness.

APPENDIX IV.

The Grand Mystic of Majorca.

A LL that we have affirmed of Nuremberg and the suggestions of its mystic environment applies with increased force to the Balearic Isles. The unfrequented by-ways of European travel, like those of European literature, have points of considerable interest to those who have the opportunity and inclination to explore them. A comparatively unknown region, not in any sense inaccessible, yet seldom visited, and that unaccountably, would frequently offer a new sensation to the jaded mind of the Continental traveller, who has exhausted the resources, or grown weary of the mind-taxing excitements of what was once called the Grand Tour. After the crowds and the splendours of the great European capitals, after the commonized attractions of the "show places" which it is the correct thing to visit, which have been bereft of half their charm by the very facilities of modern travelling, which have been "done" so often that we have lost almost the wish to do them, and the joy in the doing, it excites in the breast of the tourist a "distinct romantic flutter" to know that there is somewhere within reasonable reach—it may be, almost at his door—some place, be it town or coast, or islet, to visit which will distinguish him from the ordinary tourist, while it takes him from the beaten track which is vulgarized out of all consecration by excessive familiarity. Is he anywhere in the southern section of "serene and golden Italy," and is his constitution able to withstand the malaria of the marshes? Then he may proceed through the desolate wastes of Otranto to the forlorn city of Manfred, Prince of Otranto, and recall the grotesque incidents of Walpole's "Gothic romance," while across the long sapphire stretch of the Mediterranean, he watches the African mountains invested by the enchantment of the distance *in splendoribus sanctorum*. But if he be upon the eastern coast of Spain, in Barcelona, or in Valencia—the city of the Cid—and if he be in search of the picturesque, and of a purely intellectual excursion, more than all, if he have been "modified" by Mysticism, and if he be acquainted with alchemy, let him ship over the sea to the Balearic Isles.

A purely intellectual excursion! It is a strange term to make use of in connection with what is really only an administrative province of Spain, and involves but a short voyage which may be accomplished—blow foul, blow fair —in the space of four-and-twenty hours, and in steamers which ply regularly twice a week between the isles and Barcelona, and once between the isles and Valencia. The words, nevertheless, have been selected with due deliberation. Despite the fact that telegraphic communication has been established between Palma and the mainland, and that a line of railway has been opened up through some districts of Majorca, the chief port of the Balearic Isles is like a gate of dreams through which the traveller passes from the fever and artificiality of modern life into the picturesque simplicity of the fifteenth century. The short stretch of blue water which intervenes between the islands and the continent is the exact measure and dimensional equivalent of four long cycles of Christian progress. We are transported to a region which throughout that period has substantially stood at gaze, "like Joshua's moon in Ajalon," and is just begin- ning to awake. It requires an intellectual nature, and to some extent a cultivated mind, to assimilate the peculiar qualities which pervade the moral atmosphere of Palma, and to appreciate with accuracy the unique associations of Majorca.

There are five Balearic Islands: Majorca, Minorca, Ivica, Formentura, and Cabrera; and all of them, in respect of geographical conditions and his- torical development, are intimately associated with Catalonia. Speaking geo- logically, they constitute a prolongation of Cape San Antonia; they have the appearance of a far-stretching promontory, dismembered from the mainland in some remote convulsion of Nature, and there is little doubt that, at an earlier epoch, they formed an integral portion of the Spanish peninsula. The develop- ment of a special *Flora*, radically similar to, but formally differentiated from, the continent with which it was once united, is an interesting characteristic of the group and an indication of the antiquity of the cataclysm. Though its topography and history still remain unwritten, Balearic botany and geology are represented by a considerable literature, and scientific explorations made from this two-fold standpoint have been fruitful in valuable results. Thus, the first associations awakened by the five sisters take us back to that period when the vast continent of Europe was involved in the din and strife of earth's formative processes. But within traceable historic times the Balearic group represents, in an extremely restricted area, some singularly comprehensive landmarks in human history. It is the land of the Druid and the Moor, of Hannibal and the Bonapartes; it is the home of classic fable and mediæval witchcraft; it sheltered alchemists and magicians; it begot saints and inquisitors; it inherited from early Christianity the missionary zeal of the Apostolic Church, and it fostered the maritime spirit which gave Christopher Columbus to Portugal, and secured the New World to the blue-blooded grandees of old Spain.

Strange mounds and stranger tumuli mark the remains of the pre-historic dead; barbarous monoliths of upright, unhewn stone, some of them twenty feet high, supporting horizontal stones of equal dimensions, are scattered all over the islands, and are identical in their general character with the mysterious colossi of Stonehenge, and the rock temple of Carnac, isolated in the great plain of Auray. Imagination has ascribed them to the Druids, and the reference may, in a sense, be accepted, for, in the hands of a fanciful archæology, the name Druid received a generic significance, and was loosely applied to a number of primitive peoples whose existence can be dimly discerned in the far twilight of European colonization. In the presence of these singular remains, with their uncouth fences of flat stones, the mind naturally reverts to the origin of nations and religions; the tourist is conscious that under their influence he is lifted from the level of the common crowd of sightseers into an intellectual traveller and a *contemplateur des temps*. But while archæology has consecrated the Balearics by the supposed presence of those Druids who have been invested with the wisdom of Pythagoras and all the science of Egypt, they have also been encircled by an "amorous, silver, haze-crowned sea" of classical myth-ology, for old writers have identified them with the Fortunate Islands, with the Isles of the Blessed, the abode of the happy departed, the Eudémones, or Isles of the Good Genii, and the Aphrodisiades, or the shores of Love. Though the mediæval geographers were mistaken as to the actual locality of this nimbus of legends, the Balearics are so favoured by Nature as to deserve well of the reference. The original colonization of the islands is attributed to the Phœni-cians and Rhodians, and to this day the people of Minorca are convinced that Magon, the brother of Hannibal, founded the port which bears the name of Magon, and that Hannibal himself was a native of their beloved group.

We have said that Balearic history is still unwritten, and the materials are possibly wanting. From the time when the islands were conquered by the Romans after the fall of Carthage to the period of their invasion by the Moors is an almost unbroken blank, but they were over-run by the infidels for the space of several centuries, and, in fact, till the forces of the Crescent were demolished by John I, King of Arragon. The restitution of the islands to Christianity, and to the rule of Spain, was an era in the history of Majorca; out of that restitution there arose a great light which long illuminated the Balearics, and for two or three centuries irradiated a large area of Europe.

Now, the monoliths of Majorca are impressive, and in the mountain paradise of Valdemosa, with its rambling and picturesque village, one might imagine one's self in the Fortunate Islands. The traditions of Hannibal and the house of Hugo de Bonaparte, the ancestor of Napoleon I, are inspiring to the military mind; but if anyone wishes to understand the Balearics, and especially Majorca, he must be acquainted with the history and legends of Raymund Lully. They have given to the island its unique historical flavour—part apostolic, part monkish, part magical. From the lofty summit of Mount Randa, with its splendid central position, there may be obtained a panoramic view of the largest of the Balearics. From the moral elevation of the history of Raymund Lully, who once dwelt on Mount Randa, may be contemplated the interior genius which presides over the unbroken tranquillity of the islands, which has preserved them from all revolutions for the space of six centuries, and has kept them unspotted from the modern world in the antiquated but delightful environment of four hundred years since.

Raymund Lully is a multiform personage whose name seems to include several distinct individualities which intermingle and dissolve into one another by a species of super-incession which is in harmony with the genius of Spanish orthodoxy. "Seven and yet one, like shadows in a dream," he is at once the Prometheus, the Don Juan, the illuminated philosopher, the grand magus, the ideal lover, the missionary, and the martyr of Majorca. The central figure about which the whole cycle of fables revolves, which once filled Europe with its reports, was born, in the first half of the thirteenth century, of an old and noble Barcelona family, and his father had fought in the Moslem crusade side by side with the royal conqueror from Arragon. Courtly, accomplished, and beautiful, Raymund Lully passed from preferment to preferment, till he was installed as the Master of the Palace and the Seneschal of the Isles. Honours still more distinguished were possibly in store for him; but he was young, gay, and gallant; he surrendered himself to pleasure, and his excesses, though they did not exhaust the royal bounty, were sufficient to excite very justly the royal displeasure. His reformation was attempted by a marriage, but the experiment seems to have been a failure. Yet the nature of Raymund Lully was full of chivalry and nobility; he was generous in his disposition, and a poet after the fashion of his period, eloquent in passionate sonnets and songs wherein the ardours of love were veiled by the sombre mysteries of Spanish thought.

Great excesses, in the Roman Church, are sometimes considered to be indications of great natures, and splendid conversions have not infrequently followed on magnificent sins. Raymund Lully was the raw material of a saint, and his conversion was effected in a manner which was characteristic of himself, and to his period full of suggestion. Beautiful to all appearance, and enjoying an irreproachable reputation, Ambrosia di Castello, a young married lady of Palma, attracted the admiration of the seneschal, and he pursued her in church, and house, and palace, to say nothing of the open streets. In the end, to effect her escape, she revealed to him a cancer which had formed in her breast, and had grievously disfigured her, bidding him transfer to God the homage which he was wasting on a being who was fair only in her outward appearance.

This was the turning-point in the life of Raymund Lully. Disgusted with the illusions of things external, the seneschal of Majorca renounced the world. A man of an illimitable nature, he was precisely one of those who would do nothing by halves. *Pecca fortiter*, said Luther, and right well has he been trounced by his adversaries in polemical theology for the audacity of the maxim; but it was practised by Raymund Lully, and from a bold sinner he became a bold aspirer to the heights of Christian sanctity. With him also to aspire was to attain. He became a monk, a doctor in theology, a great teacher, a renowned preacher, a reformer, a missionary, a martyr. He founded colleges, he traversed Europe, he evangelized Africa, he invented a universal science, he planned a revolution in the arid methods of scholastic philosophy, and he died in the cause of religion, stoned by the infidels of Bugia. His conversion, his life, his labours, and his death fascinated the mind of his age; legend appropriated his history and adorned it with marvellous fables. It represented him not only as a worker of orthodox miracles, but as a magician, an alchemist who had obtained fire from heaven, a discoverer of the elixir of life, and it protracted his existence over the space of three centuries. His tomb at Palma became a place of pilgrimage; his cultus spread over the whole group of Balearics, and thence over a considerable portion of Europe.

It was essentially a popular cultus, for, illustrious as he was, the regenerated seneschal of Majorca was too much of an innovator to be quite savoury in the palate of the Roman hierarchy. The process for his beatification was, however, instituted by the Church which he adorned, but in the end it fell through. Otherwise, that authority which publishes its judgments *urbi et orbi*—to the city and the world—would have invested the doctor of Majorca with the palms and crowns of the "choir invisible," and would have apportioned him a seat in perpetuity among the splendours of that region which Shelley has termed the "Unapparent."

APPENDIX V.

SPIRITUALISM, THE SOUL'S HOME, AND THE LEGENDS OF WANDERING ISLANDS.

IT is a criticism which may seem to be severe, and we wish that we could regard it as unjust, but there can be little doubt, from our own philosophical standpoint, that a large portion of the active spiritual movement, and a still larger portion of its literature, are only a sublimed materialism. We do not here speak of what is admittedly coarse and crass in its constituent elements; we regard it even in its refined presentation as at heart material, and in nothing so much as in its demonstration of the after-life. Its furthest vistas do not bring us appreciably nearer to that which the Mystics understand by the inner life. In one of his pseudo-scientific definitions Eliphas Levi affirms that there is no spiritual world, but that there are simply various degrees of density. Unconsciously or otherwise, that is the central doctrine of the spiritualists' philosophical economy. The scope of our human correspondence with the Great Beyond is that which subsists between a transfigured physical envelope and a fantastic physical environment. A man who, like Eliphas Levi, denies the spiritual, is consistent within his own lines, though he may be vulnerable to the charge of atheism, but what are we to think of the philosophical acumen which endeavours to refine upon matter till it passes off into spirit?

> It is more life for which I pant,
> More life and fuller that I want;

but the sublimation of matter produces gas, and the tenuous existence of the spheres is not an increase of life. There all is shadowy, unsubstantial, and vague—invested in the dim splendour of the nebulous and obscured by the poetry of the half-conceived. The sunset cloud may be a parable of the soul's glory, but the soul's home is not in a clouded sunset. The soul's home is in God. It is absolutely apart from all that is objective and manifest. It is deep down, and far removed, and irredeemably withdrawn from all likeness to the home of our humanity. It is that centre of very being where the law of correspondence fails, where no similitude or comparison is possible, and where humanity is put off for ever. We neither doubt nor deny that there are such spheres in the spiritual universe as are described to us by trance and by vision, and by the revelations of the dead testifying. Therein the soul may tarry as in a phantom inn, but they are not the home of soul; they are the many mansions of the astral plane, which is contiguous to the physical; therewith communication is established with an almost fatal facility, all ages, all nations, have explored therein, to find their genius mirrored and reduplicated as in a luminous mist. It is that land of souls of which savage peoples preserve the wild traditions—thin, dreamy, phantasmal, a vaporous copy of earthly types. At times it takes shape in legend as an underworld, at times as a hidden city, and in one of its most interesting forms as a flying or wandering island, but it is essentially the same in all, based partly in material illusion, and partly upon rudimentary spiritual experience.

The phenomena of atmospheric illusion, more especially in Oriental countries, and in countries possessed of a sea-board, have materially helped in the origination of an interesting cycle of tradition, in which the marvels of wandering cities, flying palaces, and migrating islands, "prank'd on the sapphire sea," are detailed with a wealth of poetical fable which is often exceedingly suggestive. In the last case, atmospheric illusion will, however, only partially account for some of these entertaining stories. In ages when the ocean was practically unexplored, its vast waters were a world of wild romance, and the accredited home of a thousand unpenetrated mysteries. Beyond all reach and sight, the kraken had there its immemorial home; the pleasant shallows were the domain of the mer people, of the neckan, and the undine; the surface, to which the existing knowledge could assign no bounds, was a realm for the myths and marvels of sea-going humanity. There the storm-tossed mariner, buffeted by wave and wind, found shelter in strange islands, to which in subsequent voyages he vainly endeavoured to return. From this the superstition of the period would conclude that his temporary refuge had been raised from the aqueous depths, and its "bowers of starry green," by the merciful "men of the sea." Or, alternatively, it had swung serenely, following tide and moon, to another and undiscoverable region. Not improbably, the imagination was also exercised in ministering to the sense of bereavement by the creation of similar fictions. Grief for the drowned sailor may have been assuaged in his mourning relatives by the forlorn hope that he was not truly dead, but that his lost bark had drifted among "summer isles of Eden lying in dark purple spheres of sea"; and the home of the castaway, transfigured into an earthly paradise, became by an easy transition the abode of his soul in death. The latter conception was extended by that universal tradition of aboriginal folk-lore which represents the home of the departed as located in remote and favoured spots of the material earth, and the wandering island became identical with the land of souls.

Even till a comparatively recent period, very curious fables were current among the Welsh concerning certain "green islands of Ocean," or "Green Rovers of the Floods," the abode of the Tylwith Teg, or the Fair Family, who according to some accounts, are a variety of the elfin race, but are often regarded as the souls of virtuous Druids, forbidden to enter the Christian heaven, and rewarded in a paradise of their own. In either case, they are of a tricksy and troublesome disposition, and their midnight visits to the Principality mean more or less mischief to mortals. But their mysterious islands are full of spiritual beauty and have ever been desired by the Welsh people. Voyagers permitted to enter them will imagine that their visit has lasted a few hours when ages, as a fact, have elapsed. An illustrious British chieftain of the fifth century undertook, with his family, the discovery of these islands, and has not as yet returned. Should any one desire to ascertain what has become of him, the wisdom of Cambria has provided a comparatively simple means.

"If you take a turf from St. David's churchyard," says an antique legend, "and stand upon it on the sea-shore, you shall behold these Green Islands. A man once, who had thus obtained sight of them, immediately put to sea to find them; but they receded, and his search was in vain. He returned, gazed at them again from the enchanted turf, again set sail, and failed again. The third time he took the turf into his vessel, stood upon it till he reached them, and he also is there to this day."

Far beyond the supposed region of the "Green Rovers," Flath Innis, or the Noble Island, navigates the tempests of the Western ocean, and is possessed of the same faculty of vanishing and reappearing. It is likewise an abode of the departed, and is not altogether inaccessible to favoured mortals. In the wild language of one of the Bardic poems, we are told of a Druid magician of high renown, who was an adept in the difficult task of riding on tempests, and reposing on the pillow of a troubled wave. His eye, says the poet, followed the sun by day; his thoughts travelled from star to star in the night; he thirsted after things unseen, and, in spite of all his knowledge, he sighed over the narrow circle which surrounded his life. At length on a certain day of election, a storm rose over the sea, a cloud rushed into the bay, and out of its black depth sprang a boat, with white sails bent before the wind. It was furnished with a hundred moving oars, but no mariner was to be seen. The magician was seized with terror, when a voice cried through the tempest— "This is the Bark of Heroes! Arise, and behold the Great Isle of those who have passed away!" The story goes on to relate how, endued with unwonted strength, the magician entered the boat, and sailed away in the bosom of the cloud. "Seven days gleamed faintly round him; seven nights added gloom to his darkness; his ears were stunned by shrill voices; the dull murmur of winds passed him on either side." Without sleeping, without eating, and without the need of either, he endured till the eighth day. Then the waves swelled to the height of mountains, the boat rocked violently, the night deepened, innumerable voices broke into shouts of "The Isle! The Isle!" and through a vast rift in the mad whirl of waters, the peaceful home of the departed dawned in splendour on his eyes. The beauty of this spell-bound world, where the hills "did not wholly want for clouds," but each cloud was the source of a sparkling stream, gliding down verdant slopes, is described in the old poem with inspired fervour. There the magician received a crown of stars, an amaranth wand, and a girdle of melodious diamonds. Among the wildest downs of Wales, by solitary meres and broad slow streams, his presence still appears, and he offers to the chosen wanderer the mystic secret of the green isle of benediction.

Wandering islands, and their immediate relatives in tradition, those sunken cities which have the faculty of rising from the sea, are found also in Irish folklore. The paradise of the old pagan inhabitants of Erin, is as restless in its movements as the Noble Island of the Welsh. It is called Hy Brasail, and may be occasionally descried far off the western coast of Arran More. More wonderful still is the enchanted City of Hud, which is normally, but not always, submerged. It contains all the treasures of the ancient world, and the key which will open that city has been hidden in a Druidical monument. When Erin has attained to the culminating point of her misfortunes, some one will find the key, and then the moory heights of Callan will be changed into fruitful plains, the city will sink no more, and the lost splendour of Ireland will be restored. There is a similar tradition among the peasantry of Western Spain concerning the Isle of the Seven Cities, where Roderick the Goth is still believed to be alive, and where a later Spanish grandee tarried a single night, which in this case also proved to be a hundred years.

The beautiful legend of Avalon, where Arthur rests upon his arms, where the palace of Morgan le Fay shines likes the sun at noon, and where the Danish paladin Ogier dwells to this day, is depicted in Breton stories as protected from discovery by a magical power of movement. It has one point of rest, and that is in an unexplored centre of the Western ocean. It is the uttermost island of the lower earth, and the true earthly paradise, watered by the fountain of oblivion.

As much of the folk-lore of Europe has its counterpart among the aborigines of the New World, so in American traditions we find the myth of the wandering island. The Creek Indians, for example, have for several centuries affirmed the existence of a beautiful Isle of Founts. The source of the river St. Mary is said to be in a vast and mournful marsh, which is full of perils even for the hardiest hunter and is impassable to an ordinary traveller. In the winter season it is transformed by swollen torrents into a superb lake, dotted over by innumerable islets, and here the Isle of Founts may be occasionally seen. It is inhabited by women of incomparable beauty, a gentle wind always breathes around it, and the soft warmth of an Indian summer ever prevails therein. Could any one land upon its shore, he must pass through a mountain which is the abode of a royal race of rattlesnakes, who are denominated the "bright old inhabitants." They are of enormous size, their heads are crowned with a carbuncle of dazzling brightness, and by the power in their eyes they can deprive any living creature of motion. On the other side of the mountains the rocks give forth strange melodies, which float like wood-notes over the lake and enter into the heart of the hunter, till he is filled with an intense longing to attain the Isle of Founts. But his step may be the fleetest and his canoe the lightest, and great his skill with the paddle, yet, even if the wind should favour him, the most that he can do is to touch for a moment the ring of soft blue waves which encircle the place. It flies before him into the dim distance, a mist closes round him, in which he is lost for hours, and then his keel grates on the common margin of the lake. He has heard the melody of the magical rocks sounding like a choir of beautiful voices; he has seen the play of the splendid waters which fertilize the fortunate island; he is consumed on his return with a thirst which no earthly draught can satisfy, and he is found no more in battle or in chase.

Variously diversified, but always essentially the same, the legend appears in a score of other places. It is known to the inhabitants of the Tonga Islands, who tell of "sea-driven Bolooto," a mysterious place enshrouded by the will of the gods, so that the adventurous mariner will miss it without special favour. It is found in Arabian fiction as the floating island of Borico, with its earth transparent as crystal and its fountain of perpetual youth, which is protected by a guard of jinn. And it is almost unnecessary to say that modern imaginative literature has not been slow to avail itself of the same suggestive fancy. It may be added, in conclusion, that the world of natural curiosities includes the wandering island among its long catalogue of wonders. There is a lake in the vicinity of St. Omer where minute tracts of spongy earth float about upon the waves. Their dimensions differ, the largest being about two metres in extent. In some cases they have been planted with small trees, and their movements are a source of much astonishment to strangers.

INDEX.

www.ingramcontent.com/pod-product-compliance
Lightning Source LLC
Chambersburg PA
CBHW031057020726
47495CB00007B/1921